SCIENCE COMMUNICATION ONLINE

SCIENCE COMMUNICATION ONLINE

ENGAGING EXPERTS AND PUBLICS ON THE INTERNET

ASHLEY ROSE MEHLENBACHER

THE OHIO STATE UNIVERSITY PRESS
COLUMBUS

Library of Congress Cataloging-in-Publication Data
Names: Mehlenbacher, Ashley Rose, 1983– author.
Title: Science communication online : engaging experts and publics on the internet / Ashley Rose Mehlenbacher.
Description: Columbus : The Ohio State University Press, [2019] | Includes bibliographical references and index.
Identifiers: LCCN 2018051713 | ISBN 9780814213988 (cloth ; alk. paper) | ISBN 0814213987 (cloth ; alk. paper)
Subjects: LCSH: Science—Computer network resources. | Communication in science. | Internet research.
Classification: LCC Q224.5 .M44 2019 | DDC 302.23/1015—dc23
LC record available at https://lccn.loc.gov/2018051713

Cover design by Susan Zucker
Text design by Juliet Williams
Type set in Adobe Minion Pro

In memory of Sandra,
because of Brad,
and for Carolyn.

CONTENTS

ILLUSTRATIONS

FIGURES

TABLES

PREFACE

THIS BOOK can be traced back to ideas that took shape in a book chapter Carolyn R. Miller and I coauthored for Alan Gross and Jonathan Buehl's (2016) *Science and the Internet*, now reprinted in the second edition of *Landmark Essays in the Rhetoric of Science: Case Studies* (2017), edited by Randy Allen Harris. In that chapter, Miller and I explore the changing landscape of science communication with a case study of nuclear disaster at the Fukushima Daiichi site in March 2011. We look specifically to microblogs, Wikipedia, and an online database of radiation contamination readings as emerging forms of science communication online. Exploring how these platforms were used to share information in response to crisis, we advance the notion of "para-scientific genres," borrowing and expanding upon the term from Sarah Kaplan and Joanna Radin's (2011) article "Bounding an Emerging Technology: Para-scientific Media and the Drexler-Smalley Debate about Nanotechnology," published in *Social Studies of Science*.

When Carolyn and I completed our work, the world of science communication looked somewhat, although not altogether, different from the vantage we have here in early 2019. Much of what I was seeing continued in traditions to share science with broader publics, but revealed some of the internal workings of science to those who may not have previously had access. There were new actors emerging on the scene as well: citizen scientists and civic scientists, as John Angus Campbell (2015) parses them up. Much of my work has attended to citizen scientists—everyday people who participate in scientific research and not-so-everyday people who design their own grassroots research enterprises in response to technoscientific disaster. In the latter case, the situations serving as case studies in grassroots citizen science generated a more overtly political situation than we might normally see for scientific research and work. After all, the kinds of grassroots citizen science that emerge in response to technoscientific disaster often form either in the absence of professional research dedicated to the problem, or when corporate and statal entities seem to obscure the data or science that affected citizens want to know. Miller and I explored how citizen scientists worked in response to such failures following the disaster at Fukushima Daiichi. And in this book, the group Miller and I examined, Safecast, will be revisited as an example of how boundaries between experts and nonexperts continue to be complicated. However, citizen scientists are not the focus of this book. Instead, we might call those civic scientists the rhetors of interest here. Some of our civic scientists have long been motivated to engage a broader public with scientific research, and these are the civic scientists often engaged in conversations about science communication and perhaps popularization of science. There are those civic scientists, too, who are concerned with the public accessibility of data and research findings. Others find online a new way to excite others about their science and even garner support for their work. And, among civic scientists are those who wearily enter a new communicative space when partisan politics seems to stifle research.

It seems there has been something of a shift in how politically—how civically—engaged scientists are as a broader constituency. Images appearing on social media feature protestors holding up signs about the need for peer review and evidence-based policy. With the challenges that experts face in matters of vaccination, climate change, and genetic modification, it does seem we can say that in this moment something is unfolding that changes how we understand the rhetorical world that scientists inhabit, and the rhetorical strategies they will need to navigate that world.

This book puts rhetorical theory and criticism to work to better understand what appear to be evolving strategies of science communication, and I necessarily had some help charting out these strategies. Crucially, I want to express sincere gratitude and thanks to my editor, Taralee Cyphers, at The Ohio State University Press. Her dedication to the intellectual substance of the book and her editorial excellence are highly commendable and made this a stronger and more engaging book. I also owe the anonymous reviewers great thanks; their feedback was substantive and essential to the book in its current form. A number of fine research assistants kept this project moving, or other projects on track while I focused my energy on the book, including Catherine Lemer at Purdue, as well as Lillian Black, Devon Moriarty, Paula Núñez de Villavicencio, and Cailin Younger at Waterloo. Thanks also to many inspiring and motivating colleagues in rhetorical studies and allied fields at Waterloo, including Frankie Condon, Bruce Dadey, Jay Dolmage, Randy Allen Harris, Andrea Johnas, George Lamont, Michael McDonald, Aimée Morrison, and special thanks to an exemplary department chair, Kate Lawson. The Faculty of Arts at the University of Waterloo generously provided funding support for this book. Thanks also to Caren Cooper and Darlene Cavalier for opportunities on PLOS *Citizen Science, Discover Magazine's Citizen Science Salon,* and SciStarter. Also some others deserve special thanks, notably Lamees Al Ethari, Chelsea Ferriday, S. Scott Graham, Molly Hartzog, and Josh Scacco. Thanks, as well, to Sune Auken, who is conducting timely and important work in genre studies through the Centre for Genre Research at the University of Copenhagen.

On a personal note, I want to thank my husband, Brad Mehlenbacher. Our joints are now well set, and Brad's engaged and enthusiastic support contributed crucially to the completion of this book. I don't mean that with the kind of banality it invokes. Brad didn't simply encourage me and bring cups of coffee or tea at all hours (although he did pour more than his share); he also spent time listening to me talk through methodological decisions, theoretical commitments, and pragmatic implications. Brad's family has been supportive, too, including his father, Bryan, who indulged me talking about work, and Brad's late mum, Sandra, whose encouragement was energizing. Thanks also to my family for their continued support, especially Nancy, Jennifer, CJ, and Daniel, who motivated me to finish.

Importantly, I want to thank Carolyn R. Miller. It is far too early in my career for me to fully understand the gifts Carolyn has given me over the years we have worked together. My thanks are a clumsy attempt to account for what gifts I'll certainly discover as my career unfolds. I hope, then, Carolyn will forgive what I've gotten wrong in the book with the knowledge I'll likely figure it out, eventually—if only I'd listened more carefully, sooner.

INTRODUCTION

UNCLOISTERED BY the web, science and science communications are finding their way to new audiences through once unimaginable media. By playing the citizen science game Foldit while on the subway to work, recording videos of their backyards to help wildlife experts manage populations, or even funding scientific research out of their own pockets, nonexperts and amateurs can engage science in unprecedented ways at an equally unprecedented scale and rate. As science communication has moved online, a range of new forms for communicating have emerged, such as crowdfunding proposals, blogs, and databases, to name a few. Such forms of online science communication are responses by scientists to adapt their communication strategies to meet the demands of changing academic and disciplinary expectations, audiences of and participants in science, and the broader cultural climate within which scientists work. Indeed, we are steeped in science.[1] Where once the public was privy to only a taste of science's rich discourse, now scientific conversations are reaching broader audiences at a much greater volume—due, in part, to the evolution of online science communication. This book reveals how scientists can now communicate with broader and more complex audiences through online genres and, importantly, *how those audiences communicate back.*

---

1. The 2016 Science and Engineering Indicators reported that most Americans express an interest in science and technology, saying they are "very interested" (41 percent) or "moderately interested" (46 percent) in "new scientific discoveries" (National Science Board, 2016, p. 19).

Scientists have developed sophisticated, typified responses to recurrent rhetorical situations they face in their work (Miller, 1984). Creating these responses provides them with mechanisms that allow the transfer or sharing of complex technical knowledge. This transfer or sharing of knowledge is crucial for the meaning-making work that scientists accomplish through argument and for building consensus through a community effort to test and challenge what we believe we know. Without conventionalized forms of discourse, it becomes difficult to assess what information is being shared, for what purposes, and how to interpret this information. To see why this is necessary, take the example of a stock prospectus. Assuming you have no knowledge of investing, imagine how challenging it would be to look at a stock prospectus and interpret the information that is being presented to you—as you have not developed the tacit knowledge that someone who regularly reads these texts will have by virtue of immersing themselves within that discourse. Likewise, scientists are acclimated to the forms of science communication they use and encounter as they progress from students into independent researchers.

Scientists also communicate with publics, and such work has been traditionally characterized as popularizations. Material is written for a broad audience to be consumed, often for general interest or entertainment. However, the online forms of science communication previously described—crowdfunding proposals, blogs, databases, and so on—do not fit neatly into the category of popularizations; nor do these forms of science communication fit into what we might call professional scientific discourse. Instead, these forms exist somewhere between professional and popular discourses about science. We can call these emerging forms of science communication "trans-scientific" genres.

Trans-scientific genres operate alongside conventional forms of science communication without fully inhabiting either sphere. Sometimes trans-scientific genres rely on the discursive norms of professional science, and sometimes they employ strategies used to communicate science to the public. To elaborate, trans-scientific genres are characterized by their attention to a heterogeneous audience including experts and broader publics,[2] and while they operate along a spectrum of expert–public engagement, they are never wholly research-based genres, on the one hand, or popularizations, on the other. Trans-scientific genres provide grounds where we can bring scientific knowledge together with moral and ethical, policy-driven, and social discourse. In

---

2. "Publics" gestures toward the complexity of the audience often described as "the public" or "the lay audience," which is in fact composed of heterogeneous groups with differing levels of knowledge, interest, and engagement. Occasionally I let the usage "broader public" slip into the book, but here, too, I assume the kind of complexity in audience that merits more serious attention than any notion of a "general" public.

this sphere, somewhere in a liminal space between the strongly codified and normalized discourses internal to science and the more epideictic genres of external or popular genres of science communication, trans-scientific genres seem to have been called into existence.

This book investigates how genres of science communication online challenge simple distinctions between professional and public communications. By charting the unique genre features across multiple science-focused media platforms, their rhetorical purposes, and their movement in complex media ecologies, I aim to illustrate the overlapping rhetorical strategies and functions in these trans-scientific genres. Describing unique genre features, such as the inclusion of both expert discourse and also celebratory features common to popularizations, this book charts specific rhetorical strategies in written genres, and also details how other modalities operate rhetorically in these online science communications. Investigating these genres reveals a complex constellation of elements creating an exigence for their emergence and evolution. Namely, we can see how the democratization of science, challenges to expertise and expert status, new political economies, and the encroachment of professional science are shaping these complex communicative environments. We will return to the theoretical trajectories of genre studies and rhetorical studies of science in chapter 1, but before we do it is useful to survey the kinds of communication changes that have been afforded by the web, and how scientists are responding to those changes.

NEW GENRES OF SCIENCE COMMUNICATION

I provide two vignettes that illustrate some of the affordances and constraints offered by new media forms and the genres that emerge within those spaces. Situated in a broad conversational ecology, both vignettes reveal the heterogeneous audiences and purposes they serve, along with the constantly evolving nature of the genred activity in a rapidly unfolding discourse sphere. First, an example from the microblogging platform Twitter offers an interesting case of scientists engaging in political discourse. Appeals are made on the basis of conventional scientific argument as well as political argument. Although the topic of discussion is science, the focus is not scientific research alone, but also funding and support for science. Necessarily, the conversation moves into the domain of public debate, but it does not wholly inhabit a public dialogue, as the work these tweets undertake also includes an effort to marshal scientists. Second, the news and social sharing aggregation site Reddit provides an example of the complex audiences that can be found in online spheres of discourse. Reddit has a forum, called a subreddit, focused on science. In this forum, a type of post called an "Ask Me Anything" (AMA) allows scientists to engage with broader publics and answer questions about the kind of research the scientist and their team conducts. This engagement illustrates the interest of the broader public in talking to scientists about science, beyond mere popularization, and both of these examples begin to illustrate the kind of complex sphere of discourse that this book aims to chart. In subsequent chapters, these spheres of discourse are explored through a close analysis of rhetorical strategies. The following vignettes articulate some of the features of what I call trans-scientific genres.

Rogue Twitter and Trans-scientific Communication

If you want an introduction to the bleeding edge of science communication, you might very well find it in 140 characters. Although tweets from famous scientists such as Neil deGrasse Tyson (@neiltyson) could be characterized as public communication of science, there is in fact a more varied range of activity than popularization. Scientists on Twitter vary in discipline and demographics, and the purposes of their tweets encompass the conventional forms of public communication for outreach or popularization to disciplinary discourse and debate. Not without controversy, Twitter has become a tool that scientists use to communicate with each other and with broader publics.

Morrison (2019) offers a useful example of how Twitter can be used by scientists to address disciplinary issues. Her work examines "hashtag humour" as a response to sexism in science. The story begins when Nobel Laureate and Fellow of the Royal Society Sir Tim Hunt made a controversial statement about the "trouble with girls" in labs during a conference lunch toast. His comments on women in science were shared via Twitter, and these tweets generated debate about the meaning of his remarks. The exact nature and phrasing of Hunt's comments have been debated, as there is not, in fact, a transcript of his remarks. A series of tweets responded to the idea that women in the lab are distracting from the regular, professional operations of a lab. Tweets in response to Hunt's comments included images of women working in labs in camp poses, appended with the hashtag "#DistractinglySexy." The professional sphere of science is necessarily in conversation with the personal lives of women as they experience and respond to the larger sexist refrain that Hunt's comments invoke. Use of the hashtag interrogates this refrain with humor to suggest the preposterousness of Hunt's remarks. Rulyova (2017) explains that hashtags "are often dominated by irony and the carnivalesque" in an effort to "draw attention to their tweets and to provoke other users"

(p. 83). Hashtags facilitate broad conversation—conversations beyond individuals' own cultivated feeds. Indeed, Morrison (2019) explains that unlike typical social media feeds cultivated by our network of connections, hashtags facilitate a content- or topic-based conversation among users of the platform. Twitter illustrates how merging discourses may take shape in new media environments. For Morrison (2019), hashtag can movements deploy "context collapse between humour and seriousness, between pop culture and matters of law and politics" for "productive social justice work" (p. 23). In the case of #DistractinglySexy, images of women in the lab—posing in full lab gear, for instance—take aim at sexist presumptions. The hashtag functioned to broadly connect scientists from a variety of disciplines to discuss their own encounters with sexism or challenge sexist perceptions. The platform affords the possibilities for this kind of community building, and in turn, community-building functions—including keywords, sources of amplification, and expressive positions—can help us better understand the rhetorical situation to which these typified forms respond. For example, hashtags mark humor, irony, and sarcasm, along with political action or shared experience. Although a shared community is facilitated among hashtag users, a number of vituperative responses litter this seemingly progressive conversation about challenges women face in the sciences.

Devitt (2017) notes that in addition to the network-building capacity of the hashtag, there is a possibility for reinforcing certain kinds of information bubbles. Using the example of partisan political division in the United States, she writes,

> The # is potentially a new means of persuasion as it makes a statement or a joke about a person or position. But are you trying to persuade anyone if you use a hashtag that clearly marks your position? I imagine the people who use and those who search for posts with #PEEOTUS or #LockherUp have already made up their minds about the president-elect or former Secretary of State and are seeking others like them, not new input to change their minds. (para. 7)

Here Devitt recalls the importance of logos, or good reason, in the rhetorical tradition, but asks readers to reflect on the struggles of fake news. And, she explains that sometimes facts or evidence are irrelevant, saying, "It doesn't matter to some people when the evidence is shown to be false because they still believe it's true in spirit" (para. 11). Or, some use the platform to bully others into submission, a clear form of coercion and not persuasion of any sort. Devitt makes explicit the consequences of silencing effective rhetoricians, writing, "Maybe the difference today is how widespread and accepted are the less drastic means of silencing. . . . The rhetoric that persuades through logic, goodness, and positive emotions has to struggle to be heard in the midst of post-truth bullying and fearful prejudices" (para. 22). We can see promise in what Morrison (2019) describes, but Devitt accounts for those who aim, with vituperative responses, to silence others who are making an effort to engage in social commentary and discourse. Tension among these possibilities, and the silencing that occurs through these platforms, is an ongoing concern. In addition to silencing that may be motivated by certain individual ideologies, there is equally a circumstance where scientific findings will be seen as oppositional to those with power, who sometimes enact mechanisms to generate controversy and delegitimize the science to their own benefit (see, for example, Ceccarelli, 2011).

Concerns about such delegitimization of science prompted the proliferation of what have been dubbed "alt-Twitter" accounts—that is, alternative counterparts to the official government accounts responsible for communications about science, from the U.S. National Park Service (NPS) to the Environmental Protection Agency (EPA) to the National Aeronautics and Space Administration (NASA)—which appeared in response to what was believed to be government muzzling of scientists. When the 45th president of the United States enacted sweeping restrictions on federal agencies' communications, including through social media, scientists quickly responded (Eilperin & Dennis, 2017).[3] Broadly, the president's actions were seen to target environmentally oriented agencies, as demonstrated by this large-scale response on Twitter, through "alternative government" (AltGov) agency accounts. At the time of this writing, there is little scholarship on this event, and the anonymity of the accounts poses significant challenges to identifying those who legitimately have ties to government or are working scientists.

The website Snopes, a resource dedicated to verifying claims that range from urban legends to memes, contains an article that discusses the origins of these AltGov accounts and also vets which accounts seem to be run by persons with legitimate connections to the government agencies or, at least, the topics they are tweeting about. Snopes attributes the origins of these accounts to the activities of a National Park Service Twitter account. On January 20, 2017, the National Park Service tweeted about webpages on climate change,

---

3. Although some of this book will attend to these problems with an eye toward a U.S. context, the stakes exist far outside any single nation. The United States is a powerful political and economic actor on the global stage, and its powerhouse of scientists and researchers is likewise impressive, but country's activities have consequences and draw attention from around the world.

civil rights, and health care being removed from the White House website. The account was also used to share an image of the crowd at the 45th president's inaugural address, which has been the cause of much contention about just how many people attended. Reactions proliferated across mainstream media and social media platforms at what was seemingly a remarkable moment of political resistance. A meme that appeared on Reddit's r/politicalhumor forum on January 29 characterizes a refrain that would tie scientists to political contexts more broadly, using humor to deliver a serious message about the threat to democratic values this kind of censorship of scientists in federal agencies was perceived to mark: "First they came for the Scientists. \\ And the National Park Service said, \\ 'Lol, no.' \\ And went rogue, and we were all like, 'I was not expecting the park rangers to lead the resistance. None of the dystopian novels I read prepared me for this. But, cool.'" (Adam, 2017; Trayf, 2017). This meme references Martin Niemoller's poem "First They Came . . . ," which warns of the danger of being silent in response to the Nazi threat. Although adaptations have been used to critique political movements in the United States before the 45th administration, including on the political forum "Democratic Underground" in 2004, adaptations of Niemoller's poem have gained certain traction in the face of overt discrimination against certain populations (Adam, 2017). The ecology within which these activities unfold is far more complex than a single platform; it includes the political, cultural, and historical moment within which these discursive events occur.

Thinking about how genres operate in these spaces, we can look for situational, contingent typifications to help us investigate broader trends. For the AltGov accounts,[4] we can first identify those that have been verified to be "trusted accounts" by Snopes, using various and self-described "vague" methods to both shield the public from misinformation and also protect those acting in resistance (Binkowski, 2017). The accounts verified by Snopes include @ActualEPAFacts, @altHouseScience, @alt_Mars, @BadHombreNPS, @RogueEPAStaff, @altSmithsonian, and @AltYelloNatPark. Accounts responding to a particular rhetorical situation do not mark a genre themselves; indeed, the categorization or labeling of "genres" online is necessarily a fraught enterprise because of rapid changes in terms of content, use, and media form. These accounts, rather, suggest that there was widespread recognition of a rhetorical situation that called for a response, and that multiple actors responded by adopting a popular media form through which to do so.

In her study of new media users' responses to the 2013 Chelyabinsk meteor, Rulyova (2017) uses Bakhtin's (1986) notion of primary and secondary speech

---

4. Some accounts may no longer be actively used or active. When I visited the @AltWASONPS page in September 2017, Twitter returned a "page does not exist" error.

genres to distinguish between different genres occurring on Twitter. Tweets, she tells us, "could be described as individual utterances that could be either primary or secondary genres. Tweets belong to primary speech genres when they express an immediate reaction to an event or another user's utterance (the rejoinder dialogue)," and those tweets that can be described as secondary speech genres "are posted by users who have an additional intention beyond the simply informative or emotive ones, such as to reflect on or to engage with other texts or discourses, or to create hyperlinks" (Rulyova, 2017, p. 83). However, she continues, those tweets that appear to belong to primary speech genres might also function as secondary speech genres when they are collectively organized, such as by a hashtag. Rulyova identified several genres: jokes, news headlines, and commentary on the event (p. 89). Although these may seem to be rather broad categories, Rulyova makes a crucial point: while some genres may appear to be "global," they are "domesticated and localized to fit the local context by users" (p. 93). The AltGov accounts demonstrate a situated and contingent localized response—even if at a national level—with a particular cultural history and moment to which the accounts respond.

When exploring the tweets from these accounts, we could begin to look for genres such as jokes similar to the one featured in the above meme, memes themselves, news headlines, or even links to data. While this would be an interesting enterprise, it would obscure the broader implications for genre theory that this case serves. AltGov accounts do not themselves mark the creation of a genre, but rather point to a kind of situated uptake and performance on Twitter. Both #DistractinglySexy and Rulyova's study of the Chelyabinsk blast responses demonstrate the invocation of typified forms in response to a rhetorical situation. Such typified forms as those occurring across Twitter provide a repertoire of rhetorical strategies that can be repurposed to respond to the rapidly evolving discourse sphere contained within the Twitter platform, and with broader media ecologies (and, as Chelyabinsk demonstrates, material events).

Although tweets have conventionalized or typified forms, their purposes vary considerably even insofar as we can identify recurrent uses such as sharing news, resistance to systematic oppression, and so on. How new media forms allow for the discourses of science as well as a lively political engagement on Twitter is notable. Information shared by the AltGov accounts is scientific in nature—facts about climate change, for example. However, these tweets are also a public discourse governed by political norms and values. The tension between science and society places these tweets firmly in the public sphere, but their enactment and engagement by scientists moves us closer to the seemingly depoliticized world of science. What I will argue in this book is that these communications can be characterized as trans-scientific genres. As

I previously noted, these genres mark a rhetorical situation where scientific discourse cannot easily be characterized as discourse internal only to science or only a kind of popularization. Rather, trans-scientific genres describe those forms of science communication that exist within both professional and public spheres of discourse.

Reddit r/science AMAs and Trans-scientific Communication

To illustrate, however, that some forms of online communications still adhere to a popularization model—although admittedly more engaged—of science communication than a trans-scientific one, I now turn to the case of Reddit Ask Me Anythings (AMAs). Reddit is a social news-sharing website that allows users to submit news content and up or down vote the information. The basic premise of an AMA is that someone with some specialized knowledge, position, or some other attribute will answer any questions posed to them by the readers of Reddit. In a subreddit called r/science, scientists inhabit this role. Similar to the previous section investigating Twitter, this vignette is shaped by several questions to help articulate the form of trans-scientific genres. Are Reddit r/science AMAs[5] an example of genre activities that exhibit aspects of both professional and public communication of science? If they are, what characteristics might these AMAs have, or what aspects of online science communication might they illuminate for us as we explore these evolving online forms?

The r/science subreddit provides an overview of the AMA series, including a description of its purpose and rules. Examining this document is helpful because it illustrates features that might be characterized in trans-scientific genres. The six-page document includes a general introduction to the purpose of AMAs. A specific purpose and directions for the r/science AMAs are published in this subreddit:

---

5. Writing about emerging genres of communication online is challenging for a variety of reasons, many of which I will note throughout the book, but among the most difficult are those genres that seem to fail abruptly after significant success. Reddit's r/science AMAs are one such example. In May 2018, the moderators of the r/science subreddit announced AMAs would no longer be hosted. What is particularly interesting about this case is that the moderators cite a change in Reddit's post algorithms as a causal factor, saying "due to changes in how posts are ranked AMA visibility dropped off a cliff. [sic] without warning or recourse. We aren't able to highlight this unique content, and readers have been largely unaware of our AMAs. We have attempted to utilize every route we could think of to promote them, but sadly nothing has worked" (nallen, 2018). Algorithmic influence over the success or failure of genres certainly merits further attention.

> In an effort to *bring science education to the public,* the Reddit Science community (known as /r/ Science) has created an independent, science-focused AMA Series—the Science AMA Series. *Our goal is to encourage discussion and facilitate outreach* while helping to bridge the gap between *practicing scientists and the general public.* This series is open to any practicing research scientist, or group of scientists, that wants to have a candid conversation with the large and diverse Reddit Science community. (Reddit Science, n.d., p. 1; emphasis mine)

From this initial description, we can identify several familiar distinctions between scientists and publics. "Bringing science education to the public" is a typical approach to science outreach where the expert imparts knowledge to a general population, and this is reinforced with the distinction between "practicing scientists and the general public." Here the distinction between experts and the public establishes the framework for the kinds of communication that will occur in AMAs. However, later the submission guide states there are 13 million r/Science subscribers, which may include duplicate accounts, but still suggests a high volume of interest. Another characteristic of the audience is that users with advanced degrees "constitute a considerable portion of our active userbase" (Reddit Science, n.d., p. 2). However, a readership with advanced degrees does not necessarily mean users are invested in r/Science AMAs, nor that they are interested in these posts as part of their profession.

Another essential characteristic described in the submission guide is the format. AMAs are positioned against the "mainstream" press, and the authors state that one benefit is the "unique format that allows scientists to speak about their work in a manner that is not possible within the confines of traditional short-form journalism" (Reddit Science, n.d., p. 1). Indeed, the description continues to position AMAs in contrast to well-established genre forms. The document continues, "We have found these AMAs to be particularly valuable to researchers looking to clarify their findings and expand upon their results in situations where the mainstream press releases were too limited to accurately convey their work" (p. 1). Operating outside of conventional forms, r/science AMAs are positioned not in opposition to these forms, but rather as parallel to them. Phrases such as "clarify findings" indicate a perceived lack in complete reporting for conventional modes of science, which these AMAs aim to fill; yet, there remains attention to a broader, public audience. With such focus on science and engaged publics, these AMAs appear to operate as trans-scientific genres.

Eligibility is described in the submission guide, further illuminating the function of r/Science AMAs. The eligibility guidelines state that the participants who can run an AMA are restricted to "Practicing Scientists who have completed a terminal degree in their field of study," "Graduate students" (if related to a paper of which they are a primary author), and "Established science journalists working for respected science news organizations" (p. 2). There are also guidelines for the structure of the text, saying that authors should craft the "introduction paragraph to highlight the areas of research the scientist studies and to direct what kinds of questions to ask" (p. 3). Within these criteria are rather orthodox conceptions about who is sanctioned to speak on science, and these reinforce the discourse norms that distinguish internal forms of science communication from external modes.

The scientist or group of scientists participating in the AMA will answer questions posed by the r/science community, and questions can range from more personalizing matters to the science itself. In this way, we see a rather different form of interaction between experts and nonexperts than would be common in a popularization. Indeed, this is a bidirectional model of communication, and some of the threads venture into complex scientific subject matter. The level of engagement and disciplinary complexity of some of these discourse events suggest a suitable place among the other forms studied in this book. However, the discourse events here are highly contingent and the genre shape of these forms may range from something akin to Bakhtin's (1986) primary speech genres (greetings, thanks, etc.) to secondary speech genres (e.g., constrained by academic norms among practicing scientists). Crucial, among all the considerations, is the intention of the AMAs as a collection of discursive events constrained by the format, platform, and norms and values of the r/science AMA series. Although the form of the AMAs is typified, it is difficult to categorize them as simply another form of popularization, although they certainly perform similar functions. Where AMAs depart is in their efforts to engage dialogue, and in this way we can examine them through the lens of trans-scientific genres.

RHETORICAL GENRE STUDIES AND TRANS-SCIENTIFIC GENRES

The importance of a conversational model of science communication should not be underestimated, particularly one that rejects transmission and deficit model thinking (Gross, 1994; Condit, 2012) about how to communicate science to—and with—broader publics. This conversational model is not wholesale new, as science communications have long included para-scientific genres (Kaplan & Radin, 2011) and interdisciplinary efforts (Ceccarelli, 2001). Both of these communications operate in a liminal space governed by norms of science—including the innermost conversations in the pages of refereed journals and trade journals—as well as the norms of popularizations. These rather liminal spaces help us understand the complexity of genres that operate somewhere outside of external and internal spheres of discourse, but until now they have been relatively rare and rather more cloistered than the forms of science communication online.

These forms of online science communication offer valuable insights for rhetorical scholars interested in how genres of communication evolve and change. Much work in rhetorical genre studies has focused on professional or institutional forms of discourse. However, certain features of such discourse spheres leave them less susceptible to evolution and change than we might find more broadly. We learn much about genre evolution and change by exploring these emerging online forms of science communication that stand outside strictly regulated spheres of discourse. In particular, the forms of discourse explored in this book illustrate the complexities between highly codified spheres of discourse, rapidly evolving public discourse, and the intersection of media change. It is necessary to extend our perspective beyond professional, sanctioned spheres of discourse in order to advance theories of genre evolution and change. From a vantage that accounts for social and media change occurring broadly, this book investigates how online genre activities in science communication mark genre evolution and change.

Although different audiences, from scientists to publics to policy makers, have long complicated the geography of science communication, there seems to be a compelling case that our landscape for science communication is becoming all the more complicated. There are a number of reasons for this, including various kinds of organizational and institutional changes, social and cultural changes, and indeed changes to the nature of the challenging technoscientific problems we face. From climate change to challenges in health and medicine, these problems resist easy solutions, as they are embedded in complex environmental, historical, political, and social contexts. But with impressive speed, size, and ubiquity, the internet and web have facilitated communications about science in unprecedented ways.

A NOTE ON READING AND CHAPTERS

As is customary, this section includes an overview of the chapters following in the book. Another way to orient oneself, however, may be through a selective reading of chapter 1, which offers first a discussion of genre studies and rhetoric of science, and then features a discussion of what I propose are emerging forms, trans-scientific genres. In these pages, one will find the core theory developed in this book and the broad framework or methods used throughout the book's case studies. Chapters 2 through 4 follow with elaborations and refinements of the theory through empirical investigation, along with more details on the methods used in each case. Although the theoretical framework and methodological approaches are articulated in chapter 1 most fully, I have worked to include enough details in each chapter that they are reasonably informative in their own right, but it is together that these broad socio-technical sites (blogs, crowdfunding platforms, databases) most powerfully illustrate trends in science communication.

Chapter 1 introduces the theoretical framework for the book, drawing rhetorical studies, to offer an analytical approach to understanding genre evolution and change. Two subfields within rhetorical studies help explain how science communication online is evolving and provide the critical apparatus for this book: genre studies and rhetorical studies of science. Both fields currently feature research about affordances brought with the rise of the web and social media. For genre studies and rhetoric of science, the new forms of communication across a range of modalities offer a point to reflect on change, and also to take a reflexive stance on our approaches and methods. After exploring these areas, the chapter then features a discussion of current methods in these fields. Although case studies have been a staple in rhetorical studies of science, some recent critiques must be accounted for and used as opportunities to expand our methodological understandings. Relying on work in rhetorical genre studies, and allied areas of genre studies, the methodological approach developed in chapter 1 offers a blend of close textual analysis with analysis of a small sample of texts.

Chapter 2 explores how the complex networks of actors, audiences, and genres shape a new method of funding research: crowdfunding. First, the chapter examines the networked technologies and networks of people that provide a platform for crowdfunded proposals. Looking at the structure, and the communities building those structures, the book examines where crowdfunding proposals are shared, who is sharing them, and what kinds of results these efforts see. Crowdfunding platforms—from the generalist crowdfunding website Kickstarter to the niche, research-driven Experiment.com—are noteworthy because they reveal (1) the challenges in funding science, particularly those projects outside a disciplinary zeitgeist, in an era of decreased federal dollars; (2) the shift to promotional efforts in scientific discourse; and (3) the variety of voices, of scientists and students and citizens alike, appearing on these sites. This chapter notes that the importance of social networks to cultivate an audience is striking and the stakes are high—fund or fail. In contrast to usual research funding models, crowdfunding models generate a different audience, one that comprises experts and nonexperts. Given this complex landscape of experts, nonexperts, and perhaps amateur experts, the communication strategies in these proposals are markedly different from their conventional, academic counterparts. A move analysis of a small corpus of Experiment.com proposals reveals how crowdfunding proposals are written and embedded in social networks.

Chapter 3 explores databases as a central site of rhetorical work. The processes of collecting, organizing, and storing data are all negotiated in terms of a research project, and in terms of community expectations. When data are good, they can be useful to other researchers, policy makers, and citizens who are making evidence-based decisions. In the chapter, the 2011 Fukushima Daiichi disaster sets the stage for a story of how radiation contamination data suddenly became a topic of public conversation. Illustrating the complexity of data collection, the science of radiation, public education, and the tensions between government agencies and corporate entities, the case of the Fukushima Daiichi disaster is dramatic but not atypical. The chapter explores how an obscure subject area sequestered to the innermost circles of scientists (with imposing titles such as "nuclear scientist," no less) became a public conversation, and illustrates how data function rhetorically and how data sets function as a rhetorical tool for both scientists and citizens. And, when researchers and governments failed to produce these data, citizens began to compile their database. The chapter examines one of the most powerful citizen groups that emerged: Safecast, an organization that continues their work today, long after media around the world have lost interest in the ongoing disaster that unfolds in Japan. Investigating the significance of data for civic purposes, and how civically minded scientists and citizen scientists collect and put these data to work, the chapter explores the importance of this seemingly obscure form. For publics and citizen scientists collecting data, the effort to justify their methods and samples is increasingly essential, and the rhetorical work of scientists to explain and justify data must be understood to help articulate where communication breaks down between scientists, publics, and policy makers.

In Chapter 4, blogging provides a well-established case to illustrate how new opportunities to communicate with new audiences online unfold. It is unsurprising that scientists and science communicators have harnessed these affordances given the now long life of the platforms, relative to other social sharing technologies. Exploring the media ecologies in which blogging occurs, this chapter investigates the technologies that facilitate these ecologies by way of a case study of the Public Library of Science (PLOS) blogging network, a large collection of science-focused blogs written by scientists, graduate students, science journalists, and even citizen scientists. Breaking down the barriers between internal genres of science communication and public genres of science communication in powerful ways, these blogs have a vast and varied audience including scientists and publics. The uptake of blog posts among popular audiences underscores how science can be popularized using a new technology. However, blogs also serve to chart insider debate and new findings, and thus they operate outside the internal and external divisions of science communication. They offer insight into the challenging *process* of science—the debates among scientists and the characters, acts, and dramas that unfold in the theater of science. Rich, and highly rhetorical, blogs are an especially interesting site where scientists, citizen scientists, civically minded scientists, citizens, and everyone in the gradients between can communicate with one another, casting off the broadcast model of popular science genres.

The concluding chapter takes the theoretical implications and practical lessons learned about communicating with these new genres to offer insights about the rhetorical life of online genres of science communication. Audience is perhaps the most crucial element to consider in characterizing trans-scientific genres. Both the genre producers and users govern trans-scientific genres. This means that the genres we have considered here are necessarily in a liminal space between internal genres of science communication and external genres of science popularization because they are composed by and for scientists and nonscientists. But the heterogeneous audience is notable for more than its composition. In its heterogeneity, the audience has driven rhetorical conversations among blog authors, in scholarly journals, and in discussions about popularizing science. These rhetorical conversations are characterized by a rejection of the deficit model of thinking, which has plagued science communication. Science communicators and scientists trying to communicate their science talk about the value of thinking about one's audience and, significantly, engaging that audience. With new genres come new opportunities, but to effectively use these genres, communicators must contend with rapid genre change.

Overall, the book explores how we make sense of science that is presented to us online. Scientific information is immersed in an ecology and cultural moment where we are challenged by "post-truth" (once plainly called lies), "alternative facts" (once plainly identified as propaganda), and "fake news" (which Lakoff astutely explains is a dangerous modifier as it subverts the basic function of news—that is, to be *not* fake[6]). Online, we are inundated with

---

6. Qtd. in Kurtzleben, 2017.

information and claims about that information's validity and the credibility of the source. PEW found that 64 percent of American adults believe "fabricated news stories cause a great deal of confusion about the basic facts of current issues and events" (although 39 percent believe *they* are capable of spotting the fake stories), while 23 percent of respondents admit to sharing fake news (Pew Research Center, Barthel, Mitchell, & Holcomb, 2016). The stakes are high for science. Science communication has had an abiding commitment to factual information, truthful representation of established information as we generate new knowledge, and cautious and credible reporting of new knowledge for centuries. But moving into these emerging online environments, science communication leaves behind the safety of cloistered communities where trust and credibility[7] can be carefully measured and evaluated to enter the tumultuous and often-vituperative discourse communities of the web.

Science has long faced those deceivers who wish to undermine science for their own political gains, the deceivers using what Ceccarelli (2011) calls "manufactured controversy," and sometimes disguising their claims with pseudoscience. Together, scientists and science communicators face formidable political, cultural, and online social environments where they must work to establish not only facts but also credibility and trust so that they and their audiences are able to engage in discourse and debate with goodwill. Ultimately what I argue is that the large discourse community[8] composed of scientists—professional to civic to citizen, and science enthusiasts—helps us understand the complex rhetorical world of not only communicating science online, but communicating truthfully, factually, and credibly.[9] Genres create and are cre-

---

7. The majority of the American public does have confidence that scientists will act in the best interests of the public (Pew Research Center & Kennedy, 2016).

8. Porter (1986) offers a useful definition of *"discourse community"* as a "group of individuals bound by a common interest who communicate through approved channels and whose discourse is regulated. An individual may belong to several professional, public, or personal discourse communities" (pp. 38–39). Killingsworth (1992) provides a reminder to remain critical about the term, particularly owing to the positive valance that "community" tends to carry.

9. Indeed, I am calling upon an old refrain. Aristotle gave us the groundwork in his account of rhetoric as "the available means of persuasion," and specific to the matters of science, rhetoricians of science have considered the importance of trust (Gross, 1994; Miller, 2003), as have other science studies scholars (Wynne, 2006; Brunk, 2006). Trust in a speaker is central, Gross (1994) reminds us, writing, "Because the public must trust those who are trying to persuade them, central to all situated utterances is a speaker who evokes appropriate emotions and endorses appropriate values, a speaker in whose virtue, good will, and good sense the public has confidence" (p. 4). What if the source (not just the speaker) isn't trusted? Only 4 percent of online Americans say they have a lot of trust in information from social media (not that local or national news fares well, either, receiving trust ratings of 22 percent and 18 percent, respectively) (Pew Research Center, Mitchell, Gottfried, Barthel, & Shearer, 2016, p. 8). An interesting aside, however, is that 63 percent of respondents, when asked, "How closely do you follow each

ated by conventions, norms, values, and recurrent rhetorical situations with typified responses from a discourse community. Exploring new kinds of science communication helps explicate both rhetorical and technological tools that help shape discourses, even those infused with the toughest forms of argument. As new forms of science communication emerge online, the processes of creating, replicating, or modifying discourse norms are at work, but the rapid evolution of these recognizable forms has much to teach us about theories of genre and genre change.

---

type of news, either in the newspaper, on television, radio, or the internet?" reported they follow "Science and technology" very closely (16 percent) or somewhat closely (47 percent) (Pew Research Center, Mitchell, et al., 2016, p. 30).

CHAPTER 1

Theory and Method

Genre Studies and Rhetorical Criticism

IN THIS CHAPTER, the fields of genre sudies and rhetorical studies of science are brought together to establish a theoretical and methodological framework to investigate emerging forms of online science communication. First, a brief introduction to genre studies is provided for those who may be unfamiliar with the field or its more recent developments. Next, I provide a brief account of how genres of science communication have been shaped by the professionalization of science. The interplay of science communication and the organizational networks of science and institutions that form the basis for contemporary "big" science illustrate how the evolution of genres is shaped by their contexts and how genre users understand those contexts. While technology is thoroughly implicated in these developments, the interaction of genre and media forms is taken up more specifically in the next section. Treating questions of media, and new media in particular, in its own right is important because genre theorists have struggled with the implications of new media environments on genre evolution and change. Finally, I explore the theoretical underpinnings of what I call "trans-scientific genres," providing a framework for understanding those new and evolving genres of science communication online that this book investigates. The chapter concludes with the approach and methods used to test this framework. Notably, the challenges posed by case study–based research in rhetorical studies are addressed, along with a discussion of how a rhetorical approach is blended with small corpus analysis techniques from genre studies.

INTRODUCTION TO GENRE THEORY

Rhetorical genre studies[1] provide a useful set of theories to investigate how different text[2] types—genres—are used in science communication by exploring how readers and writers understand and employ those text types. Theories of genre in the rhetorical tradition can be traced back to Aristotle, who gave us three rhetorical genres: forensic (evaluating what happened), deliberative (deciding what should happen), and epideictic (celebrating what happened) discourse. Since antiquity, theories of genre, similar to genres themselves, have proliferated to include an expansive range of text types and fields of study. In scholarly research, a number of fields have used the term *genre* to characterize discourse patterns, including film studies, television studies, library sciences, computer science, literary studies, linguistics, and rhetoric. Early conceptualizations of genre can be traced to formalist approaches concerned with classical categorization and features of a text that represent a certain type (*genre*). For example, tragedy and comedy would be distinguished as different genres; or, in a more consumer-based reading, fantasy and science fiction would be distinguished as distinct genres. A dramatic turn in the mid- to late twentieth century saw formalist conceptions challenged with pragmatic approaches (Miller and Kelly, 2016), and rhetorical genre studies have followed this latter orientation.

Much of the work in contemporary rhetorical genre studies can trace its roots to Carolyn R. Miller's 1984 article "Genre as Social Action," which offers a pragmatic orientation and social theory of genre where communities of users create, refine, and reuse types of text for specific purposes. Miller tells us genres can be understood as "typified rhetorical actions based in recurrent situations" (p. 159). I have come to see genre as a conceptual framework that

---

1. For an introduction to the different traditions of genre studies, including rhetorical genre studies, please visit Genre Across Borders (http://genreacrossborders.org/). Original research introductions are commissioned for the various traditions of genre theory, translated into multiple languages, and an accompanying glossary provides an overview of key terms. See also Hyon (1996) and Miller and Kelly (2016).

2. *Text* in this sense means something broader than written text. Drawing on the semiotic tradition of *text* as utterances across a variety of modalities, we can think of text here as purposeful semiotic objects or events. "Discursive event" (Freadman, 2012), noted below, is a useful elaboration as it draws attention to the performance of discourse.

allows members of a community to interpret a given discursive event[3] through its preceding and immediate worlds—including sociocultural, material, and media contexts—and to see how that discursive event inhabits and attempts to modify the ongoing trajectory of typification.[4] Put another way, what does the immediate situation tell one about how to interpret the text? And what longer-term information can we deliberate upon or infer about this form or type of text? Understanding genre as this kind of conceptual framework illustrates how genre shapes and structures meaning by highlighting particular values, constraining expressive possibilities, and encouraging particular actions.[5] People's ability to participate in the genre, however, is dependent upon their interpretation of the situation and the possible responses they may have. As Auken (2015) writes, the "process of genre identification . . . has a strong regulative influence on how we interpret a given utterance" (p. 158). The regulative function of genre does not only apply to professional discourses.

Andersen (2017) writes:

> Genre is a particular way of seeing and understanding regularized communicative activities performed by people, and of understanding how people make sense of communicative activities in daily interactions. For this reason, I will be arguing that genre can be used as a theoretical framework to position the organization of knowledge as a communicative activity in everyday life.

He specifically considers the role of these regulative functions with respect to digital media. "Digital media," he tells us, "play rather different social and cultural roles than traditional mass media because our social and cultural institutions produce information through digital media and use digital media to communicate and structure information." For Andersen, genres in these spaces look rather different than conventional understanding of what constitutes a genre. He argues that "genres of these forms of communication are, among others, searching, arranging, friending, liking, sharing, archiving, ordering, tagging, and listing," and argues that "to google, to tag, or to like are not only verbs, they are genres." Although this understanding of genre may

---

3. A "discursive event" is described by Freadman (2012), and she advances the term as an alternative to "text" or "utterance" in genre theory.

4. Or, in Freadman's (2012) words, "generic nature of the interchange is modified by its own conduct" (p. 558).

5. An earlier version of this definition was published in Kelly (2016), but its origins are greatly indebted to Catherine F. Schryer, who introduced me to genre theory and encouraged a kind of precision in terms that becomes a necessity when working in an interdisciplinary field with many thriving traditions.

be somewhat contentious, it is likely because these forms are not wholly conventionalized by the features genre scholars are familiar with. Yet, these are the genres we deploy every day online in our lives as students, professionals, or private citizens. This expansive understanding of genre is helpful because it provides a framework to consider pedagogical questions. In the case of the genres explored in this book, the networked nature of these activities is crucial to a comprehensive understanding of genre.

As the last few sentences suggest, my account is grounded in the rhetorical tradition, where there is a strong pragmatic attunement to pedagogy. Freadman (2012) positions the commitment of the rhetorical tradition to a pedagogical mission, saying that "the pedagogical question of a rhetorical account of genre is how to bring a student to take her or his place in this history—to discover how something has been done before, and how it can be adapted to particular needs as occasions arise" (p. 547). Accordingly, the impulse to group genre activity into particular, well-defined genres serves instructional ends rather than an ontological function (see Freadman, 2012, p. 550). Otherwise, the practice of categorizing and then describing genres is a fraught mission in new media environments as change occurs rapidly and efforts to capture the "emergence" of a genre risk overstating claims. Freadman also reminds us, in a Derridean tradition, that the tension between recurrence and contingency obscures that "the 'same,' repeated on different occasions, does not remain the same" (Freadman, 2012, p. 557). Extending and advocating for such a position, Bawarshi (2016) writes that we might consider "genre difference not as a deviation from a patterned or recurrent norm, but rather as the norm of all genre performance" (p. 244). This orientation allows us to move our attention to temporal aspects of genre performance, a much-needed lens when moderating genre membership claims. Devitt (2015) suggests that combining rhetorical and linguistic approaches is valuable, allowing us to attend to both the "competence and performance" of genres, which in turn can help us explain how "genres construct writers and writers construct genres" (p. 50).

Following these trajectories in genre studies, I refrain from labeling genres and instead focus on "genre-ing activities"[6] to understand the interplay between recurrence and variation, competence and performance, and the evolution of genres. Much of what is discussed in later chapters will further illustrate the usefulness of this lens of genre-ing activity rather than genres as such. The relative newness of these online forms of science communication necessitates attuning ourselves to their instability. Despite such instability,

---

6. Sometimes genre researchers refer to "genred" discourse, but I wish to emphasize here the unfolding nature of these activities—hence, genre-ing.

however, it remains useful to describe these genre-ing activities for both theoretical and pedagogical ends. From a theoretical perspective, web-based new media environments have continually raised questions in genre theory where genre and media form are closely intertwined. Pedagogically, it is valuable to explain the kinds of writing that our students may engage. For example, as the Department of English Language and Literature and the Department of Drama and Speech Communication launch communication courses for all first-year students in the Faculty of Science at the University of Waterloo, the possibilities for science communication courses seem all the more promising from my vantage. By attending to the genre-ing activity in online, evolving forms of science communication, we do not need to identify what is "the same" but rather the similarities that reveal the recurrence and typification that show us how to respond with the contingencies that likewise situate our response.

Nevertheless, identifying criteria that mark genres allows for the characterization of recurrent situations and responses to those situations. Miller (1984) argues that to achieve membership in a genre is contingent upon "discourses that are complete, in the sense that they are circumscribed by a relatively complete shift in rhetorical situation" (p. 159). A shift in rhetorical situation is important to the forms of communication considered in this book, notably because in many cases these texts defy typification and recurrence as often formulated in approaches to genre. Scientific articles evolved over centuries, but blogs, for instance, burst onto the scene of genre studies and promptly generated a fury of debate about their status as a genre.

Although genre scholarship reaches across a range of disciplines and traditions, some commonalities have shaped much of this research, namely the sites of study for genre research. Genre researchers have explored a number of institutional and professional genres.[7] For genre researchers, the shift from studying professional communities, where genres are "stabilized-for-now or stabilized enough sites of social and ideological action" (Schryer, 1993, p. 204), to studying vernacular discourse, where genres rapidly evolve[8] in response

---

7. The systemic functional linguistics tradition has considerable scholarship focused on classroom genres, for example. In the rhetorical genre tradition, significant attention has been paid to professional genres (e.g., Yates, 1989; Yates & Orlikowski, 1992; Bhatia, 1993; Orlikowski & Yates, 1994; Schryer, 1993, 1994, 2000; Zachry, 2000; Smart, 2003; Spinuzzi, 2003b, 2003a, 2008; Swarts, 2006).

8. In our edited volume *Emerging Genres in New Media Environments,* Miller considers metaphors of genre evolution. Although the metaphor of evolution is widely used in genre studies, Miller notes there have been objections to the metaphor as it naturalizes the emergence, life, and possibly death of genres, including Applegarth's (2017) account of early anthropology, where early expressive forms allowed greater variation in knowledge-making practices by marginalized scholars. An evolutionary model, in these accounts, certainly fails to account for forms of structural oppression that shape not only genre users, but the genres we use.

to changing social and ideological actions across public spheres, is challenging. Indeed, Bhatia (1996) writes, "Non-literary genre analysis is the study of situated linguistic behaviour in *institutionalized academic* or *professional* settings" (p. 40; emphasis added). Recently, Reiff and Bawarshi (2016) challenged this preoccupation with professional sites of discourse in their edited volume *Genre and the Performance of Publics.* Attention to professional genres, at the expense of vernacular genres,[9] is troublesome because the activity systems in which genres are produced and reproduced remain relatively stable, which obscures the dynamism of genres. Reiff and Bawarshi advocate for a fundamental shift in our attention by attending to vernacular genres, which illustrate more variation in performance and evolution than in the bounded organizational settings examined (Reiff & Bawarshi, 2016, p. 4). In this book, I take up those genres that exist somewhere on the continuum between genres used by professional scientists and what we might call public or vernacular genres.

When exploring science communications, this seemingly neat distinction between professional or internal genres of science communication and vernacular or external genres of science communication is immediately complicated by genres that inhabit more liminal spaces (Taylor, 1991; Gieryn, 1999, 1983), such as the pages of popular science or trade magazines (Kaplan & Radin, 2011) or interdisciplinary writings (Ceccarelli, 2001). Excluding popular science magazines, these examples remain in academic and institutional contexts. However, there are also innumerable "meta-genres" (Giltrow, 2002), including explicit instructions or tacit acquired knowledge about how to use genres that move our publics through to experts, or at least scientifically literate publics. Now genre users must contend with the web, which provides different venues for communication. Rhetoricians of science have begun to chart these new modes of communication by looking at blogs (Sidler, 2016), podcasts (Wardlaw, 2016), comics (White, 2017), visualizations (Kostelnick & Kostelnick, 2016), and so on. Before investigating genres that exist somewhere between internal and external genres of science communication, it is useful to first explore how such distinctions arise. In the next section, the professionalization of science and the evolution of scientific communications are briefly summarized. It is important to chart the developments in science communication because it is easy to slide into a metaphor of revolution when talking about the web (Buehl, 2016). Trans-scientific genres provide a measured account of genre evolution, outside of the professional or institu-

---

9. Miller (2017) uses the term "vernacular genre" to describe "situations where users have few institutional or administrative constraints and can collectively create a way of addressing a shared exigence" (p. 24); we can also call these "public" genres, although the plurality of publics makes "vernacular" a more accurate descriptor.

tional setting that Reiff and Bawarshi (2016) identify as stabilizing elements, but still within the orbit of those stabilizing forces. Although technological change has been chartered in professional settings, what this might tell us more broadly should be met with a rather critical eye. Because of the pushmi-pullyu dynamic (Miller, 2012) in professional—corporate, business, clinical, or academic—settings, we are always given a view of technological change and genre evolution measured by sensibilities oriented toward tradition. Vernacular genres, or those genres existing somewhere on the continuum between professional and vernacular—what I call trans-scientific, for example—offer something of a different case.

AN EVOLUTIONARY TALE FOR SCIENCE COMMUNICATION

In this section, I examine the situated, material worlds as well as socioeconomic realities that shape genre use and change. Such factors provide background for understanding how a long process of professionalization has shaped scientific genres.[10] Understanding genres of science communication requires that we know something about how the communities doing the communicating are organized. For Western science, Woolgar (1988) suggests three general phases of social organization that govern science: first, there were the amateurs, and then came the academics, and finally the professionals. Amateur scientists arose somewhere around 1600 and began to dissipate around 1800, with the rise of the academic scientists. During this initial period of social organization, scientific research was not conducted in university or government research labs, but rather in the homes of gentlemen. Early scientists were financially independent and secured the resources to support their scientific research by other professional engagements. These amateur scientists began to write one another, exchanging letters about their research, thus establishing the origins of the scientific article. Here, we can identify some of the preconditions for genre development. Interest in scientific research and findings was a shared social exigence that led a group of otherwise disparate researchers to communicate. There were likely strong connections among those who were wealthy enough to engage in research during this time, and perhaps these established networks facilitated the networks among amateur scientists specifically. This model has important lessons that can be applied

---

10. This is a particular kind of tale, one that excludes genres that typically feature less prominently in the stories we tell about science communication. Although the account in this book traces common genres, this account is not comprehensive. For interesting and rich accounts of other genres of science communication, see Jack (2009) and Applegarth (2014).

to the study of how crowdfunding may work, showing not only the shape of those communications but also the economic conditions within which they arise and perpetuate. When we examine scientific genres, we are never looking at them in isolation of the community of practice, nor can we examine them without concern for the broader social, cultural, and economic conditions that also shape the genres scientists use. Indeed, the economic and social conditions leading to the growth of amateur scientists are also requisites for the development of novel genres of communication. Kronick (1976) traces the origins of the scientific periodical as developing alongside the amateur scientist. It follows that genres of science communication can develop only when an audience for the genre exists, and such an audience for specialized scientific genres was found when the economic and social conditions of the Middle Ages gave way to the fifteenth and sixteenth centuries' expanded leisure class (Kronick, 1976, pp. 34–35). This audience had also been prepared by the technological revolution that gave way to inexpensive print such as broadsides, pamphlets, and books (Kronick, 1976, p. 35), as well as antecedent genres (Jamieson, 1975) that would lead to the evolution of the journal article (see Bazerman, 1988; Berkenkotter & Huckin, 1995; Gross, Harmon, & Reidy, 2002).

Following the early development of an amateur communication, Woolgar (1988) characterizes an academic phase (1800–1940) of scientific communities that required extensive specialized training (pp. 19–20). Woolgar's sociological account reminds us that the structuring of universities along with the self-direction of the scientific research community would come to shape much of the research that took place in academic research institutions. As the institutions established themselves, and as researchers and research focus clustered around particular disciplines, scientists' roles in communities of practice began to solidify. Scientists were now responsible not only for their own work but also for the training of junior scientists to help enculturate them into communities (Woolgar, 1988, p. 20). Gross, Harmon, and Reidy (2002) elaborate on this change, arguing that the "hyperspecialization and global professionalization of science" in the twentieth century "spawned a truly international network of authors, readers, publishers, and editors," creating and supporting an apparatus for scholarly publishing as we know it today (p. 161).

Just what is that kind of scholarly publishing we know? The kind, as Gross et al. (2002) suggest, that supports "a discourse community for whom terms such as 'renormalization,' 'Fissurellidae,' 'paratolylsulfonylmethylnitrosamide,' and 'mRNA' can appear without definitions, and mathematical equations without apologies" (p. 161). Gross et al. provide a bridge for Woolgar's chronology to professional science, where not only hyperspecialization took place but also the formation of institutions and organizations that began to legislate, to borrow from Gross et al., the style and form of scientific communications. Scientific subject matter also became increasingly complex, while methods of communicating that complex subject matter became concise and clear—clear to our hyperspecialized scientists, anyway—near the middle of the last century (see also Bruss, Albers, & McNamera, 2004). Gross, Harmon, and Reidy (2002) also argue there has been a marked increase in the use of visuals in scientific articles, so much so, in fact, that they argue of their sample that "very few statements regarding new facts of explanations are made in the absence of visual evidence" (p. 201). In combination with hyperspecialized language, we can see the evolution of the research community through shared modes of linguistic and visual representations, along with an evolution in technologies that afford increasing use of visual forms, which we will learn has been a continued development with online communications. It is useful, at this point, for a short digression from our historical account to consider visual forms, before returning in a few paragraphs to the evolution of the research article itself.

Lynch's (2005) account of how visuals participate in the production of scientific knowledge offers an helpful framework for understanding how visuals are integrated into science communications: "Rather than being a discrete, well-bounded aspect of science," he posits, "visualization is inter-twined with observational and experimental practices, literary representations, [and] methods for disseminating scientific results" (p. 27). Visuals are indeed intertwined in observation, experiment, and the evolution of science as we know it—particularly as we move into the early modern period (see, for example, Lefèvre, Renn, & Schoepflin, 2003; Acheson, 2013). Visuals and visualizations have continued to be crucial to the scientific enterprise in modernity, so much so that an entire field of study called scientific visualization is concerned with advancing the visualization of scientific information and data. How visuals are used across fields varies, but strong evidence exists that, as Arsenault, Smith, and Beauchamp (2006) suggest, the "making of visual displays is of the very essence of science" (p. 423).

Visuals in online texts raise interesting questions about their situatedness—within different contexts and genres, and even different media forms. B. Mehlenbacher (2010), when looking at the use of visual models in educational studies, sums up the general notion, writing that "all the visuals displayed in a given research article are designed with a particular audience, purpose, and rhetorical situation in mind" (p. 137). So, the context for creation is essential, and the person or persons creating the visual likely have an idea for its use, purpose, and audience. Here we have a Bitzerian rhetorical situation, and the rhetorical artifact generated in response will operate under rather constrained conditions, namely the highly stabilized situation of a scholarly research article (Bitzer, 1968).

Gigante (2012), however, reminds us how the visual may change as it moves into new contexts. A visual used in a professional journal, for example, might serve a notably different purpose as it moves from one context to another, from a professional to a public audience. For example, Gigante illustrates how the U.S. National Science Foundation (NSF) International Science and Engineering Visualization Challenge encourages the production of visuals to better communicate science to the public and, even more ambitiously, to educate the public. However, Gigante's investigation concludes that without the appropriate accommodations for a public audience, visuals rather serve to engage rather than educate—and the distinction between engaged and educated is of great importance here. Gigante's work supports Fahnestock's (1986) argument that when scientific arguments move from internal to external genres, they undergo a genre shift from forensic (concerned with validation) or perhaps even deliberative (concerned with a course of action) to an epideictic or celebratory genre. Thus, Fahnestock suggests, the popular or epideictic modes tend to situate an argument as an appeal to the wonder of science or perhaps to the application of science.

Myers (1997) suggests the same problem for genres when he considers the use of visuals in textbooks, noting that a "scientific claim develops from the weakened, contingent form of its first statement and debate around it to the unmodified certainties of fact, or it gets pushed back to being a mere claim once made by someone" (p. 101). He provides us with an example of what he means, writing "from article to textbook, we move from pictures that demonstrate (providing evidence), to pictures that illustrate (showing, summarizing, defining)" (p. 101). Myers (2003) later reminds us that the question of popularizing is much more complicated than a good deal of research on the topic of "science popularizations" has suggested, and that distinctions between expert and "lay" or professional and nonprofessional audiences is a product of boundary work, a concept described by Gieryn (1983).

Visuals are created and flow within a discursive ecology, and when we examine them as a genred activity, we can learn something about the interplay of media constraint, genre affordance, and the evolving situation a particular visual might inhabit. Crucially, we do not want to imagine the visuals, or any rhetorical artifact, as a static event. As Schryer (1993) argues, genres can be understood as "stabilized-for-now," thus allowing observers to identify and investigate discursive practices, but also to remain sensitive to the requirement of historical formulation and the possibilities of future evolution. Changes can occur in a number of ways and are influenced by historical, social, and material realities of production (see, for further discussion, Jamieson, 1975; Yates, 1989). Genre change might occur through the evolution of formal features (for example, arrangement of text), through transformations in social practice (for example, who is able to invoke and use a genre), through media change (for example, a new medium where a genre is invoked), or even through relational change (for example, the introduction of new genres into a genre system, set, or ecology).

Gries's (2015) articulation of rhetoric is a useful way to describe genre change in rhetorical terms. She writes, "rhetoric, especially in a digitally mediated environment, is more like an unfolding event," and further asserts that the circulation of rhetorical artifacts is dependent upon more than the rhetorician and their craft (pp. 7, 285). Changes to the media environments in which visuals are produced and dwell require an attunement to both rhetorical possibilities and ethical positions (Reeves, 2011; Buehl, 2014). As the media environments for production and dissemination change, pedagogical work must be done to discuss not only how we create knowledge through visual forms but also how we do so ethically. Further, as we release visuals into complex, digitally mediated rhetorical ecosystems, we ought to consider what might come of them in their unfoldings. That is, we should explore what responsibilities we have to those artifacts we create and what they become as they evolve.

Gross and Harmon (2014) likewise turn their attention to the future of scientific visuals, stating, "the Internet has reinvented the scientific article and related communications," thus affording new possibilities to integrate written and visual communications (p. 267). Genre scholars, too, are beginning to theorize the role of visuals. Miller and Fahnestock (2013), recounting a workshop discussion about genre theory, raise the question of whether or not we can talk about visual representations as visual genres, observing that "visual genres may be entirely dependent on a particular medium in a way that verbal genres are not—as in the news photo, political cartoon, children's book illustration, etc. This issue raised the more general question of what the difference is between an affordance or medium or mode of communication and a genre" (p. 3).

Visuals offer important lessons about mediated space where remediations are common. If we understand a particular visual as an instantiation of genreing activity, then we can talk about conventions, communities of practice, and expectations in rhetorical terms to learn how forms travel from one context to another, from one mediated space to another. We can then ask what changes take place and what the overall changes mean to the rhetorical function of the genre-ing activity. This approach to genre offers a way of thinking about how genre-ing activities travel across online media ecologies while retaining some aspect of form or content and while also transforming (sometimes into new genres) along the way. Such questions recur as we examine crowdfunding proposals that share videos or even text as they are distributed across social networks, or blogs that embed studies or link to data while themselves being excerpted and shared online, and indeed the data and coordinating genres that encapsulate data online—issues discussed later in the book. Before exploring online genres in depth, it is useful to return to the historical account of written forms of science communication.

As the Second World War unfolded, advances in science and technology became increasingly central features for war efforts, and science became increasingly complex. Becoming *big* meant more than a quantitative change; it was also a qualitative change in the social composition of science. Woolgar (1988) suggests this change in scientific research since 1940 can be characterized as a kind of science that was "more professional than academic" (p. 120). "Professional" here does not imply that the research academics undertake is not *professional* or undertaken by *professionalized* researchers. Rather, this indicates a shift within the economic structures that support research, namely to federal and then industry funding. Woolgar writes that "scientific research has now become so expensive, especially in terms of capital investment, that only centrally located government funds can support it" (p. 120). We will return to this tension in the next chapter when considering alternative funding models in science. This shift marks the reliance of big science on federal funding for a long period, the slow erosion of that funding, and an increase in reliance over time on corporate sponsorship. It is because of this percentage decrease in federal support, and the related increase in corporate sponsorship, that scientific research is increasingly "adjudged in terms of its value for economic prosperity and security" (Woolgar, 1988, p. 120). Kinsella (2005) helps us to understand the shift in science as one of institutionalization, where all these economic preconditions and the associated social organization results in what we often think of as "big science."

Through the study of the research article, we can chart these changes to the scientific enterprise, as the work of Gross, Harmon, and Reidy (2002) demonstrates. Today, evidence of the institutionalization of science persists in the seeming lack of evolution of the online research article genre. Mackenzie Owen (2006) suggests there has been little change to the research article genre, despite the affordances of the web. A decade after Mackenzie Owen's work, change has been slow, but it has been occurring. Harmon (2016) and Gross and Harmon (2016) note there has been some evolution of the research article, including the increasing use of visuals and a complex apparatus allowing research articles to be commented on and hyperlinked within and outside of the article. However, institutional norms regarding publishing and promotion play a role in constraining possibilities for the research article, even with the affordances of the web. While we might expect to see changes driven by technology, the socialization of scientists and the institutional organization of universities slow the pace of developments in the genre. Rather, internal concerns about that process of knowledge production, the role of genres in producing aspects of that process, and institutional norms seem to be driving the most significant change.[11] For example, granting agencies are increasingly requiring that data be shared openly—even requiring that articles be published in open-access repositories. Junior scholars lament the reluctance of established journals in their fields to adopt open-access policies, and in the psychological sciences concerns about replication are giving rise to new forms of preregistered studies (see, for example, Chambers, Dienes, McIntosh, Rotshtein, & Willmes, 2015).

A product of research communities, the development of predecessors to the internet and web were essential to the future of science. Research sharing across networks and inter-networked flows were necessary for both communication redundancy and for extending communicative possibilities. In contemporary imaginings, digital networks are most readily apparent through the web as "social network" technologies—popular social media sites such as Facebook and Twitter or more specialized social networking sites such as ResearchGate.net or Academia.edu. One especially notable function of these sites is the ability to share research articles. Proliferation of these web-based tools has since had a dramatic impact on just who has a stake in sharing the findings of science. The technological functionality is apart from legal considerations regarding copyright and redistribution of scholarly works. Indeed, these sites do not restrict the uploading and sharing of material under copyright, but rather leave such obligations up to users and, presumably, publishers

---

11. Although there is a certain amount of stabilization in the research article genre, Swales (2004) reminds us that "small science" remains an active enterprise, and in small science journals, there is considerably more variation. Small science and more local publication venues (for example, Swales cites *Michigan Birds and Natural History*) are important because they may be the "first attempt at publication" for researchers (p. 217). Pedagogical lessons derived from these kinds of experiential learning opportunities are can be used for genre learning, and the genre-ing activities discussed in the following chapters, including proposal writing and blogging, likewise offer opportunities for the application of genre learning.

to monitor. Behind this idea of sharing is that researchers should be publishing the results of their work immediately online for a global audience. Academia.edu (2014), for example, writes, "Academia.edu wants to build a completely new system for scientists to share their results, one that is totally independent of the current journal system." But their vision is more than open access to research articles;[12] instead, Academia.edu (2014) believes "peer review should be done post-publication, and it should be done by the community, Reddit-style,[13] not by just two or three people." Similarly, ResearchGate (2014) announces, "We believe science should be open and transparent. This is why we've made it our mission to connect researchers and make it easy for them to share, discover, use, and distribute findings. We help researchers voice feedback and build reputation through open discussion and evaluation of each other's research." Despite these aspirations, and some generation of content through question-and-answer forums, these sites serve to redistribute established genres of science communication, namely research articles, conference proceedings, and abstracts.

Also worth noting, particularly as we look to online platforms (and the businesses that establish them) for science, economies have always been as important to the business of science as knowledge economies in terms of the former supporting the latter, but these relationships merit continued attention. When I said previously there is an emerging market for social network sites concerned with science, I intentionally framed the issue in economic terms. As with many social networking sites, for-profit companies drive these enterprises, which may be concerning as these for-profit companies are benefiting from efforts to democratize academic research, and their values may not align with the values driving such democratizing efforts (Ortega, 2016).

---

12. On the matter of open-access publication, placing research articles in a system outside of the current academic journal system is likely to raise problems for the credibility of publications. Already the "predatory journals" identified on Jeffrey Beall's now defunct "Beall's List" (2012–2017) engaged in unclear processes of peer review. Without a clear model of review, with an expert audience, it is unlikely that academic departments would take seriously articles produced and shared through social networking sites. Although there is certainly resistance to cost-prohibitive journals, particularly as budgets tighten and limit resources for faculty to perform their duties, these journals nevertheless have useful systems in place. Chiefly these rely on the credibility and trust of the journal, as established by its editor, editorial board, reviewers, and history of publishing timely and topical articles in, most often, a disciplinary framework. Even what we might call generalist journals tend to be constrained to disciplines we would find within the same department, such as, to use a humanities and social sciences example, rhetoricians and organizational communication scholars in communication departments.

13. Reddit.com is a news and entertainment aggregation service and social network site that allows users to share and comment on various kinds of materials, from news articles to personal pictures and videos. The open comment and criticism that could function to vet work is presumably the "Reddit-style" post-publication review that is referenced here.

Exceptions exist, including blog networks from the Public Library of Science, but the market within which many social networking sites participate is found equally in niche social networks for scientific research. As scientific research engages in these spaces, it will be essential to ask questions about the modes of production that are being engaged.[14]

GENRES IN NEW MEDIA ENVIRONMENTS

Tracing the term "blog" can help us understand the complex relationship between media and genre. The Pew Research Center's World Wide Web Timeline shows that the first use of "weblog" online was by Jorn Barger in 1997, who used the term to describe a list of website URLs on his personal website (Pew Research Center, 2014). While Barger coined the term, later shortened to "blog," a novel discourse activity was occurring more broadly. Genre studies have provided a number of insightful accounts investigating how blogs evolved into a popular discourse type. Because genres are marked by stabilization and typification, exploring new discursive spaces with the concept of genre can be tricky. However, the concept allows us to talk about some key ideas, including the values of a community and the kinds of knowledge that are incorporated and privileged within that community. As an analytical tool, then, genre is a useful but also challenging approach in new media environments because if genre marks stabilization of discourse, less stabilized genres such as those emerging online require some measure of caution.

The birth of blogs in the late 1990s generated significant interest among genre scholars as they attempted to characterize web-originated and web-based genres (see, for example, McNeill, 2003; Herring, Scheidt, Bonus, & Wright, 2004, 2005; Miller & Shepherd, 2004, 2009; Herring & Paolillo, 2006; Grafton & Maurer, 2007; Giltrow & Stein, 2009; Morrison, 2010, 2011; Garzone, 2012; Sokół, 2012). While genre studies investigated the blog as a genre, some questions persisted about whether blogs could be described as a genre in the first place. Two articles that address this question come from Miller and Shepherd who initially attempt to describe the cultural space under which the apparent genre of the blog developed and the rhetorical exigencies to which

---

14. Beer (2008), following Thrift (2005), notes how consumers and producers are conflated in social network spheres and how the nature of commodities changes. Scientific research is increasingly engaged in co-production between consumers and producers, so to speak, in crowdfunding and even in crowdsourcing and citizen science. These changes also mark changes in labor markets and should be held in mind while we examine the genres produced within social network sites.

blog authors responded in their (2004) "Blogging as Social Action." Miller and Shepherd's (2009) follow-up article partially attempts to understand the seeming "category error" the authors made in describing the blog as a genre, and not as a technology. Blogs, they write, appear to have "speciated," in the years since their original study, from the personal journal-like blog to journalism blogs, photo blogs, and so on. Writing that the blog is not a genre but a technology, Miller and Shepherd argue that "genre and the medium, the social action and its instrumentality, fit so well that they seemed coterminous, and it was thus easy to mistake the one for the other," as they presume they did (p. 263). Miller and Shepherd's work, as they acknowledge, underscores the problem of web-based genres. The rapid proliferation of technologies and purposes for communication create a difficult space to theorize about genre and its relationship to technology yet provides a space that demands attention. How can one understand the distinctions between technologies, technological affordances, and genres (or rhetorical motivation and action)? While Miller and Shepherd's important work begins to address questions of genre change and relationship of genre to technology, their characterization of the blog as a technology is also problematic because it simplifies the technologies employed to create blogs, diminishes the importance of typified responses to recurrent situations, and turns away from focus on the social actions "the blog" serves. Yet, their characterization of the blog as a technology is consistent with others.

boyd[15] (2006) raises questions about the definition of genre being applied to blogs, writing that "medium" is a more suitable characterization—although, as I will argue below, this is a rather significant simplification. Many researchers, boyd writes, rely on "structural definitions," and these kinds of descriptions "frame blogs as a genre that can be analyzed in temporal (i.e. post frequency) and structural (tool used, post word count, quantity of links, presence of features like calendars) terms," providing "metrics for measuring," but failing to account for the "variance in blogging practices" (para. 17). While some researchers have accounted for variation, boyd argues, others tend to compare blogging to other discursive practices, such as diary writing or journalism, failing to account for the situational and motivational differences (paras. 2, 18). However, boyd does not consider Miller and Shepherd's (2004) account. In contrast to Miller and Shepherd, then, boyd's conception of genre is narrowly situated in a formalist tradition, concerned with structure and content, not context. Miller and Shepherd are not offering formalist or structural accounts of blogs—the kind boyd rightfully challenges—but instead are

---

15. Social media scholar danah boyd writes her name without capitalization, and that stylization is replicated in this book.

elaborating on a pragmatic rhetorical account. They are concerned with social actions that blogs perform, and this concern shifts the discussion from an effort to frame research objectives (as boyd suggests) to an ethnomethodological enterprise where the recurrent practices of rhetorical actors tell us about a discursive space—the genres—they inhabit and the actions they attempt to perform.

While Miller and Shepherd offer good justification for revisiting the question of blogs as genre, it is problematic to categorize the blog as a technology, or even as a medium. Distinguishing technology and genre in this way suggests that the blog is a singular technology rather than a constellation of affordances generated not only by software structuring blogging platforms but also by the underlying cyber infrastructures and the rhetorical exigencies that call for affordances to be put to use in a typified way, even across modalities (for example, video blogs). Nardi, Schiano, and Gumbrecht (2004) describe the considerable variation in technologies with open-source/free software and proprietary/closed software platforms, and even hand-coded HTML blogs. Blogging software has moved from being "primarily textual" to including image-based blogs and video blogs (Nardi, Schiano, & Gumbrecht, 2004, p. 222), employing visuals in significant ways. This is true in microblogging spaces such as Twitter as well, where the incorporation of images and videos continues to proliferate. Even when these platforms were primarily text-based, and where the length of a post is limited to a certain number of characters, the conventional uses of the genres and platforms are recursive. Recall a time when Twitter retweets (sharing a tweet, or short post) were accomplished by the hand-typed prefix "RT." The platform has long since automated this process, creating interesting technical consequences such as the ability for original posters to delete their content, which is then removed from the feed of the person sharing. When blogs first began appearing, the infrastructure to support blogging as an activity was much less specialized than today. Now blogging platforms provide a list of features and some direction in blogging as a conventionalized practice. Moreover, as with many contemporary web platforms, the need for technical skills is sizably smaller than it once was. Users can set up a blog that will format text, allow embedded images and videos, create menus, tag posts, and share materials in broader social networks with a few clicks through a user-friendly interface, one designed to let them perform these tasks with minimal consultation of a manual. Blogs of yore and blogs of today differ profoundly in terms of technological affordances. Even now, the difference between starting a blog with a platform such as Wordpress and a platform such as Drupal demand different kinds of expertise, experience, and skill levels. Equating all blog technologies creates obvious problems when theorizing about the relationship between these technologies and the kinds of affordances they offer our genre users.

Technologies of the web afford different kinds of audiences, sharing, and possibilities for creating arguments, but their inhabitation and disciplining provide a recognizable and recurrent rhetorical form. This inhabitation and disciplining has occurred through decisive rhetorical action by motivated rhetorical agents. While the technological affordances provide space for new rhetorical possibilities, and help to shape these possibilities, they have also been shaped and constrained by prior rhetorical knowledge and perceptions of community-driven norms. However, it is not simply online users who drive technological development; likewise, technological development does not alone drive what kinds of social actions online users perform. Gries (2015) makes the case powerfully, and her account is worth quoting again: "rhetoric, especially in a digitally mediated environment, is more like an unfolding event—a distributed, material process of becomings in which divergent consequences are actualized with time and space" (pp. 7). Her lesson is an important one, reminding genre users that as they engage rhetoric in these digital spaces, the circulation of rhetorical artifacts is dependent upon more than a rhetor's crafting.

When Miller and Shepherd (2009) argue that "genre and the medium, the social action and its instrumentality, fit so well that they seemed coterminous" (p. 283), they gesture toward a fundamental distinction that is impossible to uphold in rhetorical accounts of digitally mediated spaces. Infrastructures that establish the basis for particular platforms or blog software, for instance, create a novel space for circulation, limit the nature of visuals and videos that can be shared due to technological constraints, or provide new affordances such as the ability to share original scientific research near-instantaneously around the world from the moment of publication. The social actions we might participate in are dramatically altered by our cyber infrastructures. The rapid proliferation of technologies, and their affordances, means an equally rapid proliferation of genres, or proto-genres—or, better yet, genre-ing activity. Technological development is not predicated only on the affordances or constraints of our cyber infrastructures, but also on social exigencies.

Among these exigencies are changes to scientific communities, publications, and engagement with broader publics. Science blogs—a phrase used by science bloggers to describe a constellation of activities aimed at sharing science-related knowledge more broadly than, say, research articles—are a useful site to explore these changes. While scientist blogging and science blogs can be understood generally, Shanahan (2011) argues that numerous types of science blogs can be identified, including those that review recent studies, analyze science news, focus on particular fields, report autobiographical accounts, and serve pedagogical functions (p. 904). Stepping back and looking at the platform of science blogs, Shanahan asks us to consider what affordances science blogs as a medium provide. Specifically, she asks us to think about the way science blogs may operate outside of conventional boundaries of science communication, writing, "What then is the role of science blogging as a medium? Does it support traditional transmissionist boundaries and merely provide a new venue for translation or does it represent a new boundary phenomenon?" (p. 905). To answer these questions, she proposes the concept of a "boundary layer." Building on the ideas of boundary work (Gieryn, 1983, 1999) and boundary objects (Star, 1988, 2010), Shanahan (2011) takes up the general concept of rhetorical boundaries, the rhetorical work needed to maintain them, and rhetorical objects that can cross them, but she rejects some of the ways we imagine boundary crossing occurs. Unlike boundary objects, she argues, "blog posts are not created for the purpose of meeting shared goals—the interactions that they spawn may or may not result in any concrete action—and they do not grow organically out of work needs" (p. 909). Thus the need for a concept to describe discourses that interact across audiences in a less collaborative and goal-driven way: a boundary layer, which "is a place where members of boundary social groups are both present and have an influence on one another" (p. 910). When the audiences and information are "heterogeneously mixed," there is a boundary layer. So, science blogs afford a space where "transmissionist and translationist metaphors" can be challenged (those metaphors that suggest repackaging and delivering content); instead, questions of *interaction* among audiences and information become paramount (p. 917).

Rejecting further the idea that blogs function similar to popularizations, often informed by those transmissionist and translationist models, Riesch and Mendel (2013) suggest that science blogs engage in more boundary work to keep good science from bad science, or pseudoscience (p. 53). Similar to Shanahan (2011), Riesch and Mendel find boundary work is a difficult concept to apply in the case of science blogs and, further, that a number of different types of science blogs can be identified (p. 55). Likewise, Trench (2012) argues that the internet/web opened previous "private" (or internal) spheres of scientific discourse to broader publics, allowing for discourse that "blurs the boundaries or restructures the relations between these spheres" (p. 274). This follows from his 2008 suggestion that the internet/web is "turning science communication inside-out" (p. 185). Among tools blurring the boundaries between internal and external spheres of discourse are blogs, Trench (2012) suggests, and "blogs, with their personal, even intimate, character appear strong candidates for facilitating this 'inside-out' process" (p. 274). Evidence exists that science bloggers are attuned to these changes. Mahrt and Puschmann (2014) found that bloggers identified multiple audiences for whom they write their posts, including professionals and publics at once. Complex audiences are a key feature of trans-scientific genres; specifically, complex audiences that are composed of experts, nonexperts, and those along the continuum are central to these genres. However, more than audience and form characterizes trans-scientific genres. In the next section, I explain the theoretical foundations for trans-scientific genres.

TRANS-SCIENTIFIC GENRES OF SCIENCE COMMUNICATION

Kaplan and Radin (2011) describe another kind of genre at work: para-scientific. Scientists use these para-scientific genres to argue, to persuade, but they do so outside of the gatekeeping mechanisms one might find in, for example, peer-reviewed journals. Kaplan and Radin examine the trade journal debate between K. Eric Drexler and Richard Smalley in *Chemical & Engineering News,* about what possibilities nanotechnology may hold. Because *Chemical & Engineering News* is a trade journal, and not subject to the same institutional gatekeeping through peer review that one would find in a research journal, Kaplan and Radin suggest that this kind of publication is a site where boundary work may occur and can be described as "para-scientific media."

Carolyn R. Miller and I took up this idea of para-scientific communication and broadened the definition to include emerging genres of online science communication (Kelly & Miller, 2016). In our account, para-scientific genres are those genres that function alongside conventional genres of science communication in that they borrow scientific authority and knowledge structures from the realm of science, but they operate outside the conventional models of gatekeeping and reporting found in internal science communication. In other words, para-scientific genres borrow some features from the internal discourse of science without the whole complex of features upon which the epistemic authority of science depends. However, these genres, unlike popular science genres, often forego the rhetorical accommodations outlined by Fahnestock (1986), such as appealing to "wonder," as previously noted. Rather, the para-scientific genres are concerned with the construction, collection, arrangement, or application of scientific knowledge in spheres of discourse formally external to, but somehow involved with, the scientific community (and, I will argue, catalyzing new communities).

The work of nuclear physicist Alvin M. Weinberg is helpful in theorizing how these genres are not sanctioned, not entirely stabilized, and not entirely within the network of scientific genres. In 1972 Weinberg published "Science and Trans-Science" in the journal *Minerva,* coining "trans-science"; he expanded on this work in his 1987 "Science and Its Limits." In 1992, he followed up this work again with a book entitled *Nuclear Reactions: Science and Trans-science,* devoted to the issues he had raised decades earlier. In these works, the idea of trans-science describes difficult interactions among science, technology, and society; questions arise that have a factual scientific answer, but that science cannot answer. Put in Weinberg's (1972) terms, trans-science describes questions that are within the epistemological domain of science and are "questions of fact and can be stated in the language of science," but they are also "unanswerable by science; they transcend science" (p. 209). Adopting Weinberg's term, I also adopt some of this thinking as the epistemological grounds for trans-scientific genres. These genres may use the language of science, they may discuss matters of scientific fact in that language, but they also transcend sanctioned scientific discourse because they must attend to not only the epistemological but also the axiological. That is, these genres transcend the narrow epistemological grounding of typical scientific discourse, which has been crafted in the service of scientific methods and the progress of what Kuhn (1970) calls "normal science" (the kind of research that builds up a theory once the general theoretical framework has been established). Instead, these genres of science communication expand the epistemologies to which they are accountable, and notably engage in axiological programs, thus entering the difficult problem space that Weinberg outlines. That is, this is a problem space where the answers to scientific questions of fact also mean engaging questions of value, which may be dependent on certain cultural, social, or community norms. For example, questions about the probability of an improbable but catastrophic nuclear disaster would require a refocusing of efforts away from some other problem and a decision about what is valuable. In this example, part of the problem is that it is well nigh impossible to calculate all the scenarios. So, what is the probability of a nuclear disaster on the East Coast of the United States? This is a trans-scientific question because of the numerous factors a risk analyst[16] would have to account for, requiring significant resources to research all the possibilities; as such, it would be necessary to make a calculation of where such resources ought to be allocated (that is, a social or economic, not strictly scientific, decision). Concretely, it is possible to determine several likely scenarios and calculate the risks of disaster. However, risk assessment is never exhaustive because such an effort

---

16. See also Danisch and Mudry (2008) on the rhetoricity of risk assessment and how it reconfigures publics' relationships with objects of scrutiny.

would outstrip the resources to perform such an assessment. Further, at some point, taxpayers providing the funds for the assessment would be furious at the expense and the diminishing returns on a continued calculation of risks. Someone needs to assess not only risk but also the degree to which risks will be measured. Weinberg (1972) offers an analogy to simplify the importance of broader engagement through trans-science, saying, "The obvious point is contained in the saying that he whose shoe pinches can tell something to the shoemaker" (p. 218). Aristotle argued a similar position in *Politics*: "The maker might not be the only or the best judge, but where those who do not possess the art also have some knowledge of its works. The maker of a house, for example, is not the only one to have some knowledge of it, but the one who uses it judges better than he does, and the one who uses it is the household manager; and a pilot judges rudders better than a carpenter, and the diner, not the cook, is the better judge of a banquet" (Aristotle, 2013, III, 1282a, ln 18–24). While experts have significant domain knowledge, and indeed are crucial to these conversations, when we talk about science in society, we are talking about the implications of science for society itself. In a democratic nation, Weinberg suggests, these implications are going to be taken up in more open, deliberative spaces.

How can Weinberg's discussions of epistemological grounding of science and the axiological matters of trans-science help address the problem of emerging genres of science communication? Reconsider the description of para-scientific genres above—genres that operate "alongside traditional genres of science communication in that they borrow scientific authority and knowledge structures from the realm of science but operate without the gatekeeping and traditional reporting forms of internal science communication" (Kelly & Miller, 2016, p. 221). Perhaps, instead, trans-scientific genres can be said to operate alongside conventional genres of science communication. Trans-scientific genres borrow values from science, such as the factual and reproducible nature of science that establishes its authority. These genres, however, also borrow values from the larger cultures within which the genres operate, such as the right to make health decisions as an individual or for one's family. For trans-scientific genres, then, established forms of gatekeeping and reporting of science need to be set aside to allow for an expanded deliberative space. In this way, trans-scientific genres are concerned with the construction, collection, arrangement, or application of scientific knowledge to promote more inclusive deliberation about complex techno-scientific problems and their social corollaries. These trans-scientific genres are the same as the "para-scientific genres" Miller and I previously considered (Kelly, 2014, 2016; Kelly & Miller, 2016; A. R. Mehlenbacher, 2017), following Kaplan and Radin (2011). But the change of phrase here is somewhat more pragmatic. Although "para-scientific" is a productive way to think about the range of genres employed in scientific spheres of discourse, the prefix "para-" (meaning "alongside") paired with "science" can invoke some unintentional readings and implications. Most notably, a number of pseudoscientific organizations and research agendas have adopted "para-scientific" as a descriptor. "Trans-scientific genres," in contrast, is a convenient category to set apart some of the new and evolving forms of online science communication from conventional genres, such as scientific research articles or research grant proposals or popularizations, without unintentionally confusing those with pseudoscience.

Because what I am characterizing as trans-scientific genres are so new, there are a number of challenges in studying them—among them, challenges in the instability of the genres, or proto-genres, under investigation. How does one go about studying genres that are less likely to be highly conventionalized, or that may be rapidly evolving, or that are difficult to situate in a particular community of practice? In the next section, I bring together rhetorical genre studies as well as approaches from allied fields in genre studies to build a methodological approach to investigate these challenging genres. As well, I draw from recent critiques and discussions in rhetorical studies of science in an effort to build a robust approach that balances the close, deep reading of rhetorical approaches with somewhat larger data sets.

METHODS AND APPROACH: CASE STUDIES AND SMALL CORPUS ANALYSIS

Each chapter that follows describes the particular methods employed within, but a larger rationale for the particular approaches at work shapes the book. Following the critique that genre studies have too narrowly confined research to professional or institutional contexts, a number of coterminous methodological problems arise. Notably, studies attending to professional spheres of discourse tend to focus on stabilizing elements of genres, with momentary disruptions such as technological innovation, and not an ongoing lifeworld of texts. Graham and Whalen (2008) illustrate how methodological approaches used in conventional rhetorical studies of genre in new media environments understate the complexity of studying genre in new media forms, particularly undertheorizing the relationships between media forms, the rhetorical situations calling for a response, and the genres themselves. When studying new media forms, genre researchers tend to employ two distinct types of methods, Graham and Whalen (2008) argue: "the postmortem" and "the situational" (p. 70). Postmortem studies are those relying on the collection of genre artifacts, often exemplars, in an effort to characterize situated genre conventions and use. Situational studies attend more specifically to genre evolution through a study of situational (often media) change. However, it is likely in professional contexts that the social and ideological space remains "stabilized-enough" (Schryer, 1993), such that the genre change is quite gradual—a consequence of the pushmi-pullyu dynamic that arises when balancing tradition and change in the realms of technology, rhetoric, and, indeed, professional settings (Miller, 2012). Graham and Whalen (2008) argue the central problem with postmortem and situational approaches is they attend to artifact, audience, or user analysis, but less frequently to the "impact, demands, and exigencies of audiences, contexts, cultures, and genres" in the design process and ongoing distribution process (p. 71). Attention to such unfolding is useful in new media environments, particularly when the genres exhibit a kind of hybridity or "gestalt-shift," where, in Graham and Whalen's case, a genre is put to use for multiple purposes. Further to the point, the kind of evolution in genres online makes the project of conducting a postmortem analysis challenging and largely unfulfilling, as the case of blogs later in the book will illustrate.

Overall, this book draws from several online platforms to offer a number of exemplary cases, crossing disciplines and the expert/nonexpert divide. Such a methodological approach better accounts for the "interplays between genres" (Bawarshi, 2016, p. 247) and the dynamic nature of genre evolution, while attending to, but not focusing on, the singular invocations that mark genre recurrence. Within each case, methods attending to the interplay and hybridity of genres are tailored to help illustrate not only conventions but also argument strategies. Adapting Swalesian move analysis provides machinery for examining a collection of texts that have a similar rhetorical situation and similar typified forms, but may operate within a larger genre set (Devitt, 1991), system (Bazerman, 1994), ecology (Spinuzzi, 2002, 2004), or genre repertoire (Orlikowski & Yates, 1994). Variation in performance can be understood in the context of genre formation, and move analysis can help us explain some of that variation. Such work combining the methods of rhetorical genre studies and more linguistically oriented approaches is valuable in both its analytical power and for pedagogical practice (Devitt, 2015). *Moves* are made in texts, and these moves are functional units of text (Connor, Upton, & Kanoksilapatham, 2007, p. 24), sometimes with certain identifiable linguistic features. John Swales (1990) identified several "moves" that work in concert to provide the basic argument structure for research article introductions, and his model applies broadly to what he calls research process genres (grant proposals, abstracts, and articles). Identifying features across genres within a particular discourse community neither invalidates the highly typified form of the article nor does it discount relations to or blurring with other genres. It is noteworthy that what Swales charts is a way to identify and describe typified forms that recur. Such abstracted patterns are realized differently in each instantiation, and the aggregate of particular instantiations comes to shape genre expectations, and thus conventions. When exploring dynamic, evolving genres, a combination of rhetorical and linguistic methods in genre studies is a useful approach that allows flexibility to mark recurrence and typification while describing argument strategies with some precision.

Rhetorical genre theory has long intersected with rhetorical studies of science, and this study follows in that tradition. Segal (2000) describes a "rhetoric of the professions" emerging in Canada, where "rhetoricians of science are not easily distinguishable from genre rhetoricians" (p. 66). Situated in this tradition, and following work in genre studies to better account for public or vernacular genres, this book engages both the rhetorics of the profession (science) and public rhetorics. These are certainly in line with the developments in the nearly two decades since Segal's assessment, and still rhetorical genre theory and rhetoric of science are intersecting. Two important considerations arise from the intersection of these fields: the first is the attention to visual modes in texts, which rhetoricians of science are increasingly called to account for in their analyses; the second is a broad methodological concern about the use of case studies. Of the former, rhetoric of science brings valuable questions to genre studies, asking us to consider the use of visuals in text and their suasive functions. Of the latter, genre studies offers worthy lessons on this question of case studies, showing how a marriage of case analysis and close reading paired with corpus analysis offers an epistemologically powerful approach.

Case studies have served as the most common method of analysis in rhetorical studies of science. With the recent release of the second edition of *Landmark Essays on the Rhetoric of Science: Case Studies* (2017), edited by Randy Allen Harris, the ongoing relevance of case studies for the field has been reaffirmed. However, there is some question about when case studies are a strong method and when they may have significant limitations. Bazerman (2016), in the afterword of the edited volume *Science and the Internet,* writes, "Each of the chapters has taken up interesting cases—that is, cases where novel or previously unexamined or previously unappreciated changes seem to be occurring," and tells us that an advantage of this approach is "to expose small signs of bigger things to come" (pp. 269–70). The punch line, however, is less flattering. Bazerman suggests the selection of interesting cases is "not surprising" because "the novelty of one's findings often depends on the novelty of one's cases" (p. 270). When looking for broader trends, Bazerman argues, "particularly at a time of hypothesized change where there are many experiments and many different choices being made," case studies may not be a particularly strong approach (p. 270). Instead, Bazerman suggests approaches that involve larger samples and possibly even statistical approaches. S. Scott Graham and Kirk St. Amant raise similar questions in their 2019 special issue of *Technical Communication Quarterly* on durable and portable research in technical and scientific communication. Certainly there have been strong works in rhetoric of science that combine case studies that examine larger data sets, including Bazerman's own work, but the case study remains a common approach. I do not mean to say there is a problem in rhetorical studies of science because of this approach, but rather to suggest, as I believe others have, that there is room for a broader range of approaches to the problems that interest rhetoricians of science. In this study, a combination of case studies and move analysis from genre studies are used to provide a broader analytic approach.

Chapters two and four put to work a modified version of move analysis to study crowdfunding proposals and science blogs. For these chapters, the move analysis is followed by a more conventional rhetorical approach. Each chapter begins and ends with discussion concerning how to rhetorically characterize the texts examined by considering the exigencies and audiences to which they respond, the ways in which such responses are designed, and the affordances and constraints for these responses in their current form and as they shape the future performance of the genred space. In each chapter, I have also included an extended discussion of an exemplary case from the data set to help illustrate the broader trends identified in the data. The focus of move analyses is discernable discourse fragments, and what those tell us about broader discursive trends and norms. In the third chapter in the book, focusing on database documentation, the modes of communication investigated are markedly different. Instead, chapter 3 adopts tools from rhetorical criticism to study a case that is exemplary but also generalizable.

Selection for the cases varies according to each chapter's contribution to the book's overall argument, and so a brief overview of these decisions may be useful. Broadly, the selection of cases is meant to represent communities that are actively constructing spaces for both new modes of science communication and reflective practices and genre-ing activities that help direct these emerging forms. Take, for example, Experiment.com, which is a crowdfunding site devoted exclusively to science. Elsewhere I have examined crowdfunding proposals on Kickstarter.com (A. R. Mehlenbacher, 2017), owing to the particular case of crowdfunding I studied, the Safecast initiative (Kelly,

2014, 2016; Kelly & Miller, 2016). However, it became clear in the course of that study that Kickstarter's generalist model meant choosing examples from a small selection of proposals tagged as science or technology, although even in this category lines blurred with more creative projects (for example, a documentary about some scientific topic). Experiment provides a dedicated space to examine crowdfunding proposals for science and has longevity and staying power on its side.[17] Experiment, then, is a useful case because it demonstrates a range of science-specific adaptations of crowdfunding models and platforms, and unlike other examples has gained enough traction that the site remains operational. Five years or so of operations might seem trivial when stacked up against the annals of the Royal Society, founded in 1660, but for start-ups, lifespan is normally counted by months.

For chapter 3, which examines databases, the case selection was a little more complex—because databases and their related ecologies are complex. Attending to matters of form and style, and argument, the chapter examines a hard case for science communication. The case study helps explain how something so seemingly disconnected from the average person's everyday life as a scientific database can have significant social implications and, crucially, utility to the broader public. Admittedly, this case, Safecast, was selected not for its typicality but rather because it is an exemplary case. In 2011, my research focused on how publics were able to participate in decision-making processes around nuclear energy in North Carolina (Kinsella, Kelly, & Kittle Autry, 2013). At a utilities commission hearing—regarding funding for a nuclear project—held just days after the 2011 Tōhoku earthquake and tsunami, a number of members of the public questioned how events in Japan would affect the United States. Few had a good idea of just what was happening beyond knowing the Fukushima Daiichi nuclear-generation site had taken a devastating double hit, first by the earthquake and then by the giant tsunami that overtook the seawalls and flooded the plant. "Meltdown" sat on everyone's lips, even without knowing if that was likely, or just what that meant. Amidst the global confusion, from those on the ground in Japan to the international atomic energy community, groups of scientists, citizens, and publics all tried to understand what was occurring. Among these groups, an unprecedented collective effort by a group known as Safecast, only called into being following the accident, responded with an impressively large data collection and sharing operation. Safecast stands among the giants of grassroots response to this natural and technoscientific crisis, and their efforts to collect and share complex radiological data are not only a technical feat but a rhetorical one as

---

17. At least as of writing this in late 2018.

well. Master communicators, Safecast shows us what complex data mean in their scientific and social forms.

Despite being one of the oldest forms of social media, blogs continue to fascinate genre researchers. To take a broad look at science blogs, and to understand what genre activities are at work in these spaces, the case I have chosen in chapter 4 is the Public Library of Science blog network, which is composed of different kinds of science-focused blogs, about different topics, written by different kinds of authors. Although there are numerous blog networks, including from *Scientific American* and *Discovery Magazine,* such large and successful science blog networks are published by rather traditional publishers. The PLOS blog network is unique and interesting because it is a born-digital effort, with a commitment to open-access publishing, and was a direct response to problems with conventional models of publishing.

Together these cases present a meaningful story about how the web has energized science communication, expanded the audience for science communications, and crucially, expanded the range of actors who may participate in creating communications about science. It is an exhilarating time for science, and together these cases help illustrate the innovative ways that complex scientific programs are being researched, shared, and used. Critical approaches in this book rely on the pillars of rhetorical criticism and genre criticism; thus, a model of building a larger case with either a small corpus or collection of cases is sensible for trying to understand both the particulars of each rhetorical act and their recurrent forms.

CHAPTER 2

Crowdfunding

Genres for Funding Research

GENRE STUDIES demonstrate historical, cultural, and technological conditions that shape the rhetorical world in which genres evolve. Today, this culture consists of increasing pressure for faculty to secure external funding in a climate where such funding is difficult to obtain. Scientists work hard to coordinate funding from various national granting agencies and foundations to support their research—often a difficult and time-consuming task. There is a good deal of advice to help researchers draft their proposals. A search through an online bookseller shows numerous options, including Crawley and O'Sullivan's (2015) *The Grant Writer's Handbook,* Li and Marrongelle's (2013) *Having Success with NSF,* or Schimel's (2012) *Writing Science: How to Write Papers That Get Cited and Proposals That Get Funded.* Online, many websites offering advice on how to write grant proposals are hosted by academic and government institutions. Workshops and webinars are presented by funding agencies, and research faculty often have access to specialized staff who support efforts to secure research funding. All of this interest in how to write effective proposals and grants is unsurprising. Despite the significant time and effort many researchers will devote to drafting and revising proposals, their requests for support will go unfulfilled. In search of new mechanisms for funding, some researchers have moved to a new trend: crowdfunding.[1]

---

1. Academic authors are a restricted subset of the population writing these proposals and the population funding proposals. For an academic scientist or citizen scientist, then, it is

Crowdfunding is a way to secure support for a project by appealing to a broad audience that might be interested for various ideological or practical reasons. As the name implies, a crowd provides funding. Imagine a hundred people each giving you five dollars for your research project—their *gift* to you, in the hopes that your research will have positive outcomes. Investigating crowdfunding for science is important because it can tell us about the changing nature of science communications afforded by the web. This chapter investigates crowdfunding proposals for science by charting rhetorical strategies, antecedent genres, and closely related genres. Specifically, conducting a move analysis to illustrate the appeals at work in these proposals illuminates the relationship between crowdfunding and conventional research funding proposals. And, appeals might be shared across proposals, further revealing the ways in which crodfunding science adheres to disciplining, reflecting norms of science or where significant departures may appear. Move analysis is also helpful for understanding the media form through which genre-ing activity is enacted. Guiding this chapter is the question: how does crowdfunding illuminate broader changes to science communication and genre evolution in complex new media environments?

BACKGROUND: CONVENTIONAL FUNDING AND CROWDFUNDING MODELS

One of the more interesting differences between conventional funding proposals and crowdfunding proposals is that the latter engage in a deliberative space and must appeal to a wider audience than almost any traditional proposal. For example, if a researcher submits a proposal to a National Science Foundation (NSF) funding stream, experts will review it. Whether experts have specialization in the same area as the proposal author or expertise in a different area of research, they will still have the appropriate academic training

---

imperative to understand the typical composition of the population funding proposals. The Pew Research Center provides useful insights about the typical backers for crowdfunding proposals, although it is difficult to ascertain how applicable these numbers might be to crowdfunding science in particular. However, some numbers do provide good evidence that crowdfunding is not such a niche market that only a select few have participated. Of adult Americans, 22 percent have backed a project, with slightly more women than men providing support. Younger people are more likely than their older counterparts to back a project. Among those ages eighteen to twenty-nine, 30 percent have backed a project, and among those thirty to forty-nine, 27 percent have. However, only 18 percent of older adults, ages fifty to sixty-four, have backed a project, and even fewer, 8 percent, among those sixty-five or older. High-income, highly educated, and urban individuals are more likely to back projects than their peers (Pew Research Center & Smith, 2016).

to assess the proposal. Crowdfunding proposals, in contrast, may be reviewed by a broad public readership, from friends to publics interested in science, as well as colleagues and other experts.

Another interesting feature of crowdfunding proposals is that the audience is partially a result of the platform itself that is used to share the proposals. Crowdfunding platforms both create and inhabit networked spaces. The platform creates an arena for users to gather and fund projects on an ongoing basis, and it is also embedded within a broader media ecology where proposals can be shared via social media or emailed to possible supporters who are not already using the platform. These spaces are also situated with and connected to a company that runs them, such as Kickstarter, Inc., which runs Kickstarter.com, but it is the front end of the platform, the public-facing website, that provides a place for supporters to gather and is thus of interest here. This space merits investigation because the genre system appears rather different from research or grant proposals one might submit to a federal funding agency.

Consider the genre system for proposals in large organizations such as the Natural Sciences and Engineering Research Council of Canada (NSERC) or NSF. Organizations such as these will first issue a request for proposals (RFP); this is the first genre in our genre system. An RFP describes the kind of funding that will be supported and the research questions and concerns that are of most interest to the organization in the granting cycle. For large organizations such as the NSERC or NSF, there are further documents to assist researchers in drafting their proposal, such as a grant guidelines handbook, a handbook or instruction genre that includes what information belongs in a grant proposal for the NSF and also the ways that this information should be formatted.

In addition to these established genres, researchers might employ interpersonal genres, such as calling or emailing grant officers to begin a conversation about their work, such as how to address a specific RFP. In the case of NSF proposals and other proposals going to large granting organizations, a research office at a university will help applicants develop proposals and ensure that their proposals are compliant with content and formatting rules. Often this kind of work begins with a pre-awards office. At my current institution, the University of Waterloo, we have dedicated staff at both the faculty/college level and at the university level that provide pre-awards support. This is similar to the support offered at many research-intensive universities across the United States and Canada. Support is often not limited to federal grants and extends to include foundation and industry proposals, too. Contact with the pre-awards office might begin with an email, often elements of an introductory or greeting genre deployed, and then perhaps turn into a phone call or in-person meeting. During this time, the primary investigator may complete a proposal worksheet or a cover sheet, genres that help identify critical information and requirements for the proposal, and this may initiate the generation of a "Financial Conflict of Interest" document, if applicable. Soon the pre-award specialists will assess the RFP and its associated guideline genres. A notable constellation of genres, the timeline or schedule and other project management planning genres are developed to ensure a package is submitted by the deadline. Genres embedded within these large grant proposals deserve some attention, including biographies, customized résumés or curriculum vitae, budgets, and budget justification documents. Much of this negotiation will be to develop an accurate budget that accounts for the costs of hiring students, buying equipment and supplies, and travel. But the budget is not a mere list of costs and includes a budget justification that, as the name suggests, explains specifically and in some detail why the outlined costs are necessary. Other documents may need to be generated throughout this process, including any materials for subcontracts if researchers from other institutions are involved. Letters of support from communities, institutions, or other research sites indicating researchers are welcomed and their work is valued, supported, and needed might be included. All of these materials are then gathered and submitted to the granting agency for review.

But the constellation of genres generated around a research funding proposal does not end with the submission of the proposal package. At the granting agency, a number of genres will be employed to review the package. Some of the genres include requests to reviewers indicating that proposals related to their area of expertise are ready for review. In some cases, a group of reviewers might hold a conference call or meet as a panel to discuss proposals, and ultimately reviewers will provide reports indicating the strengths and weaknesses of the proposal and their recommendations regarding funding decisions. For the sake of continuing our example, let us assume that a given proposal is funded (allowing us to bypass the rejection letter as a well-known genre).

Genred activities that follow the success of a proposal include the notice to proceed, the notice of award, contracts, genres of negotiation around contracts, terms and conditions, technical reports, receipts and balance sheets, cost projections, and numerous genres of coordination between administrative units. Other genres might be employed, including mandatory reporting, evidence for regulatory compliance, invention or intellectual property disclosures, and any materials associated with training. From this work might follow patents, white papers, conference proceeding papers, research articles, and so on, but genres employed in the grant process alone are many. This is not a definitive overview, but rather a general case from a major research university in the United States or Canada. It is from this context—the highly structured world of proposals—that this analysis turns to instead examine the less stabilized crowdfunding model.

Crowdfunding Science through Experiment.com

Crowdfunding proposals are embedded within a platform and a set of related technologies, including microblogging and blogging platforms, social networking sites, and even social news-sharing sites. The networked technologies and networks of people that provide a platform for crowdsourced proposals are useful to understanding crowdfunding, and media platforms and the communities building those platforms are central to understanding how these technologies are deployed. While early crowdfunding platforms such as Kickstarter had a more general, or at least arts-focused, orientation, specialized platforms for crowdfunding of science and research currently claim a share in the market (see, for a list of platforms, Cadogan, 2014). For example, Petridish.org was a platform specifically for funding scientific research. Similar to Kickstarter, Petridish was a for-profit company. The system worked on an all-or-nothing funding principle and supporters were provided with rewards. However, as the past tense indicates, this platform is no longer active. A number of crowdfunding platforms specializing in scientific research are now defunct, but one platform has persisted in this niche market: Experiment. com (formerly Microryza, established in 2012).

Experiment is also a for-profit company and earns a percentage of the funds of successful proposals. Reporting 653 projects funded (and 749 that failed), and a total of US$7,160,029 pledged by 36,916 backers, the site has a steady stream of projects (Experiment, 2017a). A backer is someone who has donated to your cause, and according to Experiment (2017b), "Anyone with a credit card can become a supporter of science research."[2] On average, a project will secure US$4,313, and the average pledge is US$136 (Experiment, 2017a).[3] While these numbers are lower than large NSF or NSERC grants,[4] the amounts

---

2. It is worth noting, as well, that projects in art and design and the social sciences, along with science, technology, engineering, and math (STEM) disciplines, appear on the platform.

3. The Pew Research Center found the majority of supporters on crowdfunding sites have only contributed to a small number of projects, noting that 87 percent of adults who have backed crowdfunding projects have contributed to five or fewer projects (Pew Research Center & Smith, 2016). The numbers Experiment reports seems to be higher than one might expect on more general crowdfunding sites.

4. NSERC's *2017 Competition Statistics Discovery Grants (DG) and Research Tools and Instruments (RTI) Programs* reports that early researchers' average grant in 2017 was Can$25,409

align with seed granting, and the numbers of researchers participating suggest many have turned to crowdfunding as a means to support their research. Statistics on the amount of scholarly content generated within the crowdfunding platform are also interesting in that they offer some insight into the ongoing conversations taking place in these spaces. Consider the more than 6,306 lab notes written or the 19,987 comments made by backers and supporters. In addition to the content internal to the crowdfunding site, 31 papers associated with projects funded through Experiment have been published (Experiment, 2017a). Further integrating with scientific publishing norms, Experiment is able to assign Digital Object Identifiers (DOIs) to each successful proposal.

Beyond the commercial model Experiment uses, the company has positioned itself in some rhetorically distinct ways. Unlike many crowdfunding models, backers receive no physical rewards, but rather, they benefit from advancing scientific research. Interestingly, this adaptation mimics an older model of patronage. Experiment (2017a) suggests that "the real value of research is in the process," and so the rewards for the donors are, instead, updates that show what work has been accomplished. While the level of disclosure is up to the researcher, the site encourages the idea that the donors should be made aware of how the funding is being put to work. The products of this kind of funding are beginning to appear in conventionally sanctioned spheres of scientific discourse: research articles. In early 2014, Experiment announced in their blog that a peer-reviewed research article from a project funded through the site had been published (Experiment, 2014). The article was written by Jaffe et al. (2014), who had collected over US$20,000 from 271 donors through the site and published an article in the journal *Atmospheric Pollution Research*. This is a notable achievement for crowdfunding, but perhaps not so for the university. The donations were indeed *donations*, meaning that the university would not claim the typical overhead for grants. While the researchers were able to complete their work, and had other funding sources, this source functions institutionally in a different manner than an NSF grant might. In the case of donations, the researcher's work is supported while the institution does not receive funding for overhead or indirect costs from the award. Such overhead support is valuable to universities to cover expenses associated with infrastructure, maintenance, and oversight. Despite the minimal contributions that $50,000 might make to a major research laboratory,

---

($34,948 for established researchers) for discovery grants (Natural Sciences and Engineering Research Council of Canada, 2017). In this model, other funding mechanisms are available for purchasing equipment and other expenses, but still the average grant size is higher than the average on Experiment. The NSF profile, too, offers greater support, with the average annualized award size for research grants in 2016 reported as US$117,100 (National Science Foundation, 2016) and US$177,700 for 2018 (National Science Foundation, 2018).

the site suggests the support offered is meaningful for researchers, providing travel expenses and equipment. These seemingly minimal funds would in fact be significant to an unfunded researcher starting out or even to researchers in the humanities and social scientific disciplines. In cases such as these, crowdfunding is a viable source of supplemental or even seed funding for academics.

If crowdfunding is a viable alternative (or supplement) to standard research funds for scientists, then the implications of the model must be explored. For example, novice researchers may be less likely to have the well-developed professional networks from which their more senior counterparts benefit, which would make securing funding more challenging. Indeed, Kickstarter has noted that existing networks play a key role in initial funding support. Experiment's FAQs tell us that "the researcher's professional and personal networks play a large role in getting the project off the ground" (Experiment, 2014). While the discussion goes on to suggest that otherwise identifying the audience is important, and that social networking sites including blogs and microblogs may be helpful, some questions still need to be raised about the value of previously established social networks. Assuming a junior researcher has a network of colleagues, and the appropriate ethos to energize their network to support their work, one can ask questions about the scholarly and economic status of the network's members. An economic reality of academia is that junior researchers, especially postdoctoral scholars and other non-tenure-track scholars, are less likely to have disposable income to help support their colleagues. Early- and late-career researchers, then, may have different resources to draw upon in their effort to support research through crowdfunding. Variation among disciplines is likely to play a role in how well established and financially stable a network might be for a given researcher. Consider, for instance, the differences between researchers at private and state institutions, the sorts of networks they might be embedded within, and the variations among those networks' financial capacities.

Experiment's Platform

Experiment.com's home page features an imperative to "Help fund the next wave of scientific research," which is further supported by a quotation from Microsoft founder and philanthropist Bill Gates stating that the platform "helps close the gap for potential and promising, but unfunded projects" (Experiment, 2014). All the standard ways of interacting with a website are available, with a link about "How it Works" and a sign-up/login link. Further down the page, you will find a section entitled "Featured Experiments" (for example, "Using Cell Penetration Peptide to Enhance the Delivery of Antibody-Gold Nanoparticles for More Effective Radiotherapy," "Dear Ticks, Show Me Your Metal!," and "Identification of Pancreatic Cancer Specific Tumor Markers for Early Detection"). Information about partner institutions, more categories, and further links to site information follow. But it is in the proposals themselves that some of the key features of the genre are found.

Opening any proposal you might come across while browsing the various categories, perhaps ecology or even paleontology, the first information you might notice is an image or video for a given project. Images could be pictures taken of the researchers, a dig site, or even an illustrated graphic. They appear in place of videos, which otherwise are featured prominently at the beginning of the proposal, following the title, principal investigators (PIs), and backers. The image, the title, and the PI's name and affiliation appear alongside the project's funding information, including the number of dollars pledged, the pledge goal, the number of days remaining to back the project, and a link to "Back This Project" (allowing you to donate funds). An open-access button optionally appears when the researchers promise to disseminate the results of their research through open venues.

At the time of finalizing this chapter, below the image or video appear links to four different tabs: "Overview," "Methods," "Lab Notes," and "Discussion." The overview tab is the default tab to open when you choose a project and begins, as the title indicates, with a short overview of the project and, along with a textual description, sometimes a video, hosted on the video hosting service Vimeo. Below this general introduction is what was formerly (c. 2014) included under an "Abstract" tab in the navigational menu. Following the abstract is the budget overview, including a doughnut chart to visualize the budget breakdown, and a rationale for the expenses. Endorsements follow the budget, which allow researchers and supporters to testify to the importance of the research or the competence of the researcher. Some projects then include a project timeline, but it does not appear to be mandatory. "Meet the Team" appears as the next section, which provides an image of a researcher or researchers, affiliation information, and a short biography. Lab notes are linked to at the bottom of the proposal, followed by a list of backers and related statistics, and then a site-wide menu. Our final two menu items allow for interaction among the researchers and project backers. The "Lab Notes" section might include updates, further elaboration on the project, statements about the funding goals, and even links to related published materials. "Discussion" allows supporters or prospective supporters to ask questions or to provide encouragement.

Structurally the proposal platform is unique, but many of its features simply codify the written and unwritten rules of the traditional research funding proposal genre. The overview's budget and biography are features one can find in almost any research funding proposal, including guidelines from major federal granting agencies, although some variation in the register of these biographies can be identified. Characterizing funding proposals in terms of a singular genre obscures the complex discursive ecology that in fact composes a completed grant proposal package. Lab notes and comments, alternatively, provide spaces for writing that are not codified in conventional research funding proposal writing. Lab note updates might provide preliminary results or links to products such as publications. Comments can include words of encouragement from supporters or questions about the project. Both of these tabs provide atypical (for a research funding proposal) spaces for writing, but these are interactive spaces. Interactive spaces are crucial for crowdfunding because, as suggested above, they are deliberative spaces, and deliberation requires shared reflection and consideration.

EXPERIMENT: AN EXAMINATION OF RHETORICAL MOVES

Early studies in the rhetoric of science provide some account of proposal development.[5] Greg Myers's *Writing Biology* traces the life of a proposal as it moves through systems of review and feedback. Myers (1990) demonstrates how funding proposals are not transparent accounts of scientific work, but rather carefully constructed documents that frame the author's ethos through disciplinary affiliation and expertise, and shape the kinds of research conducted with respect to different kinds of granting mechanisms. Early work in technical and professional communication also helped chart the discursive strategies of proposals, and contextual matters, including competition for funding dollars, have long shaped this genre (B. Mehlenbacher, 1992, 1994).

---

5. Early work in rhetorical studies of science and genre studies focused on the scientific research article, notably the work of Bazerman (1988) and Berkenkotter and Huckin (1995). Interest in the scientific research article continues in rhetoric of science studies, particularly in light of online sharing of journals and articles, and the emerging open-access movement (Gross & Harmon, 2016; Casper, 2016; Harmon, 2016). We could posit a number of reasons for this, including the difficulty in accessing both successful and unsuccessful proposals for comparative analysis. Journal articles are considerably easier to access for large-scale analysis than grant proposals, and it is then unsurprising that they are infrequently being studied. Or we might note the relative importance of the research article to all academic disciplines, whereas funding needs vary considerably by discipline.

More recently, genre studies have contributed several meaningful studies about proposals (Fairclough, 1993; Bhatia, 1998; Tardy, 2003; Feng & Shi, 2004; Ding, 2008; Moeller & Christensen, 2010).

Connor and her colleagues (Connor, 1998, 2000; Connor & Wagner, 1998; Connor & Mauranen, 1999; Upton & Connor, 2001) have conducted several studies that offer empirical analyses of proposals. In their studies, they advance a model of proposals using move analysis to identify different strategies at work. Beginning with the work of Swales, Connor and her collaborators identify both the typifications we see in proposals (what makes them a genre) and the variation across proposal types (the particulars of a genre performance). Relying primarily on the work of Swales (1990, 2004), and the work of Connor and her collaborators, my earlier work explores science-focused crowdfunding proposals on Kickstarter (A. R. Mehlenbacher, 2017). In that work, I adapted move analysis to attend rather specifically to the kinds of complexity that interest rhetoricians, including the polysemy of moves. In move analysis, a "move" is "a segment of text that performs a specific communicative function" (Connor, Upton, & Kanoksilapatham, 2007, p. 23). For the purposes of a rhetorical analysis, we can say that moves are segments of text that help build an overall argument. Think of a move this way: It is an identifiable segment of text at the level of a phrase, sentence, or even paragraph that constitutes part of a large-scale argument. For example, in Swales's "Creating a Research Space" (CARS) model, based on his analysis of research article introductions, *Establishing a Niche* is a move that builds toward an argument for the importance of a research study at the level of a research article. Moves are part of the gestalt of a research article. Moves, as parts of an argument, create meaning by coming together to form the whole argument (what we often talk about as the contribution in research). For trans-scientific genres, moves may overlap with traditional genre moves but might also include moves that seem to align more closely with strategies in popular or vernacular discourses.

The trans-scientific genres or genre-ing activities examined in this chapter are also rapidly evolving, which means that identifying moves can be something of a challenge. Although moves do not necessarily appear in a particular order, in Swales's CARS model, the moves do appear in a relatively well-established order. However, Swales (2004) revised his model to simplify the first two moves and further complicate the third and final move. In his original framework, there were three possible steps involved with move one, and four possible steps in move two and move three. In his revised version (Swales, 2004, pp. 230, 232), the model is streamlined and, importantly, iterative (see table 1).

TABLE 1. Swales's Revised Create a Research Space (CARS) Model

MOVE 1: ESTABLISHING A TERRITORY (CITATIONS REQUIRED)	Topic generalizations of increasing specificity
MOVE 2: ESTABLISHING A NICHE (CITATIONS POSSIBLE)	Step 1A: Indicating a gap
	Step 1B: Adding to what is known
	or
	Step 2 (optional): Presenting positive justification
MOVE 3: PRESENTING THE RESEARCH	Step 1 (obligatory): Announcing present research descriptively and/or purposively
	Step 2 (optional): Presenting research questions or hypotheses
	Step 3 (optional): Clarifying definitions
	Step 4 (optional): Summarizing methods
	Step 5 (probable in some fields): Announcing principal outcomes
	Step 6 (probable in some fields): Stating the value of the present research
	Step 7 (probable in some fields): Outlining the structure of the paper

For traditional proposals, studies show that the moves in the body of the text, while consistently appearing, do not necessary appear in a consistent order. This seems sensible because different funding mechanisms will provide unique structures or styles, but generally expect the same kind of appeals. In addition to this varied distribution of moves in traditional proposals, in my own study of Kickstarter proposal (Mehlenbacher 2017), I posited that moves in crowdfunding proposals might be more varied because the genre space is less stabilized (see also Schryer, 1993) than its conventional counterparts. Because moves may be more nebulous in less stabilized forms such as the crowdfunding proposal, allowing for some flexibility in how we characterize them helps us understand what may be crystalizing, or typifying, without making claims about genre membership. However, moves also provide a way to remark on texts that appear to be responding to similar rhetorical situations, even though there may be some variation in particular instantiations. That is to say, if we take a Milleresque theoretical position and understand that genre membership is marked by "discourses that are complete, in the sense that they are circumscribed by a relatively complete shift in rhetorical situation" (Miller, 1984, p. 159), then attempting to categorize different genres of crowdfunding proposals is not especially instructive. Instead, it is useful to attend to the rhetorical work these invocations serve to accomplish, and to do so I have collected a number of proposals to examine.

Data Collection and Analysis

To first develop the moves in a pilot study, five proposals were collected in July 2014, with the criteria that these proposals were the most recently listed on the page and they were successful. An additional sixty proposals with the same selection criteria were collected in February 2018 for detailed analysis, including of new features such as endorsements.[6] Three questions framed this initial data analysis: First, what kinds of moves are made in these proposals? Second, how are these moves made? Third, how do these moves seem to function rhetorically to persuade a prospective backer?

First, I examined the sections contributing to the overall structure of these proposals, including the short overview, abstract-like questions, budgets, and so on. Then, using the moves identified in scientific and proposal genres, I analyzed the different sections to better understand their independent functions and relationships to one another. Table 2 provides a summary of the moves and steps I have identified, which address these questions. In the following section, I will detail the findings that suggest this summary of moves is a useful characterization of the strategies used in crowdfunding proposals for science.

Building on the study of research proposals (Swales, 1990, 2004; Connor, 1998, 2000; Connor & Wagner, 1998; Connor & Mauranen, 1999), my own study of Kickstarter proposals (A. R. Mehlenbacher, 2017), and the qualitative and case analysis here, table 2 provides some basis to describe the rhetorical work occurring in crowdfunding proposals. Although all of these moves may not appear in each proposal, and different platforms (for example, Kickstarter versus Experiment) will have different affordances, it seems as though the basic heuristic that these moves provide is sufficient to understand some key issues shaping the rhetorical work in crowdfunding.

Establishing a Territory, in Swales's (2004) revised model, calls for citations, but these are less common in crowdfunding proposals. However, the overall rhetorical strategy is similar and can be adapted here. In my analysis of Kickstarter proposals (A. R. Mehlenbacher, 2017), I suggested that Swales's original CARS model might require some modification for crowdfunding pro-

---

6. If you were to open a tab and look at the website in 2014 and then in 2018, you would find since the time of pilot data collection and even full study data collection for this chapter, there have been several major changes to the platform. For example, the abstract has been moved to the overview, and "Methods" is an interesting new category as it provides a dedicated space for what is perhaps the most essential information provided in a funding proposal for scientific research. These changes matter because they may alter some of the characteristics of the proposals. However, the genre-ing features in these proposals remain typified and can help us chart moves made in the crowdfunding proposal.

TABLE 2. Moves Found in Crowdfunding Proposals

MOVE	DESCRIPTION	STEPS
ESTABLISHING A TERRITORY	Establishes the rhetorical situation to which the proposal responds through geographically, disciplinarily, temporally, or communally grounded means.	Step 1: Topic generalization
ESTABLISHING A NICHE	Establishes the appropriate rhetorical and material response to the exigence, and may overlap with Swales's *Establishing a Niche*.	Step 1A: Indicating a gap *or* Step 1B: Adding to what is known *and* Step 2 (optional): Presenting positive justification
OCCUPYING A NICHE / PRESENTING THE RESEARCH	Indicates the contribution that the project intends to make to respond to the exigence and may outline the rhetorical or material plans.	Step 1 (obligatory): Announcing present research descriptively and/or purposively Step 2 (optional): Presenting research questions or hypotheses Step 3 (optional): Clarifying definitions Step 4 (optional): Summarizing methods Step 5 (probable in some fields): Announcing principal outcomes Step 6 (probable in some fields): Stating the value of the present research
JUSTIFYING EXPENSES	Explains monetary expenses associated with present research and why those costs must be incurred.	Step 1: Listing expenses *and* Step 2: Outlining necessity *and* Step 3 (optional): Appealing for support
OUTLINING MEANS	Includes methods, procedures, plans of action, and tasks required to occupy the niche.	Step 1: Stating methods or approach *and* Step 2: Detailing protocols and/or process *and/or* Step 3: Outlining project timeline and/or tasks

MOVE	DESCRIPTION	STEPS
CLAIMING IMPORTANCE	Underscores the centrality of the anticipated results or outcomes of a study in a value-system relevant to either the backers or a real-world issue.	Step 1: (Re)Stating significance *and* Step 2: Identifying who stands to benefit
CLAIMING BENEFITS	Explains the intended or projected outcomes that contribute to advancement of knowledge in the public domain.	Step 1A: Stating intended engagement activities *and/or* Step 1B: Stating intended policy influence
STATING ACHIEVEMENTS	Describes the proposed or accomplished results, findings, or outcomes of the study for either the project and/or the community supporting the project.	Step 1: Stating intended research outputs *and* Step 2 (optional): Stating previous accomplishments *and/or* Step 3 (optional): Stating intended further research
CLAIMING COMPETENCE	Contains statements to the effect that the proposer is well qualified, experienced, and generally capable of carrying out the tasks set out. May also suggest some personal attributes.	Step 1A: Stating specialization or expertise *and/or* Step 2: Stating credentials such as university affiliation or degrees *and/or* Step 3: Highlighting publications, previous studies, and awards *and/or* Step 4 (optional): Stating relevant personal history

Adapted from Swales (1990, 2004), Connor (1998), Connor and Wagner (1998), and Connor and Mauranen (1999); see also A. R. Mehlenbacher (2017) for initial adaptations.

posals, and indeed, this bears out in this analysis, as it also did in Swales's own (2004) work on academic genres. The abstract questions map onto John Swales's original CARS model well: *Establishing Territory* ("What is the context of this research?"), *Establishing a Niche* ("What is the significance of this project?"), and *Occupying a Niche* ("What are the goals of the project?"). As we will see, this is not the first time these moves might be made, but this is certainly a significant codification of the model into the structure of the proposal. When we consider the kinds of projects that emerge from the growing cadre of students (including high school students) and citizen and civic scientists—including do-it-yourself biology (DIYBio) researchers—the rhetorical situation for these projects is not necessarily a disciplinary question. The growing number of groups involved in scientific research or experimentation expands the range for trans-scientific genres. In many cases, these researchers are driven by problems in their communities and show that civic engagement may take shape as scientific thinking and work.

Another complicating factor for the projects on Experiment involves research efforts responding to challenging problems, which may not frame research within Swales's CARS model. For example, some of the projects might be highly multidisciplinary and involve multiple disciplinary trajectories that need to be integrated. As new kinds of investigators and new configurations of teams move into the mainstream of scientific research, it may be that the moves to establish the research space vary somewhat. Perhaps most essential, the norms of the Experiment proposals also seem to favor an introduction that will appeal to a broader audience than we might imagine for research process genres, such as those Swales studied.

Beginning with the overview, the CARS-style introduction did not appear as strongly as might be expected in a conventional proposal, but it was present in a variety of combinations. For instance, one strategy is to state the niche that is being occupied initially and then explain the territory and its significance (for example, "The *goal* [*Occupying a Niche*] of this project is to initiate archaeological survey and excavation at the Alabama Site in the Stann Creek District of southern Belize. Little work has been done at the site, but it is an ideal place to investigate Ancient Maya urbanization and trade [territory and niche established]") (Schake & Peuramaki-Brown, 2014). This example reorders the three moves that constitute the CARS model.

However, other examples follow the model offered by Swales quite closely. Consider these project descriptions from the "About the Project" section:

> Jamaica is a highly biodiverse island in the Caribbean, but its ecological resources are threatened by climate and land-use changes. To conserve

Jamaica's flora and fauna, we need a better understanding of how the island's species responded to past climate and human impacts. Funds raised through this campaign will help us collect sediment cores to develop a 10,000-year long environmental record of vegetation, fire, climate, and human impacts in Jamaica. (Williams & Gill, 2017)

Otters are immigrating to the Greater Yellowstone's historically fishless Beartooth Plateau as a side effect of sport fish stocking as well as climate change. As an "invasive species" in this alpine environment, these predators could have serious consequences for native species. Our team of citizen scientists will collect data on this new population for monitoring and hypothesis testing, and we will share results through both technical and popular formats. (Cross, 2018)

In both examples, the authors first *Establish the Territory, Establish the Niche,* and then *Occupy the Niche* with their research. Although these examples are brief and do not include many optional steps detailed in the CARS model, they do adhere to the foundational moves outlined by Swales. These two examples are typical of those found in the sample, with minor variations appearing in some of the descriptions, such as Williams and Gill (2017) clearly stating why funding is needed for the proposed work and Cross (2018) omitting this step. In these examples, the influence of traditional strategies suggests that genreing activity found in crowdfunding proposals is influenced by professional, internal scientific genres.

CARS-style moves are also made in the "Ask the Scientists" (formerly "Abstract" page) section of proposals, further demonstrating the influence of professional scientific genres. Three questions posed by this template ("What is the context of this research?" "What is the significance of this project?" and "What are the goals of the project?") frame the content. In each proposal, the CARS model followed within the first two questions and the final question typically involved *Outlining Means.* This is interesting because it suggests that the norms of the scientific community have been imported to this broader social context. For many, the rhetorical situation may indeed be similar: a researcher in need of funding (certain exigencies such as funding a major lab is beyond the capability of crowdfunding). But will these questions, the framing imported from science, be most likely to reach a broader audience? We might propose the following hypothesis: the CARS approach is not necessarily functioning exclusively in academic disciplines but perhaps in transscientific genres, too, and so the general nature of the questions may very well be appropriate for a broad audience of researchers. As well, looking especially closely at the question of significance in a large sample of both successful and unsuccessful proposals, controlling for research products and disciplines, we might further suggest that appeals to wonder or other public accommodations (Fahnestock, 1986) have begun to appear in the proposals. But for the purposes of our exploration here, we will set questions of reception aside and, instead, revise the model of moves that might give us some strategies to work with in developing proposals.

Justifying Expenses is a move crucial to the crowdfunding proposal as it provides the account and rationale for how funds would be used. Proposals from Experiment are highly structured, and while justification of expenses might be included in abstracts or methods, they most frequently and obviously appear in the budget. In the proposals examined, the budgets consisted of two obvious parts: a list of budget items and a justification. This is consistent with the kinds of features we would expect in a conventional grant proposal. Budgets and the justifications that come along with them have long been part of proposal writing, but usually occluded and accomplished with significant support of research staff. In crowdfunding proposals, the efforts needed to undertake this work become visible, as does the work a budget accomplishes, and thus both become a significant point of departure from conventional proposal writing discussions. In the budget justifications, then, we sometimes find a third and optional step, as listed in table 2, where an appeal for support is made. For example, in the budget of one proposal, the authors write, "Your contributions will allow us to significantly improve our understanding of long-term climate and environmental changes in the tropics, which contain some of Earth's most biodiverse regions" (Williams & Gill, 2017). In another proposal, the author writes, "Your donation is essential and would be greatly appreciated to help this project follow through by funding its longest leg and seeing it to completion" (Jiang, 2017). Only a small percentage of proposals include these appeals, but their appearance in at least 9 of the proposals indicates some recurrence. It is also a notable step in the *Justifying Expenses* move because it suggests movement beyond a conventional budget proposal, where such appeals would be uncommon.

Often a research office at a university will provide budget templates and assist researchers with explaining and justifying budgets. In many cases, researchers also have to ensure they are following a number of rules about how money can be spent when drafting a budget for a specific granting agency. For example, they might be able to hire students and pay their salary, but not able to buy themselves out of teaching by including their own salary in the budget. Crowdfunding changes this model, and we see that explaining what the money will be used for becomes a crucial strategy in securing funding. But this kind of writing is difficult. Do you explain all the tools you will need (glassware and samples?) or travel costs (for either students or yourself?), and what about where money will *not* be spent (summer salary for faculty)? All of these moves are made in the five sample proposals. One strategy proposal writers use in crowdfunding proposals, similar to traditional proposals, is to provide as much transparency as possible: how the money be spent and, if they are academic researchers, what commonly funded lines will not be included (for example, salary supplements). Transparency in budgets is certainly crucial in academic research contexts, but the justifications are often much more occluded than the rest of the proposal writing.

Outlining Means occurs most obviously in the methods section of proposals, although not all proposals provide significant detail here on the methods to be used. Before looking to the methods pages, however, it is instructive to look at the landing page for a project, where the main proposal elements are located. Although there is more room to describe the means for completing research on the methods page, readers are likely to first encounter the project through the landing page. In a project's timeline, *Outlining Means* functions more obviously and consistently than in other areas of the proposal. Authors provide a description of the methods and tasks they will perform, along with a timeline with rough estimates of when work will be completed. For example:

> I plan to arrive on Cumberland Island on June 1st, 2017. Although field work can sometimes depend on weather and the cooperation of the research animal, my plan is to spend 6–8 weeks searching for, counting, tracking, and monitoring the Gopher tortoises on Cumberland Island (while giving updates to this group). I will then spend the Fall semester analyzing and writing up the results for publication and to orally present at scientific meetings.

> MAY 08, 2017 Project Launched
> JUN 01, 2017 Arrive and set-up equipment on Cumberland Island
> JUN 15, 2017 Complete Island Survey for burrows/tortoises
> JUN 20, 2017 Set-up motion cameras, radio transmitters, and temperature monitor discs on select burrows/tortoises
> JUL 18, 2017 Monitor tortoises for 4 weeks, then collect all equipment and data
> DEC 01, 2017 Analyze and write up results (Gagne, 2017)

Detailing the means for the research, however, entails other sections of the proposal. For example, in the budget section, Gagne (2017) writes, "Each piece of equipment will be used in the daily surveying, tracking, and monitoring of the tortoises throughout the summer of 2017." But it is in the "Methods" section that the details are elaborated upon, to help outline means:

> Cumberland Island will be surveyed for gopher tortoise burrows using the standard line transect method. Once a burrow is found in [sic] will be classified as active or inactive and scopes using the burrow cameras to note occupancy. Once found, burrow dimensions will be measured and a GPS point will be taken for GIS mapping.
>
> Tortoise will be caught using the bucket trap method. Once caught, tortoise measurements and gender will be quickly taken with subsequent release. Six tortoises (3 adult males, 3 adult females) will recieve [sic] a radio transmitter and temperature monitor and tracked for 1 week, after which, 6 different tortoises will be chosen and tracked. This process will continue for 4 weeks.
>
> In addition, each tracked tortoise will recieve [sic] a 24hr motion camera at its burrow entrance to record daily entering and exiting, with time stamps. (Gagne, 2017)

It is not surprising that this move is meaningful in a science crowdfunding proposal, and each proposal has varying implementation, but each works to explain how the study will be accomplished, much as we would expect in a conventional funding proposal. However, there is a plain language to many proposals that makes the methods more broadly engaging than we might expect from a traditional, disciplined proposal.

Claiming Importance is a move that can be found throughout the proposal, including in the endorsements, which are written by someone other than the proposal author(s). In the proposal body, examples of *Claiming Importance* commonly appear in response to the framing question "What is the significance of this project?" For example, in one proposal, the authors explain the importance of this research in both the context of research itself as well as its possible implications for on-the-ground, real-world work:

> To this point, no studies have assessed long-term vegetation changes in Jamaica in the combined context of the island's climate and human land-use histories. This research will fill an important knowledge gap in Jamaica's environmental history, and the findings will create new possibilities for both ecological and archaeological research on the island. Ultimately, this will expand the information available to Jamaican natural resource managers

about the causes and effects of environmental change on the island, which will provide significant benefits to local biodiversity and habitat conservation efforts. Overall, our project will promote the advancement of ecological research in Jamaica, and will provide a platform for future studies about prehistoric environmental changes on the island. (Williams & Gill, 2017)

In this example, we see that resource management is a main output for this research, as well as broader advancement of ecological research, as the authors tell us. In this move, a refrain is called, one invoked by *Establishing* and *Occupying a Niche,* where the significance of the research is first articulated, and here expanded upon. In this example, the strategy also moves toward *Claiming Benefits,* as the importance of this research is extended beyond academia.

Claiming Benefits allows us to understand the implication for research beyond a disciplinary conversation, and works particularly well with *Stating Achievements,* a move that attends more specifically to the academic contributions of a project. In these two moves, we learn about research outputs for the public, policy makers, and other researchers. In Experiment proposals, research outputs are often and clearly stated. Public engagement, resource management, policy implications, and a range of nonresearch outputs are included, too. Consider the following example, from the "What are the goals of this project?" section of a proposal, which describes the project's intended outputs:

I expect to send one or two manuscripts for publication in peer-reviewed scientific journals with the results of this project. Also, I will share the findings with local environmental authorities and other stakeholders, such as community leaders and NGOs [nongovernmental organizations] related to the conservation of the great green macaw in Costa Rica. (Molina & Monge, 2017)

Here we see expected references to publishing in peer-reviewed journals. Interestingly, the authors also note several other stakeholders with whom they hope to share their research, including community organizations, NGOs, and resource or environmental management. How these stakeholders will be engaged is not described, however. Such outputs, while certainly gesturing to the broader engagement that trans-scientific genres mark, are not unique to crowdfunding proposals, and we would expect to see similar gestures in traditional proposals. Marking another commonality between academic proposals and crowdfunding proposals are the strategies to generate the requisite ethos to persuade funders the researchers are indeed capable of producing these outputs.

Claiming Competence appears in its most full, complex form in the "Meet the Team" section of an Experiment proposal. Usually the biography will frame the research focus of each member of the team, provide some account of their education, including where they studied, and may list some information about previous research or publications. The move to claim competence in these proposals often cites personal reasons about why researchers are interested in a particular issue. Many of these bios are rather lengthy, as you might expect for the number of moves included here, but they remain consistent in many ways with what we would expect to find in conventional proposals. Understanding where a researcher has been trained, the field and methods they have cultivated expertise in, as well as their past record of accomplishment are all essential factors in assessing the credibility of these prospective funding recipients. A concise example that illustrates these features is instructive for how these moves function together. Using an image of the researcher standing in front of a wintery landscape, looking toward the camera smiling, and wearing a red coat and a brown hat, the "Meet the Team" section quickly establishes this is Tom Glass, an MSc student, University of Alaska Fairbanks (Glass, 2018). First the bio lists two other team members, both reportedly taking on advisory roles, and then it moves into the description for the PI:

> I have a B. A. in biology from Whitman College, and I love wolverines. I'm conducting this research for my MSc at the University of Alaska Fairbanks, with Dr. Knut Kielland. I have spent the last four winters working with wolverines, on the Wolverine and Winter Recreation Project in Jackson, Wyoming, the Wolverine and Industrial Development Project in northern Alberta, and most recently this project, in northern Alaska. I believe that this is one of the most critical unknowns in wolverine biology today, and has widespread implications for the management decisions we make, especially in light of climate change. (Glass, 2018)

The steps may not appear in order, but they are present. Many of the longer bios also feature a more extensive description of what led a researcher to a particular topic. For example, "Back in the early 90's I read a book called 'Neotropical Parrots in Crisis' and I realized that this family of beautiful, smart and charismatic birds were in great danger of extinction but we knew very little about them. So, I decided to dedicate my career and my life to study them in the wild and captivity and to promote their conservation" (Courtenay, Brightsmith, Trauco, Regelmann, & Boyd, 2018). It is also common to see a further narrowing of the field and research topic. For example, "I have been curious about rare and endangered cacti, the habitat in which they occur, their adaptations to particular soil substrates and soil textures and their unique morphology" (Breslin, 2018).

For many major granting agencies, a standardized biographical sketch is used to establish the expertise, and therefore the credibility, of a researcher. Typically, these will include the affiliation of the researchers, where they completed their studies, a list of several publications they have authored, and perhaps some additional work they have completed, such as editing major journals in their fields. Another interesting inclusion in these kinds of biographic sketches is a list of collaborators, including doctoral advisors. Ethos-building work occurs in other sections of a conventional proposal, certainly, and we might find mention of how well suited a particular researcher is to complete a project. Ethos building operates in a similar manner in Experiment proposals. In these proposals, authors make claims about their expertise, they request that other researchers endorse them, and in this work, there appears to be a variation on the biographical sketch. However, the biography offered in an Experiment proposal has social media–influenced profile features, including photographs of the researchers. A photograph is not required but may be included, and in the sample texts there are a variety of photos, ranging from professional quality portraits to candid shots or self-shot portraits ("selfies") of the researchers. Beyond the photos, a range of strategies might be employed, including providing standard academic affiliation, but also notes that are more personal in some of the proposals, including what motivated researchers to engage in a particular project or line of research. Some even include hobbies outside of their research agenda. These examples show how blends of both professional and popular genres have influenced the strategies found in crowdfunding proposals. With these combinations of genre-ing activities, the complicated rhetorical unfoldings of trans-scientific genres is further illustrated.

Drawing on one's professional network and the credibility affiliated with more senior or distinguished scholars is also at work, in a similar manner to what we might see in more conventional funding models. *Claiming Competence* appears in the recently added endorsement ("Endorsed by") feature. Allowing others to publicly note support for your project, the claim to competence here is made by first establishing you hold credibility within a research community. Finer points, such as the excellence of researchers or their unique ability to conduct a project can be made; for example, "Mario and Jacquelyn are uniquely equipped to accomplish this project" (Bush, qtd. in Williams & Gill, 2017), "Sofia does excellent work" (Nowak, qtd. in Lora, 2017), and "Saethra is uniquely qualified to carry out this research" (Foster, qtd. in Ha & Fritscher, 2017). We might identify this as a kind of *Claiming Competence,* with a step that allows the endorsement "stating uniqueness or excellence of a researcher/team" (this step is not included in the above Table 2). This step, part of the construction of the proposal author's ethotic work, further parallels traditional proposals. In many academic proposals, external reviewers will provide not an endorsement per se, but an assessment of the work and the PI and team's ability to complete that work. It may be there are similar strategies at work between these kinds of assessments and endorsements. However, more likely is that endorsements have similar features to letters of reference or support.[7]

Taken together, the moves detailed here present us with a collection of rhetorical considerations and strategies that might usefully be applied when drafting a crowdfunding proposal. Or, at least, they might be useful conceptual categories to entertain in pre-proposal brainstorming. The context for these proposals differs from conventional academic research funding proposals, entering the complicated landscape of trans-scientific genres. Discounting lessons from expert writers of academic research proposals is unwise, but discounting the lessons from expert community fund-raisers may be a more serious mistake. Because crowdfunding proposals operate in a different rhetorical space than research proposals written for major granting agencies, and because we know that social networks are crucial to crowdfunding success, understanding the distinct rhetorical situation to which a researcher responds is useful. That is, in addition to *how* researchers communicate with an audience, *cultivating* an audience is crucial to the success of crowdfunding proposals (see: Byrnes, Ranganathan, Walker, Faulkes, 2014). Perhaps the most essential factor in successfully funding through a crowdfunding proposal is the crowd, the audience (A. R. Mehlenbacher, 2017). Until you have an audience to persuade, there is not much sense in developing persuasive strategies. And in the twenty-first century, in an "attention economy," as Lanham (2006) has dubbed it, securing that audience is crucial to one's success. Thus the moves we have outlined here are only part of the artistry a rhetorician must employ to first call into being an audience and, only then, deliberate on what means of persuasion are available and most appropriate for their audience. To better understand how these moves function within that broader rhetorical artistry, the next section explores an in-depth case of a successful grant proposal.

---

7. In Canada, when a student applies for funding through those federal or provincial scholarship programs previously noted, their supervisors and other faculty provide letters of support. Such letters include features that promote the value of the study and the student's capability to conduct and complete the project. Parallels between these different genres would likely inform a productive study of endorsements on Experiment.

CASE ANALYSIS: AN EXPERIMENT.COM PROPOSAL

To explore how this move analysis might be applied, let us consider one case as an illustration, complementing our small corpus analysis. This exemplary proposal is titled "How Do Post-industrial Landscapes Affect American Woodcock Breeding Success?" (Farley, 2016), and the proposal makes full use of the 2017 configuration of Experiment. Methods are detailed, lab notes include nine updates, and there are fourteen comments in the discussion—only missing are results, which is expected given the proposal has only just been funded at the time of writing this analysis.[8] In addition to using most of the features of the platform, the proposal is also well detailed. Kathleen Farley, who is a PhD candidate in biology at Rutgers University, launched the project and secured US$5,050, with an initial goal of US$4,570.[9] Finally, then, this case was chosen because it was successful in generating support.

Under the project's "Overview" tab and then "About This Project," we are offered what appears to be a typical general introduction to the research effort. Before the written introduction, however, a video is showcased. The two minute and twenty-nine second video is a combination of visual interest and storytelling. It features visuals of the landscapes to be studied and an interview with the proposal author, who describes the work she is undertaking in accessible terms (for example, describing the woodcock as "the shore bird that decided to live in the woods" and "early successional forest" as being "like fields with shrubs in them") (Farley, 2016). But Farley is also describing more technical or methodological concerns (for example, discussing singing ground surveys or noting there is a decline in woodcocks of "about 2% per year"). Finally, she makes the pitch for the significance of the research at 2:29:

> We have these abandoned, industrial landscapes that wildlife are beginning to move into. I'm curious to know what cost or benefit do Woodcock gain from choosing post-industrial sites, and to hopefully build that out to the population level to see, as a whole, can using post-industrial habitat help the species, because there are also half a million post-industrial sites throughout the US right now. If we could capitalize on land we degraded, for wildlife, it could really turn things around. (Farley, 2016)

Like other multimodal forms in these emerging spaces for science communication, this video underscores how the ways we report science, argue for the

---

8. January 15, 2017.
9. The average Experiment project is funded at US$4,313 (Experiment, 2017a).

value of research, and relate research to broader audiences is fueled by the platforms we are afforded. Specifically, this platform not only affords a form for presenting research, modes for interacting with one's audience through the discussion, and a way to share a video promoting one's work; crucially, it also embeds the proposal within the larger Experiment network.[10]

The overview text aligns with the kinds of moves Swales identifies in his CARS model, with the notable absence of some features, such as in-text references. However, as a more general introduction to a research proposal, this is not particularly bothersome.

> I study American Woodcock breeding success in post-industrial habitat to see if human altered habitat can be beneficial for wildlife. To do this, I will be placing radio transmitters on woodcock to monitor them throughout the breeding season. This will allow me to determine their health, survival, and return rates. Studying woodcock can help us better understand other species (Ruffed Grouse, Golden-winged Warbler, etc) that are severely declining due to significant habitat loss. (Farley, 2016)

Breaking this down with the moves identified above, three introductory moves appear to be at work in this text:

> Move #1 (*Establishing Territory*): "I study American Woodcock breeding success in post-industrial habitat to see if human altered habitat can be beneficial for wildlife."

> Move #2 (*Establishing a Niche*): "To do this, I will be placing radio transmitters on woodcock to monitor them throughout the breeding season."

> Move #3 (*Occupying the Niche*): "This will allow me to determine their health, survival, and return rates. Studying woodcock can help us better understand other species (Ruffed Grouse, Golden-winged Warbler, etc) that are severely declining due to significant habitat loss."

---

10. I do not mean to suggest any kind of reductionist, technologically determined motivation for the forms of science communication we are seeing online. Rather, different kinds of affordances online are allowing scientists and science communicators to engage in new methods of delivering communications about science, collaborating in knowledge-making processes, and even reaching new audiences of nonexperts in response to new demands for academic researchers.

The "body" of the proposal, or at least the lengthier discussion, is found in what previously appeared under the "Abstract" tab. Now it is embedded within the "Overview" tab and structured with the same questions: "What is the context of this research?" "What is the significance of this project?" "What are the goals of the project?" Here we can see not only some of the broadened introductory moves but also some additional elaboration on what the project is meant to accomplish and how it will do so.

What is the context of this research?
On-going research in Liberty State Park lead [*sic*] to repeated observation of American Woodcock in the highly polluted interior forest. As a PhD student, I was brought on board to investigate this phenomenon. First I needed to answer: Are woodcock in Liberty State Park a random occurrence or indicative of a greater trend?

I conducted a pilot study in 2016 across 30 non-industrial and post-industrial sites in northern New Jersey and it's clear that woodcock are making use of these former industrial sites. We now need to quantify this behavior in terms of what proportion of populations are using each habitat for courtship/breeding, and what impact this has on regional woodcock population trends. New Jersey is the most urbanized US state making it ideal for this research. (Farley, 2016)

At work in this passage are several moves. For instance, we see a move that can be mapped as *Establishing a Territory* at the outset of the paragraph that starts, "On-going research in Liberty State Park lead [*sic*] to repeated observation of American Woodcock in the highly polluted interior forest" (Farley, 2016). The particular researcher's role is added to further clarify the exigence of her proposal when she writes, "As a PhD student, I was brought on board to investigate this phenomenon." Several efforts are detailed here that can be categorized as *Stating Achievement,* namely the products of a pilot study: "I conducted a pilot study in 2016 across 30 non-industrial and post-industrial sites in northern New Jersey and it's clear that woodcock are making use of these former industrial sites." Then we are provided with the move *Establishing a Niche*: "We now need to quantify this behavior in terms of what proportion of populations are using each habitat for courtship/breeding, and what impact this has on regional woodcock population trends. New Jersey is the most urbanized US state making it ideal for this research." The next section further elaborates on this move.

What is the significance of this project?

Post-industrial landscapes already replace much former forest and field habitat for North American wildlife, particularly in the east. The 450,000 post-industrial sites in the US include old rail yards, landfills, former industrial complexes and superfund sites.

We know when woodcock succeed so do New England Cottontail, Golden-winged Warblers, Ruffed Grouse, Hognose snakes and Brown Thrashers, among other species. When woodcock populations thrive, we have hope for the larger community.

While woodcock have been declining since the 1960s, this change in habitat selection is new. If we can identify species that thrive in modified habitats, we will have better insights for conservation management in highly urbanized regions that have few pristine areas. (Farley, 2016)

By midway through the paragraph we see a shift to *Occupying the Niche*: "If we can identify species that thrive in modified habitats, we will have better insights for conservation management in highly urbanized regions that have few pristine areas." Then we turn to an explicit and more detailed account of how this will be accomplished.

What are the goals of the project?

In 2017–2018, we will study woodcock on 2–3 post-industrial and non-industrial sites. Data collected includes determining age and sex, a quick health assessment, and attaching the radio transmitter allowing continued monitoring through the season and into the following spring. Monitoring the radio frequencies will allow us to determine if males incur a cost for performing courtship displays in post-industrial habitat, survival rates of nestlings in post- and non-industrial sites, and if returning woodcock change habitat selection based on previous choices. Monitoring the population over multiple years will allow us to begin understanding population trends based on habitat selection. (Farley, 2016)

In this final section, details about the research are given, including what data will be collected, how the monitoring of radio frequencies (the niche for the research) will be carried out, and further articulation of why these efforts are important and the contribution that the research will make to understanding of population trends and habitat selection. Taken together, the moves here offer a rather standard account of how a scientific project will be described, with some departure to note—for instance, why a junior researcher would be pitching this research on Experiment.

In the "Overview" tab, the budget provides a space for a paragraph description of expenses. In the example, a rationale is provided for paying hunters with dogs that can track woodcocks and for purchasing radio transmitters. An itemized list of expenses provides further details. A visual provides a doughnut chart breakdown to further supplement the list of expenses. Part of the persuasive appeal here is one of transparency: providing clear information about how monies will be used allows backers to make a decision about whether or not they believe their funds will be used responsibly. However, to make such decisions may require some insider knowledge that a scientist would have but not a broader public. For example, the itemized list includes "Additional Nets & Poles for Mist Netting (4)" and "Additional Banding Kit Supplies" (Farley, 2016). At 152 words, the budget justification takes up a relatively small percentage (nearly 14 percent) of the proposal text within the overview, which is about 945 words, exclusive of the budget.

As previously noted, it seems apparent that endorsements align well with *Claiming Competence*, although someone other than the proposal writer makes the claim. But recall that this move involves "statements to the effect that the proposer is well qualified, experienced, and generally capable of carrying out the tasks set out" (see table 2). These are ethotic appeals and help to establish the credibility of the researcher; establishing this credibility through endorsements chiefly relies on the status that the endorser brings with them. One of the individuals endorsing this project identifies himself as an associate professor; his status as a faculty member and within a university helps to establish the credibility of the junior researcher proposing the work. But a closer examination of this endorsement illustrates that the rhetorical work being accomplished extends beyond establishing the ethos or credibility of the researcher.

In the US, post-industrial landscapes are found wherever people live in significant numbers. How they develop as nature takes hold again affects the environment around a large fraction of the population. Woodcock are normally an "indicator" species, meaning that their presence is associated with other kinds of wildlife. Kathleen is asking if woodcock on post-industrial sites have normal behavior and ecology, in which case their presence suggests a thriving ecosystem. Her research will help us manage our urban and suburban "human habitat." (Farley, 2016)

Here the research itself, not the researcher, is centrally framed. Contextualizing the research and its importance this way helps underscore the purpose of the funding, which is indeed the research effort as a means to improve understanding of population trends and habitat selection among woodcocks. However, the other endorsement on this project takes a different approach, speaking to the researcher's credibility and ability to accomplish the work set out:

> Kathleen's passion for birds and they [*sic*] role they play in an environment are inspirational. I can't imagine another person to run this project, she is intellectually creative, hard working and loads of fun to be around. I expect great things from her and this project! (Farley, 2016)

Also from a university faculty member, this approach is certainly distinct from the previous endorsement, and suggests a range of rhetorical strategies. Certainly, it is worth further exploring the role of endorsements in scientific crowdfunding proposals, although it is likely early in this features implementation to make strong claims about the role of endorsement broadly in science crowdfunding proposals.

Under the "Team Bio," two more senior researchers use predictable rhetorical appeals to establish their credibility:

> Claus Holzapfel, PhD: 20+ years in community ecology investigating novel communities created by fusion of exotic and native species. Holzapfel began the urban biodiversity monitoring outreach program at Rutgers Newark in 2012.

> Barb Gilbert: Leads data collection for Montclair State University's American Kestrel Monitoring Program in Sussex County. Gilbert will be leading field collection for two sites to expand hands-on science opportunities for her students. (Farley, 2016)

Referring to a degree in the field and citing institutional affiliations, these two bios look similar to those we might expect of academic biographies. Likewise, our project leader offers a similar collection of strategies to establish her credibility:

> Kathleen Farley I'm a PhD Candidate at Rutgers-University in Newark, NJ. My interests are changing landscapes focusing on the long-term population changes in avian communities. I have worked with banding and mortality

databases in urban regions and endemic cloud forest species in the tropics. (Farley, 2016)

Farley offers a more extensive bio, which I will not quote at length here, but it is a typical example of a biography for a scientist, establishing credibility through her degrees and experience in the field. The implicit appeals across all of these biographies are that the institutional affiliation indicates participation in a certain community of practice—and there is most certainly a transfer of prestige associated—and the experience cites past success to indicate some basis for assessing whether or not further success is likely. In-field experience is crucial, as it suggests the kind of expertise required to successfully execute a project. These claims fall into the *Claiming Competence* move, which clearly has some conventional instantiations for scientists, as references to institutions, degrees, and specialties indicate. All of these claims are made explicit for this project by establishing strong methods.

In the "Methods" tab, a lengthier account of what exactly the research involves is provided. At about 750 words, or nearly four thousand characters, the section appears similar to what we would expect to find in an academic proposal. Different aspects of the methods are explained, including aims, challenges, and details on data collection and analysis, complete with in-text references. Rather than providing the text in full here, for the sake of space, I will point to some of the strategic moves made within the text and describe its general structure. The methods are divided into three major sections, "Summary," "Challenges," and "Pre Analysis Plan"; these labels are provided by the Experiment platform. Within this particular exemplary proposal, the summary includes two aims,

Aim 1: Determine whether courting males can distinguish differences in habitat quality between post-industrial and non-industrial early successional landscapes.

Aim 2: Determine whether post-industrial landscapes are source, sink or ecological traps for offspring.

Each aim is further described, complete with in-text references to research. In these descriptions, the researcher details how she will complete this work, *Outlining Means*. Following this section, in "Challenges," the researcher begins identifying limitations, beginning with a statement about the overall difficulty of the task: "American Woodcock are cryptic species, meaning that they can be incredibly difficult to find" (Farley, 2016). But also, the research is further detailed by *Outlining Means*: "However, as they are also a game species, there has been considerable interest in their population status for decades," and then the researcher provides an account of how to improve this method (Farley, 2016). All told, the methods section appears typical of such a section for a research project, particularly if we consider how a methods section will be framed for a more general audience as research funding proposals often are, assuming multidisciplinary review panels.

Lab notes work to supplement the proposal itself, and they ensure an ongoing site for engagement with backers. With nine lab notes posted, the range of topics includes posts that further explain or inform ("What is a woodcock" and "Why New Jersey?"); a thank you to backers midway through the campaign ("Thank You [2016 Edition]"); and at the end ("Today is a day to celebrate!"), holiday wishes ("Happy Holidays!" and "Peent,"[11] two, one. Happy New Year!"), a post about conference going ("#SciComm through Art"), and two guest posts about field work ("The True Beauty Behind this Research" and "On a First Taste of Fieldwork"). These notes include creative, promotional, or illustrative visuals that help chart the multiple rhetorical purposes notes may serve. In her lab notes, for example, Farley includes playful images of woodcocks sending Yuletide wishes. Images of Farley's tweets are embedded in another lab note, along with a video of an American woodcock "dancing," linked from YouTube, and completed by The Champs' "Tequila" for the soundtrack. Farley herself appears in one lab note describing how her work had been visualized as a biosketch (see, on Twitter, @sketchbiologist, aka Abby McBride, or #biosketch).[12] Images of the landscapes describe the woodcock itself, and scientists completing field work also appear in Farley's lab notes (see figure 1).

This is an exemplary case by virtue of the proposal's success in acquiring funding, and it demonstrates the wide range of uses of visuals in crowdfunding proposals. Promotional uses are clear, certainly, but these visuals do more than simply make promotional appeals. They make a case for the research, for the value of science, and tell engaging stories of the natural (and postindustrial) world. Although it might seem such work is at the popularization or public engagement end of the science communication spectrum, some of

---

11. "Peent" refers to a sound, a cry that the male woodcock makes when courting.

12. The feed has been archived on Storify if you're interested in exploring these "biosketches." On the point of art, science, and Twitter, there is a growing and vibrant community on Twitter of enormously talented artists creating science-based or science-inspired work (#SciArt). For an introduction, see the work of @FlyingTrilobite (Glendon Mellow) and @Symbiartic on Twitter (online at Symbiartic.com or the Symbiartic blog archive on *Scientific American*'s website).

FIGURE 1. Lab Note Images from an Experiment Proposal. Lab notes vary in their form, but attention-grabbing images can be used to help generate an audience. Once a reader clicks through one of the images (as illustrated above), they will find a variety of information, from updates on research progress to details about publications. It may be that lab notes serve a similar function to blogs, including broader uses in the social science–sharing ecology—for example, tweeting a link to a post to generate attention for the research.

these images, including the visualized biosketch Farley holds, provide a window to the life of the scientist, attending a conference and engaging her peers, and continue such engagement online (Twitter engages a robust community of scientists, to be certain).

Maintaining lab notes is one way to further connect with backers or potential backers during the campaign, but they also provide a way to update supporters once the work has begun. Although it is certainly too early to expect that of this proposal, the multiple purposes for lab notes create an interesting rhetorical space, as these notes may serve informational or promotional ends and, perhaps, highlight the continuing and concurrent nature of the project work as well.

The "Discussion" menu tab holds the comments section of the proposal, where backers ask questions about what the woodcock eats and other questions about the project or provide encouragement, well wishes, and congratulations. The proposal author provides responses to the questions posed. As lab notes afford the opportunity to remain engaged with the audience of backers, so too does the discussion, which allows for the backers to likewise remain engaged with the project. The degree to which this engagement is sustained is a matter that could be debated, but the two-way model of communication in the proposal is certainly an affordance unlike anything one would find in conventional proposals.

When results become finalized, they are shared through the "Experiment Journal of Results." On this page, there are links to project result pages, which include peer-reviewed journal articles, posters, theses, and some more descriptive accounts of the work completed, including images. Interestingly, what is achieved on this page attends to the world of professional, sanctioned science. These are academic activities and remind us there is, indeed, an emphasis on peer-reviewed research outputs for projects, including the raison d'être of the academic world, research articles in disciplinary journals.

SUMMARY: EVOLVING CROWDFUNDING STRATEGIES

Emerging as a typified form of online science communication, the crowdfunding proposal takes on a different rhetorical life than its conventional academic counterparts, inhabiting a space alongside traditional scientific genres. Take, for instance, the average annualized research grant award at the NSF: US$167,800 in 2014 and US$174,900 in 2015 (National Science Foundation, 2016). Typically, this level of funding exceeds the size of the average successful crowdfunding campaigns on Experiment. Although an important distinction, this does not suggest that crowdfunding is simply a poor substitution for such large-scale funding (although it is a poor substitution for robust, publicly funded support for scientific research). Instead, the function of crowdfunding seems to be to provide small-scale support for projects that cannot secure funding elsewhere. There are numerous reasons that funding may be unavailable to some researchers, and this is especially true for our citizen and otherwise independent or grassroots scientists, as well as for less experienced or junior researchers.

Understanding the role of one's own network and the funding platform's network is crucial to successful campaigns. Requests for support through crowdfunding platforms change the response asked of the audience. For conventional grant proposals, a successful bid would be paid through federal, state, or corporate funds. Crowdfunding proposals request that personal funds be used in the support of research—and, it should be noted, this has critical implications for the kinds of research that are funded, or indeed the researcher who is funded, as I will discuss below. Thus, budget justifications are essential and should be carefully considered and explained with a good deal of transparency: Will equipment, travel, or salary be covered? What other monetary expenses will be incurred? But there is also a clear requirement of trust on behalf of those providing support. Presumably this is where endorsements assist in establishing the credibility—and trustworthiness—of the researcher.

Matters of trust are likely at play when we consider that one's own network is often a source of financial support. On the matter of social networks, the amplifying function they serve is likewise meaningful. Put simply, sharing the page with one's own social network amplifies the number of views, and with some luck the number of supporters, that a proposal might obtain. This also means an inequitable distribution of research dollars may be perpetuated based on the socioeconomic status of one's already established peer network. The audience provided by platforms such as Experiment.com may, in part, alleviate such disparity, but further study in the economics of these networks is crucial to better understanding these implications.

Crowdfunding also contributes in economically different ways to its federal funding counterparts (for example, from the NSF or National Institutes of Health in the United States or NSERC in Canada). Indirect costs or overhead payments taken from an awarded grant by the university to pay for facilities, equipment, and administrative costs are not permitted to be collected by the crowdfunding platforms and companies that we have examined here. This means that the financial incentives for a university are much lower in the case of crowdfunding, which typically awards the funds to a PI as a gift, and subsequently the incentives for a researcher are lower. In fact, the stakes for this seemingly obscure academic practice are so high they have even garnered some attention in the mainstream press when President Obama sought to place restrictions on how much overhead universities could claim from federal funding. *Boston Globe* reporter Tracy Jan wrote in a March 2013 article that "Harvard, MIT, and a coalition of other powerhouse research institutions have thwarted a reform proposal by the Obama administration to slash the amount of government research money each school receives for overhead costs," noting that Harvard received 69 percent, with the national average sitting at 52 percent. Put simply, crowdfunds do not represent the same fiscal benefit to universities that federal grants do because the overhead (indirect costs) that would typically be included in the grant amount for these purposes no longer exists. This being so, the institutional prestige of securing such funding must be understood as not only qualitatively, but quantitatively, different from federal grants. With less institutional prestige and fewer financial benefits to an institution, researchers are less likely to benefit directly in terms of tenure and promotion for their work on a crowdfunding proposal than on a major national grant.

Crowdfunding is also a one-time—that is, nonrenewable—grant. Many granting agencies allow researchers to renew grants, which makes the funding of labs more stable and predictable. Naturally the cost of running many labs is also far outside the capacities we would expect of crowdfunding. Thus, crowdfunding becomes a supplemental form of funding, perhaps more central to new investigators or un(der)funded investigators. This last point should not be underestimated. The implications for novice researchers or researchers following what might be otherwise unfunded research are complex.[13] We have at once a new way to supplement and support research that federal agencies, for one reason or another, will not fund. However, because crowdfunding has less prestige associated with it, some might ask: Is it worth spending the time writing and managing crowdfunding proposals? This will depend on the research it allows one to conduct and the associated institutionally valued products that one will be able to produce because of the research.

Although crowdfunding proposals may not exhibit all of the strategies common to a proposal for a government-sponsored competition, this is not for a lack of rhetorical sophistication. Rather, rhetorical sophistication allows successful crowdfunding proposals to reach a broad enough audience to secure funding. For crowdfunding proposals, an appeal to a large audience requires accommodating one's rhetorical efforts to this audience of experts, amateurs, engaged publics, and others. The complex audience for crowdfunding proposals requires a shift in the rhetor's position; thus, a change in rhetorical strategies and style is warranted (for example, stating implications in such a way that they are obvious to a nonexpert, while also retaining precision of language and appropriately restricting claims about significance or implications). Indeed, it is not simply a "public" audience reading these proposals. While a proposal does not undergo the same process of review, it is likely that

---

13. Despite these concerns, crowdfunding currently offers a helpful supplemental tool for research funding. This is especially true for novice and otherwise un(der)funded researchers in the sciences. That is to say nothing about the importance that crowdfunding might play in the humanities and social science disciplines, which sometimes require funding for travel to archives or other kinds of field work, but which have become largely undervalued. Indeed, it is not simply our contemporary STEM focus that undervalues the work of the humanities and social sciences. Rather, there is a deeper contempt for modes of intellectual inquiry that threaten to operate outside of product-based research and discourses of innovation and progress, focusing instead on critical democratic issues. To illustrate this point, we need only look to the NSF's criterion for political science research (it must advance national security or economic interests) or to the cancellation of the political science grant cycle in 2013 (Mole, 2013).

writers will be acutely aware that their peers may be reviewing (that is, reading critically) their proposals. Crowdfunding proposals, then, inhabit a deliberative space comprised of an audience of peers and publics, placing these proposals in the sphere of trans-scientific genres.

CHAPTER 3

Databases

Genres for Knowledge Production

AT THE CORE of scientific research are the data used to support claims. A complex apparatus of communication tools is used in the collection, coordination and organization, and dissemination of data. Research methods have a lot to do with designing studies that collect good data, but these efforts do not end with collecting the data. Data must be organized and stored in some way that is useable for particular kinds of research efforts. Methods of organizing data have always been central to scientific research, but we have increasingly complex methods of organizing, accessing, and re(using) data in these databases. As science becomes more digitized and digitally reliant, data and databases remain central to the enterprise of knowledge production but increasingly inhabit more public spaces in the dissemination of knowledge. We might ask what kinds of rhetorical activities, and possibilities, data afford. Databases are, in their simplest form, structures that assist in organizing, storing, and retrieving data.[1] But not all databases are the same, and a number of

---

1. It is a noteworthy distinction, as well, particularly for those less familiar with databases, that the *database structures* I am exploring here are not the computer code underpinning databases themselves. Elsewhere Brock and I have explored rhetorics computer code and how code is governed by certain world-building logics that, while distinct from natural language, are not independent from natural language. In our analysis, we employ a genre approach to explore the norms and values that shape certain projects. Specifically, we suggest rhetorical features of code "exist within its articulation of components (e.g., through naming of variables and functions in code files), through its structure (e.g., by promoting certain procedural logics of how

decisions go into their design, including field- or subject-specific decisions. Further, the kinds of texts that operate in support of databases must respond to the disciplinary norms and values of the specializations they inhabit. Databases, by their design and use, are rhetorical artifacts, and serve as a source for understanding science communications online. In this chapter, I explore a range of discursive activities that support such artifacts.

Notably, there is an increase in open models of data sharing in many scientific fields, and this creates a more complex rhetorical situation to which databases and their associated texts must respond.[2] Making the move to more open data requires critical attention to documentation strategies as the constellation of genre-ing activity that support databases grows to include not only help documentation but also sophisticated approaches to managing metadata. With open data, the database moves from a particular research project, research laboratory, or even institution to a broader base of users. And when these databases are aggregate sources or rely on a number of different users and institutions to compile the data set, the coordinating genre activity proliferates, and the complexity of the database ecology increases. In this reading, the rhetoricity of databases is found not simply in a collection of data or the container that holds it, but in the careful negotiation of database logics and construction. This is to say that databases are not simply a media or platform, but rather a kind of cyber infrastructure. A cyber infrastructure is

---

to compute data), and through its process of iterative development (e.g., as multiple contributors create and edit those files)" (Brock & A. R. Mehlenbacher, 2017, p. 4). Lewis (2016) has also used a genre-based framework to investigate the rhetoricity of code. While attention to code and its rhetoric is a growing site of study, what I am focusing on in my analysis is the database structures. They are, however, mediated by code, and certainly the choice of database tool and its code base will influence the kinds of data structures that can be chosen from and implemented.

2. Centrality of the database to open data, and subsequently open science, might seem obvious given that the database stores requisite information for studies, as well as any follow-up studies or efforts to reproduce results—all to say nothing of efforts to collaborate on original research. However obvious it might seem, it is worth explicating the assumptions and underpinnings that shape databases, data use, and genres affiliated with databases. Although the norms of science have deep roots and are well canonized, efforts to broaden research teams into multidisciplinary spaces, to include citizen scientists, and to share data with broader publics require we make explicit the implicit. Through sociocognitive apprenticeship models, scientists develop tacit understanding of discourse norms, and these norms need to be made explicit (see Berkenkotter & Huckin, 1995, on the matter of sociocognitive models as related to genre knowledge). Put rather simply, as the number of people interested in using scientific data expands, we need to make explicit rules and norms about how the data should be used and what they can be used for to produce sound science. Because some of the people who might be interested in using the data are not professionally trained, thinking about how we craft databases and their attendant genres for a broader audience becomes crucial to ensure strong scientific work continues.

"the set of organizational practices, technical infrastructure, and social norms that collectively provide for the smooth operation of scientific work at a distance" (Bowker, Baker, Millerand, & Ribes, 2010, p. 102). Bowker et al. (2010) argue, "It is not enough to put out a new technical infrastructure—it needs to be woven into the daily practices of knowledge workers" (p. 110). In studying these emerging cyber or information infrastructures, Bowker et al. are also calling for new approaches and methods that help manage scale and complexity with an "integrative view" (p. 113). These lessons from critical data studies help illustrate how data are put to work socially, and how their very conceptualization and construction have powerful social influences (Gitelman, 2013; Dalton & Thatcher, 2014; Iliadis & Russo, 2016). Such cases illustrate the ways that data operate in political economies, how labor practices influence how we constitute data, and the applications of data for governance and surveillance as well as sites of resistance. As well, the agents and actors who collect, share, use, and are used by data are merit consideration in studies of data—notably, in the ways data are seen and function to authorize or sanction epistemological vantages (Jasanoff, 2017).

In this chapter, databases and the broader media ecologies within which they are situated are investigated as part of larger information infrastructures scientists are developing to share data. This chapter examines what kinds of rhetorical work occur in the construction and management of data sets. The framing question for this chapter is: What does tracing genre-ing activity illustrate about the rhetorical activities involved in the collection, organization, and dissemination of data sets? Another guiding question asks: How can we understand the governing logic and rhetoricity of databases?

BACKGROUND: DATA COLLECTION, ORGANIZATION, AND DISSEMINATION

Rosenberg (2013) helps us untangle the complicated history of the term "data," a history that affords us insight into the term's twenty-first-century use. First used in English in the seventeenth century, "the rise of the concept in the seventeenth and eighteenth centuries is tightly linked to the development of modern concepts of knowledge and argumentation" (p. 15). Because the conditions of our knowledge production are grounded in the kinds of arguments we make (wherein we situate facts and evidence), data are part of this rhetorical process. But what is shaping the kinds of arguments we make; that is, what shapes the possibilities for lines of argument—data? Rosenberg helps us understand this point by aligning facts as ontological, evidence as epistemological, and in a profoundly important move, data as rhetorical (p. 17). It is in his etymological enterprise in studying data that he tells us the word's uptake in English, from Latin, came with a more restricted sense than the donor language. In English, Rosenberg writes, data "emphasized the argumentative context as well as the idea of problem-solving by bringing into relationship things known and things unknown" (p. 20). Data presuppose argument in this sense, and are not true or untrue or aligned with reality or not, but rather are part of how we build truth and reality (p. 37). By the eighteenth century, data saw something of a "semantic inversion" where they came to be thought of as the "result of investigation rather than its premise," and it is in this framework that the twentieth- and twenty-first-century notions of data aligned with numerical form. However, "still today we take data as a premise for argument" (p. 33). That is, data "went from being reflexively associated with those things that are outside of any possible process of discovery to being the very paradigm of what one seeks through experiment and observation" (p. 36). This account provides us an understanding of data as rhetorical, being "that which is given prior to argument"; thus, "the meaning of data must always shift with the argumentative strategy and context—and with the history of both" (p. 36).

Data collection employs a number of different coordinating genre activities that work to define the exigence for the research, establish a fitting response and boundaries for the data-collection efforts, open lines of communication for organizational and administrative work, and outline expectations and rules to govern data-collection processes. A particular genre may serve multiple functions at different points in the development of data-collection procedures, but in many of these cases, the genres are consistent in their social exigence, such as the event invitation or the team meeting. Along with these genres, we see multiple communication technologies employed, and this reminds us of the role of communication technologies and their relationship to genres in coordinating social activities and actions.

Working through an example, partially fictional and partially based on the activities of researchers following the disaster at Fukushima Daiichi, we can examine the interaction of genres, technologies, and social activities to understand some of the work done to design data collection. Establishing the grounds for an exigence is a crucial first step for a research project. Understanding not only the context that led to the research interest but the particular issues one is responding to actually takes a good deal of conceptual shaping. In these early stages, the nature of the problem must be identified. One might ask, for example, if increases in certain kinds of cancers are tied to environmental pollutants. Understanding baseline cases, environmental conditions and changes, and other possible conflating factors is all work that requires some parsing out of interacting elements. From there, precise research questions can be established, and a team will often negotiate this kind of work, including citing the existing literature in the respective fields (for example, public health or environmental sciences). Field variation is a useful point to consider for database designers, and illustrates the rhetoricity required to design such systems and the rhetorical situations to which they respond.

While in some academic fields sharing data in an open manner is well established, not all disciplines have the same approach to data sharing. The norms of a discipline may make construction of a large, aggregate data set difficult. However, as federal funding agencies around the world begin to mandate sharing of data, this may change, although attention to disciplinary norms currently remains a concern (Nelson, 2009). Some disciplines share data freely, while others make decisions about whether data should be shared pre-publication or post-publication, if at all. Practically, these variations in norms mean that some disciplines have a number of different concerns they must attend to in the design of large database repositories. Rhetorically guided criticism attends to design questions. For example, "What kinds of data will be included?" leads to considerations that will illustrate the norms and values of the field as arguments about what data counts or doesn't, and how the data must be conceptualized.

Multiple communication technologies might be used for the purposes of this initial coordination and negotiation, including telephones, email, video chat applications, and research databases. Established genres correlate with these technologies, including telephone conversations, email threads, meeting agendas, and research articles in research databases. It is likely these genres, many of which correspond to Bakhtin's (1986) notion of primary speech genres—simple genres characterized by "unmediated speech communion" (p. 62)—should not be characterized as "trans-scientific" in that they are well-established and well-used genres of communication across the sciences and academia. Those that correspond more closely to Bakhtin's idea of second-ary genres, composites of primary speech genres into more complex genres, such as the research article, are equally well established. But these established genres are valuable in the development of trans-scientific genres.

Because genres do not exist in isolation, they help us to identify appro-priate and *possible* responses to a situation. As Miller (1984) argues, we must use socially appropriate ways to respond to a situation. In the sciences, this fitting response will typically concern the kind of research methodologies and approaches that will be employed. These kinds of decisions are negotiated through a number of organizational and institutional as well as administrative genres.[3] By organizational and institutional genres in this case, I mean those genres used to enforce policy and norms. For example, institutional review board (IRB) forms serve to enforce policies regarding the ethical treatment of humans and other animals in the course of research that involves human and other animal subjects. These genres might also be those used to enforce norms and policies of a funding agency, including the grant proposal itself, which we learned in the last chapter varies across funding agencies.

As a research effort moves from establishing a fitting response to executing the response, the communication technologies and genres employed take on more regulated forms. For example, the negotiation that eventually results in a grant proposal is likely to establish methods and procedures for data collection in general terms, but specific details and associated documentation for technicians and research assistants may be developed. As databases evolve, and as the open-data movement progresses, the technologies employed to coordinate and collect data change, too. With these changing technologies come genres that help explain the procedures and processes for data storage and retrieval.

Genre-ing activity at work to support the creation, maintenance, and use of databases includes data management plans, help documentation, and FAQs, among other text types, including metadata, protocols for contributing and accessing data, and various kinds of software interfaces. Data management plans will be familiar to academic research proposal writers as they are a crucial genre for explaining how one will handle data throughout a research project, related publishing, and also the archival efforts that will be undertaken. For granting agencies, such as the NSF, data management plans are crucial supplemental documentation. NSF data management plan guidelines suggest including the kind of data that will be collected, data and metadata standards, the digital formats in which data will be stored, privacy and security policies, provisions for access and sharing, reuse and redistribution policies, and also provisions for storing and archiving data.[4] The exigence for this docu-

---

3. By administrative genres, I mean those genre activities that are used by the team to negotiate the terms of the research within their own team and with the institution they operate within (which could certainly overlap with the organizational and institutional genres). In its early stages, a grant proposal does not serve to persuade a research agency to fund a project, but rather serves as a site where the research response is negotiated. This is an important alternative function of the genre: it works to better establish the function of the genre as an internal consensus-building document rather than an external and perhaps slightly promotional document to appeal to an external funding agency.

4. See, for example, NSF, "Chapter II—Proposal Preparation Instructions." Grant Proposal Guide. http://www.nsf.gov/pubs/policydocs/pappguide/nsf14001/gpg_2.jsp (Jan. 2014).

ment is often a grant proposal.[5] Given the growth in data size and complexity, we might speculate that this genre will gain increasing attention. A good data management plan is especially essential for the purposes of open data if we consider any sensitive data that might be shared. Ensuring that data have been handled properly and anonymized, and that it is not possible to connect anonymized data to identifying information is crucial. This document, then, serves to coordinate and also archive data. Data management plans lead us from the collection of data to organization and through to dissemination and use, and provide an overall framework and argument for the use and purpose of a given data set. A data management plan is a required text to understand the broader framework within which a data set has been crafted. However, data management plans are not yet what we might call trans-scientific genres, although the push toward open data can certainly help them become part of these genres.

Moving into data organization, a hypothetical case can help illustrate the process, institutional norms, and genres at work in data management. In this hypothetical case, a research team is designing a study to collect human subject data. The team has filed appropriate institutional paperwork to conduct a research project involving human participants; the IRB board has approved the study and enclosed a letter of approval in an email response to their proposal submission. This, however, only happened after much coordinating among their team submitting the proposal (emails, phone calls, chats in the office hallway, video conferences) and with the IRB office and the granting agency, perhaps. Soon after, the team won a grant, which included a data management plan, and they were able to collect data in a timely and efficient manner. Now the database serves as the fundamental site of organization, but it is not the only site. Supporting genres and technologies, including metadata, protocols, and help documentation, surround the database. Supporting documentation becomes increasingly meaningful as data are shared widely.

Researchers who may never have met those researchers who collected the data may use their open data. As such, data must be organized in an intuitive and easy-to-understand manner. If a researcher needs to access data five years after a project has finished and, for one reason or another, cannot contact members of the original team, that new researcher should be able to use the data set anyway. It is important to conduct this work to advance research, which is achieved by more researchers looking at these data sets rather than spending time duplicating efforts. One way to ensure that other researchers

---

5. Although it is unlikely to be required of crowdfunded proposals as we discussed them in the previous chapter, this document is required for many other proposals supporting academic and scientific research.

can use your data is to have good metadata. Metadata functions in a descriptive capacity, compiling information about the data, how the data are structured, and how to use the data (Strasser, Cook, Michener, & Budden, 2012). Creating a database that will be widely useable requires contextualizing the data collected so that someone who had not previously participated in the project would be able to quickly understand not only the strengths of the data but the limitations. Users must consider when assessing a prospective data set whether or not it can answer their research questions at all, and to what extent it can fully answer said questions. A number of documents or documentation efforts can help users answer these questions, including logs listing changes to the data set, details about how and when the data were collected, what software and hardware tools were used to prepare or process the data, critical methodological decisions and their rationale, how such decisions affect the quality of the data, unit and format information, and so on (Strasser et al., 2012). The particular kinds of information that will be included, and how that information should be included, will depend on the discipline or granting agency, and in this way, we can trace the conventions in an instantiation.

Finally, dissemination includes a number of conventional academic genres, including research articles and conference proceedings. But the genre-ing activity that occurs in trans-scientific modes of communication may also be put to work to share the results of analysis from some data set or even information about the data set itself. For example, blog posts can be used to share information about how a data set was collected, solicit feedback during the development process, or talk about struggles in developing a particular part of the data set or database. As well, a concern about accurately representing data exists, particularly in charts that a general audience may be unfamiliar with interpreting. This concern is a rhetorically interesting aside because it reminds us that even when we have data, their representation shapes how they can *mean* and how they can mean differently.

Data lead a peripatetic life, and many genres exist to support not only data storage but—crucially and chiefly—retrieval. Some technologies such as the Application Programming Interface (API), a tool that helps developers access a database, for instance, and the associated genres of help documentation allow developers/users to easily extract the data they need. In addition to help documentation, interactive genres designed for user support exist, such as user groups. User groups may be designed to help users understand processes for archiving and for making available data in a particular platform. Some of the issues that might be addressed are indeed technological, but others may address more theoretical or even ideological issues surrounding data archiving and sharing. Organizing around questions of data management is an important activity, if we take data to be rhetorical. Indeed, such organizing suggests that what we are looking at is a community attempting to negotiate highly rhetorical spheres, and this rhetorical essence of data positions arguments made from that vantage in interesting and powerful ways. To better understand the specific kinds of rhetorical work and the rhetorical possibilities of data and databases in science and open science, I now turn to a case study of a project focused on the collection and dissemination of data to a heterogeneous audience.

CASE ANALYSIS: A CITIZEN SCIENCE DATABASE

The Safecast project illustrates how these genre possibilities can be translated into social action. Specifically, its story is one of constructing data to share and use with a broad audience, on the continuum from experts to nonexperts. Elsewhere I have written about this citizen science initiative,[6] a group that devised an impressive method for organizing citizens to collect data following the 2011 Fukushima disaster, and then compiled an equally impressive data set, with millions of readings. Over the years that I have written about Safecast, I have updated the number of readings and the range of areas in which they are engaging, only to continually fall behind on their tireless work toward collecting and sharing better data and supporting informed decision making.

Safecast's story begins in 2011, following the massive earthquake and subsequent tsunami that damaged the Fukushima Daiichi nuclear generation site in Japan. Safecast's story is compelling: A few friends begin coordinating to find out what happened to loved ones following the disaster, and soon found that getting information was extraordinarily difficult. With significant creativity and industriousness, they formed what is now known as Safecast, a large collective of volunteer technicians and scientists. Safecast's efforts to collect radiation measurements are consistent with a scientific interest. In Japan, a sensor network managed by the Ministry of Education, Culture, Sports, Science and Technology (MEXT) provided data to the Japanese government, which in turn provided data to the International Atomic Energy Agency (IAEA). Following the disaster—but not during the initial crisis—the IAEA established the Fukushima Monitoring Database (FMD) through their Inci-

---

6. This section draws from my doctoral dissertation (Kelly, 2014), which examined Safecast's database as part of a larger study of Safecast as an exemplary case of citizen science or grassroots science. Predating my dissertation, although published after its deposit, Carolyn R. Miller and I suggested Safecast's database might be examined as a genre (Kelly & Miller, 2016). As well, I have explored the ethical motivations behind Safecast's open-data efforts (Kelly, 2016).

dent and Emergency Centre (IEC). The FMD provides information to both IAEA member states and the public and includes data from MEXT as well as from member states (International Atomic Energy Agency, 2014). In addition, the Preparatory Commission for the Comprehensive Nuclear-Test-Ban Treaty Organization (CTBTO) monitoring system network contributed to this effort by the IAEA for the FMD. Given the significant global efforts to address the disaster at Fukushima, including data collection and analysis, the work of Safecast should not be understated. The group not only collected data like these other sources but collected a more significant data set in terms of sheer quantity.

We can call this citizen science or community-based monitoring, but these labels tend to downplay the great achievements of the group. Often citizen science efforts are top-down, run by scientists recruiting volunteers, but Safecast was built bottom-up by nonexperts who became amateur experts, then experts. And as far as community-based monitoring is concerned, typically the label applies to geographically restricted areas. Safecast is a global effort, and certainly nuclear disaster reminds us that with respect to the environment, natural disasters, and technoscientific disaster, we are indeed a global community. So rather than apply these labels, I might rather say Safecast is a research and monitoring effort that puts to work the kinds of communications charted in this book in an exemplary manner—truly a project by civic scientists.

Safecast provides a striking case for the value of databases as a form of science communication, not merely a technical tool or apparatus, but instead a mode of science communication at the heart of the tension between media, genre, and the socio-rhetorical creators and consumers of databases. Indeed, one crucial matter for Safecast is material access to data, provided through both media and legal modes. Technologies themselves provide some affordances, such as sharing data online around the globe, but we must also consider the kinds of legal affordances we might find and employ to really put those technological affordances to work. Data Safecast aggregates are published under a Creative Commons dedication that places their work in the public domain (CC0). Safecast cofounder, director of the MIT Media Lab, and vociferous proponent of open data Joi Ito argues for the importance of publishing such data sets under a CC0 dedication because of the complications in attribution when many volunteers participate in data collection efforts: "if each person with each sensor had to be attributed and our data got rolled up into a massive analysis of all historical sensor data to find megatrends, it would be impossible to provide attribution to every single provider of data" (Ito, 2011). This does not deny the value of attribution or suggest that it should not be a consideration when using CC0 dedicated data; rather, he continues, a distinction should be made between what is "ethical or normatively true and what is legally true." Ito emphasizes that even when sharing data under a CC0, one may still ask for attribution, and given the ethical norms of science, it is likely most researchers would make an effort to attribute sources of data. Figshare (2014), a data repository used by scientists, similarly notes that while "CC0 doesn't legally require users of the data to cite the source, it does not take away the moral responsibility to give attribution, as is common in scientific research."

Distinguishing open databases from their closed counterparts is not a purely technical matter but rather a rhetorical one. The audience—and in the case of the database, users and contributors—potentially becomes larger and broader when data are openly available and not restricted to a team, a lab, or a particular field or scientific community. Yet Safecast's work to compile a large data set is constrained by disciplinary norms and the values in academic science. Safecast has worked with universities, and experts in those institutions, to design data collection and sharing efforts and, thus, they offer an interesting site for analysis. Their efforts are noteworthy because they must make moves to signal their scientific authority without relying on traditional institutional affiliations or training and apprenticeship models of academic professionalization (see, on apprenticeship models and professionalization, Berkenkotter, Huckin, & Ackerman, 1991; Ding, 2008; Bazerman, 2009; see also, on pedagogical approaches in particular, Freedman, 1993; Bawarshi & Reiff, 2010).

Safecast has used a number of genres to coordinate their data collection and dissemination. When the group began, use of oral genres via a Skype video conference call session helped organize their efforts, and they also relied on email, including a Google Discussion Group for device support. Software is also supported through a software development service called GitHub, which provides information about the device, including schematic designs; about the API used to interface with the Safecast data set; and also about the iOS app that can be used. Although much of this support is technical in nature, Safecast has several other sources of support to render their data set useful to broader audiences. Chief among their documentation is their blog, which details efforts to map and understand their data. A more formalized version of their findings has been published as a report, which provides "readable summaries of important news and research" (Safecast, 2017). A number of genres are at work in Safecast's efforts to document and support their data-driven research, as well as a number of technical platforms. With such complexity, it is unlikely that all interested parties toward the nonexpert end of the continuum would be able to fully participate. In this way, it is clear that trans-scientific genres demand a certain motivation that broader audiences work to understand scientific and technical discourses. The difference, however, between these genres and genres of expert scientific discourse is that trans-scientific genres make an effort to bridge expert knowledge to the amateur or novice.

Further, while other professional scientific sources are building data sets, Safecast identifies two essential niches to occupy. First, they see other data collection efforts as too geographically broad, not taking into account the granularity of radiation contamination. Second, they recognize that no single source of data is as useful as multiple sources. The latter contention expresses not merely distrust of a particular government source, but rather a scientific norm that suggests a single source is not authoritative because it claims to be credible, but because the data and analysis of the data bear out the source's credibility. Credibility is central to establishing why one's data should be considered at all. Questions about the quality of citizen science data abound, and with politicized matters such as nuclear energy and nuclear disaster, this is certainly the case. Safecast's standards ensure that the data in the data set are consistent with the design and purpose of their database, requiring specific temporal and geographical stamps, device IDs, appropriate metadata for the data, and normalized measurement practices and units (Bonner, 2014). These efforts ensure that the database contains a consistent set of data. But this list of standards also reveals the ways in which the database is constructed. The kinds of information that must be contained within the submissions tells us about what was determined to be required information and how that information must be collected (for example, the units of measurement must be taken in counts-per-minute only).

To better understand the forms of data considered here, and how specific kinds of data are included in a database, looking specifically at the structure of Safecast's data is useful. There are several examples of a bGeigie log provided on Safecast's GitHub page, including:

\$BNXRDD,300,2012-12-16T17:58:24Z,31,9,115,A,4618.9996,N,00658.4623,E,
   587.6,A,77.2,1*1A
\$BNXRDD,300,2012-12-16T17:58:31Z,30,1,116,A,4618.9612,N,00658.4831,E,4
   43.7,A,1.28,1*1D
\$BNXRDD,300,2012-12-16T17:58:36Z,32,4,120,A,4618.9424,N,00658.4802,E,
   428.1,A,1.27,1*18
\$BNXRDD,300,2012-12-16T17:58:41Z,32,2,122,A,4618.9315,N,00658.4670,E,
   425.5,A,1.27,1*1B

\$BNXRDD,300,2012-12-16T17:58:46Z,34,3,125,A,4618.9289,N,00658.4482,E,
426.0,A,1.34,1*13
(Scheibler, 2014)

This is an example of the "radiation data sentence," or a "basic message containing the geo-located radiation measurement," and embedded within this excerpt is much more (Scheibler, 2014). But how can we understand this information as nonexperts? Must we wait for the data to be visualized for us in order to be useful? Safecast provides supporting explanatory documentation through their GitHub account that helps to explain the structure of the data sentence.

GitHub is a web-based platform that facilitates software development with a version control system that allows projects to be split into different streams, merged, and even forked off into new projects. Such sites allow for documentation about how software works and how data are structured (as in our example here), and are thus a valuable site of genre-ing activities when we examine how digital, data-driven projects can be constructed and broadly shared. Data corresponding to the above sentence appear in square brackets (these were indicated as differently colored text boxes on GitHub, and although some changes have been made since 2014, the following provides a useful illustration for our purposes):

Header : BNXRDD

Device ID : Device serial number. [300]

Date : Date formatted according to iso-8601 standard. Usually uses GMT.
[2012-12-16T17:58:31Z]

Radiation 1 minute : number of pulses given by the Geiger tube in the last minute. [30]

Radiation 5 seconds : number of pulses given by the Geiger tube in the last 5 seconds. [1]

Radiation total count : total number of pulses recorded since startup. [116]

Radiation count validity flag : 'A' indicates the counter has been running for more than one minute and the 1 minute count is not zero. Otherwise, the flag is 'V' (void). [A]

Latitude : As given by GPS. The format is ddmm.mmmm where dd is in degrees and mm.mmmm is decimal minute. [4618.9612]

Hemisphere : 'N' (north), or 'S' (south). [N]

Longitude : As given by GPS. The format is dddmm.mmmm where ddd is in degrees and mm.mmmm is decimal minute. [00658.4831]

East/West : 'W' (west) or 'E' (east) from Greenwich. [E]

Altitude : Above sea level as given by GPS in meters. [443.7]

GPS validity : 'A' ok, 'V' invalid. [A]

HDOP : Horizontal Dilution of Precision (HDOP), relative accuracy of horizontal position. [1.28]

Fix Quality : 0 = invalid, 1 = GPS Fix, 2 = DGPS Fix. [1]

Checksum. [*1D] (Scheibler, 2014)

Here the exact details of what information may be submitted to the database are described. We can see that the information is highly contextualized, and what is ultimately included in the database is explained through these definitions. Those genre-ing activities taking place in the support documentation noted above help a novice understand the significance of the data Safecast collects. In different sources, Safecast explains why granularity of location is crucial, which is identified by the latitude, longitude, hemisphere, altitude, and East/West measurements. Knowing the particular device used helps in assessing differences in measurements. Other features such as the Checksum and GPS validity ensure data quality by checking for technical errors caused by digital devices. Our core data are the radiation counts, but all of the contextualizing data are necessary to make meaning of the radiation counts. Data here are given meaning through their interrelationships with other points of data. Design decisions are necessarily embedded, including the way that radiation counts are measured (there are several different units of measurement that can be used for radiation detection). These design decisions are wed to the technologies that gather these data, and the designs behind both are informed by disciplinary norms and expectations. All of this is governed by expectations for how data are to be used. Because data are so crucial to knowledge production in the sciences, the arguments they advance and will be used to advance require careful evaluation.

Harris (1997) explains the centrality of evidence and argument in the sciences, writing that for scientists, "standards of evidence are frequently more rigid than those of other arguers, and they are so good at arguing that they won't let each other get away with weak cases for very long, and the ultimate matter of their arguments is so concrete that we can stub our toes on it" (p. xi). Argument in this sense is the careful work of negotiation, testing, challenging, and working toward consensus to ultimately produce new knowledge. We can think of the work that scientists do in research articles to help persuade their colleagues that their research contributes meaningful, new insights. Presentation of research is rhetorical in that it abides by a conventional style of argument that sets boundaries around how evidence is presented, including the degree to which the evidence is shown and explained. A good deal of rhetorical work is also done before these results are ever shared. Conventional-izing the forms for databases are the products of argument as well, to ensure that the data are stored in such a way that they can be used appropriately and effectively to advance research. Further, I want to suggest that databases are not only the products of argument and negotiation but are also arguments themselves about ways of knowing.

Visual Genres and the Case of the Safecast Project

Safecast's case extends to the dissemination of data, too, and it illustrates how trans-scientific visual genres function to produce and communicate scientific knowledge outside of the internal/expert and external/public binary. Rather than focusing strictly on the visual analysis of the final products, this discus-sion will explore how group discussions about the production of visuals and their rhetorical attunement to their audience shape the final visual product. Comparing print visualizations with their digital counterparts in newspa-pers and with Safecast's visualizations, Wynn (2016) concludes that although the computational infrastructures making complex visualizations online are "widely available," the "accessibility alone could not account for the unique character of Safecast's risk visualization strategy" (p. 216). Specifically, compar-ing the interactive visualizations of the *New York Times* and Safecast, which we might think would be functionally the same, he found that "differences in the goals and audiences of institutional and noninstitutional risk visualizers play a critical role in shaping visual choices of risk communication" (p. 216). This indicates that the technological affordances in new media environments are only technological possibilities until put to work in response to some exigence or, at least, perceived exigence. While the technological underpinnings are integral, the community of genre users (for example, Safecast) plays a pow-erful role in establishing the conventions of visualizations and the audience likely to engage with their visualizations. Here Safecast exemplifies that the heterogeneous audience that marks trans-scientific genres is, then, not only self-defined but also cultivated by the rhetorical work of genre creators and users.

Safecast collects data through a combination of fixed-sensor networks and mobile monitoring. Volunteers collect data and share their results through an online platform created and hosted by Safecast. All of the data are made freely available to anyone who wishes to use them. For those who are less interested in or capable of using the raw data, Safecast provides a number of ways to visualize the data, including measurements, interpolation, and overlays. From a rhetorical vantage, what is particularly interesting about Safecast's work on mapping is how critical they report this aspect of their work to be. As Sean Bonner (2011a) writes,

> We think about maps a lot here at Safecast. In fact, it's probably one of the most frequent topics of conversation. Especially maps with a lot of data and especially making that data understandable. But more than understandable, it needs to be useful. Understanding what data a map is showing you is one thing, understanding what that data means is a whole other story.

Bonner's account of the importance of data visualization through maps suggests that the author of these artifacts understands the difficulty not only in representing data but also in making data *understandable* and *meaningful*. And, indeed, being understandable and meaningful is crucial to both generating and communicating scientific knowledge. To create visuals that are understandable requires that they are meaningful. Bonner helps illustrate this point as he describes how Safecast team members talk about developing maps. He reminds us that radiation is an abstract subject to most people and, further, that the business of measuring this imperceptible phenomenon is doubly so. To make information understandable, it must, to a great extent, be meaningful to the audience. This is not to suggest that the audience must care about a particular subject; rather, we learn from Safecast, they must have some kind of reference point to which they can relate new information (data, visuals). Bonner (2011a) puts it this way: "If you and I both know what the weather was like yesterday, and you ask me what it's like today and I say it's hotter—you instantly know what I mean." Extending the idea that meaningful visuals will be understandable visuals, he asks, "What if we could do that with radiation as well?" Safecast thus decided a baseline reading would be useful in providing a reference point. This is complicated business, and deciding what ought to be a reference point requires considerable thoughtful attention, but Safecast's general design principles offer a useful insight into how difficult it is to present visual data that are both understandable and meaningful.

If you browse through the Safecast blog, you will find numerous updates about how their maps are progressing as they develop or employ different kinds of visualization techniques. Evolving technique and application of visualization technologies is not particular to Safecast's enterprise. Scientists around the world work to develop better visualizations, but Safecast faces different challenges. Several significant factors distinguish Safecast's rhetorical work from that of other scientists. Rhetorical choices Safecast must make differ from those of most scientists working in the field because Safecast works outside of the field, so they are not afforded the same community norms and genres to help shape their work. Safecast is a heterogeneous group of experts working on monitoring and mapping radiation contamination. In effect, this means that Safecast must be highly rhetorically aware of their design decisions because they are not working in a prescribed discourse sphere. Further, the work Safecast engages is not designed only for research scientists interested in, for example, radiation contamination, the dispersion of radioactive materials, or modeling how the contamination travels through ecologies. Certainly, their work is partly designed for researchers interested in those problems, but it is also designed for nonexperts, citizens of affected regions. Once again, our dual purpose reveals a heterogeneous audience, and thus we can understand the kind of visualizations that Safecast produces as trans-scientific.

The progress of Safecast's visuals is certainly worth considering briefly, and some of their visuals are replicated here to show the evolution of their efforts. First (figure 2), we have an early visualization that plots all of the Safecast data collected at the time onto one map, obviously before the automated efforts had been undertaken, which is unsurprising given the image was shared on May 29, 2011, only a little over two months after disaster first struck Fukushima Daiichi. A group at Keio University with the "Scanning The Earth" project produced the visual (Bonner, 2011c).

Numerous data points are represented, but a large area remains unaccounted for. (This would change over the next several years.) At the time, these data, though admittedly sparse, were some of the first publicly available. In a color version of the image, the data points represent not only where measurements were taken but also contamination levels through colored points (green for low, red for high, and a range in between). Also represented on the map is the disaster site, with the hazard symbol for ionizing radiation and four concentric circles that mark the exclusion zone used to force or recommend evacuation. Here the data suggest the concentric circles of the exclusion zone do not correlate well with the worst contamination (Aldrich, 2015). That is, the contamination was not evenly dispersed near the site, but rather a plume contaminated outside the immediate exclusion zone in a northwestern direction.

Over time, Safecast developed more tools and maps for their audience, and others used their data to create maps, too. The group produced the Safecast map, a full data set map, drive maps, a fixed sensor network map, and an aggregate map. The Safecast map served as their primary map, with all of their data in an easily readable grid. With their full data set map, Safecast provided their data with granularity. Drive maps contained aggregate and singular drive data, and the fixed sensor map rendered data from Safecast's

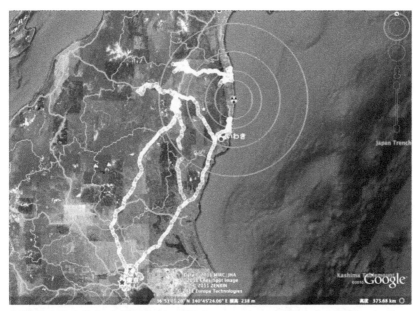

FIGURE 2. Early Safecast Visualization. This image was generated early in Safecast's efforts by the "Scanning the Earth" project at Keio University in Japan. Although it is difficult to see in this black and white reproduction, elevated readings appear in numerous points on the map, including outside the immediate evacuation zones. This figure illustrates how complex, abstract data can be made meaningful to a broad audience while retaining features that make them interpretable to an expert audience.

partnership with Keio University's Scanning the Earth project and their stationary network of devices. The aggregate map included all the data Safecast obtained as well as data collected from other sources (Bonner, 2011b). And so the narrative continues, documented in their blog, explaining how maps are developed, how they changed, and where the data are sourced. In their blog, they reveal the rhetorical and design decisions that have rendered their project so successful. Certainly the group has members with remarkable proficiency in hardware and software development, but also in design, and it seems that here attention to design is fundamentally driven by attention to the audience. Safecast's work is for the public, exampled by their commitment to putting data into the public domain, and by their blog posts that document their thoughtful attention to how visualizations are created and used. For example, the group was interested in providing data that could be used for localized interpretation (figure 3).

But, it is challenging to visualize data when you do not have complete coverage. Even with highly granulate coverage, such as that Safecast has surrounding the disaster site, gaps exist in the data. Visualization here can create

FIGURE 3. Safecast Interpolation Map. Although mapping particular data points can be valuable, it is difficult to obtain comprehensive coverage. Interpolation allows for data points to be generated on the basis of current data. In this figure, this approach provides fuller coverage, allowing individuals in affected areas that were not directly measured to assess the relative risk in their location. Bringing these complex ideas to a public audience has been a feature of Safecast's work, and the immediate application of their work to affected citizens demonstrates the rhetorical effectiveness of their data-driven approach.

a continuous image of measurements and predicted measurements. Thus, in figure 3, Safecast provides an example of this effect, achieved through interpolation. Essentially, interpolation is a mathematical method by which existing data points are used to create new ones. Dolezal (2015) provides an extended discussion about how Safecast went about constructing their map. The act of describing the process, challenges, potential pitfalls, and problems with interpolation is rhetorically significant because it makes the technical and scientific decisions clear to the audience, which in turn suggests a technically capable audience. However, certain features of the discussion open it to a more general audience, where readers such as me, not familiar with these techniques, can gain some insight into the process they have used and the decisions they have made. The blog posts seem to be trans-scientific, but are the visualizations? Two competing uses suggest they can be characterized as trans-scientific.

First, Safecast's visuals, like their data, are designed for public use. Safecast reports that their motivation for the project is to get data into the hands of the people who need it most: the people affected by the disaster, and loved ones at a distance who want to know what is going on. Government and other official data, where they existed, were inaccessible. Safecast's work to redress the lack of data is a project concerned with civic engagement. With these motivations, we might suggest that Safecast's audience is an external or popular one. But the group's data and maps have also been significant for internal or scientific audiences. The group was invited to the 2014 IAEA expert meeting on radiation protection following the disaster at Fukushima, which provided an audience of experts. It is also clear with the level of detail provided for hardware design, the software used, and the visualization strategies that an audience with some technical or scientific proficiency is anticipated. With these features, the efforts mapped here can be characterized as trans-scientific in that they operate alongside and intersect with conventional genres and discourse spheres of science.

Bringing us back to the question of how these images function rhetorically, now we have established they are rhetorically designed, we can look first at the genre and then at the argument made within the visualization. In the case of the genre, we see the way data are visualized with various norms to the map genre. There are geographical and topological markers, transportation markers, and land and sea differentiation, and overlaid on this are the data collected by Safecast and an associated legend. In their web-based visualization (figure 4), the conventional features of a map are overlaid with navigational tools to scroll into or out of the visual, with the Safecast logo, hyperlinks to information about the project, and menus to select different maps.

We can see that as the map is transported across contexts and platforms, from the Safecast website to a mobile device to a newspaper article, the map carries with it meaning, and that meaning shapes and structures how other genres will incorporate the map and, in turn, how those genres might persuade by use of the visualization. We also see a kind of rhetorical reasoning at work here in the way that the measurements are reported. While the color version of the image helps us see the range of readings, we can see even in gray scale there is variation. The variation in readings functions as a kind of *accumulation (accumulatio)* where data are piled up to mean. We also find a kind of visual *climax (gradatio)* where the readings build from high to low, with corresponding colors, a deep blue for low readings moving through red into a yellow for high. The visual effect in color is stunning, the location of the Fukushima Daiichi site bright yellow. In this we also find a kind of visual argument that the region is badly affected, which opens a space to reflect on the risks. Indeed, the existence of the map itself is an argument, not only about the visualized risks but also about the importance of having access to good, reliable, and significant data.

FIGURE 4. Safecast Web Map. In addition to representing complex data to a heterogeneous audience, Safecast also capitalizes on the affordances of the web to make their data representations interactive. Here we see a screen capture of Safecast's web-based map, including tools to zoom in and move around on the map. How data are represented on the map, and what aspects of the data, can be manipulated by the user to suit their needs, thus showing the way such data might be used to respond to different rhetorical situations (situations where data must be represented, and possibly shared) while appearing in a familiar, stabilized visual genre of the map.

All told, Safecast's visuals represent only one of the many possibilities of trans-scientific genres. They are, however, a reminder of the power these visuals have to do more than simply inform a public. Shortly after Safecast's map was released, the evacuation zone was reconsidered. In Bonner's (2012) account, Safecast released their maps, and it soon became obvious that the concentric circle evacuation zones did not cover the most severely affected areas and that some were needlessly displaced. Whether Safecast's data or other data and their visualized counterparts, it seems obvious that having these data exist in both internal and external spheres led to some different questions and deliberations about how evacuation should occur—certainly a trans-scientific matter. This reminds us of a key point about the rhetoricity of data as data sets move us from science into the realm of rhetoric. Those representations may be crafted in visual graphics or charts, but structures of our data representation permeate more deeply, into the organization of information itself. Because the organization of data itself is a rhetorical act, it is useful to articulate how decisions are made about how data will be represented.

Broadly, in the example Safecast provides, we can find a recurrent rhetorical situation in the representation of risk. Because risks associated with radiation and radiation contamination are complicated and not always well understood, there are ongoing efforts to understand what the data mean either alone or in relation to other data. As well, since the disaster at Fukushima has been an ongoing event, there are new data to be collected, included, and represented. These representations of data and risks participate in genre-ing activity. Understanding how these representations do so provides a theoretical lens to trace the antecedent forms. Further, understanding how these representations operate as genre-ing activities provides a framework to understand the complex, and sometimes competing, nature of the situation to which these data collection efforts respond—namely, a confluence of institutional, statal, and public demands relating to risk assessment, regulatory structures, and also environment, health, and safety concerns.

Safecast's database, when understood as an artifact that participates in genre-ing activity, tells us something about the ways genres and technologies interact to co-constitute one another. Further, this approach helps us explore the rhetorical logics that govern these processes of design, development, and use. Because the kind of data and the use of the database are all determined by design *decisions,* including anticipations concerning the audience/user, kind of work being done, institutional or social context for the work, and the available means that the rhetor/designer perceives, there are clearly more constraints than technical feasibility alone at work. For example, in Safecast's story the exigence itself, the need to respond to a quickly evolving situation, shaped the iterative and agile design processes that resulted in their development of new devices and a large database. Constraints of the devices shaped the database, too, as there were too few devices, which changed the way they would need to be deployed. Further, rhetorical dimensions include metadata. Without good metadata—that is, descriptive contextual information about the data set and how it was collected and structured—the data may essentially be useless. To share data broadly, the information that helps to contextualize the data, and especially its limitations, is crucial to developing a useful and usable data set.

Approaching the database through the lens of genre-ing activity helps illustrate the ways that design is embedded with not only the database creation but also its ongoing use. Thus, to echo Lanham (2006) on the matter of rhetoric as oscillation, looking both at the data and through to the structure is crucial to understanding the database as a rhetorical object. The dynamic functionality of the database, and the multitude of forms and functions databases have, must distinguish them from antecedents that appear to have similar functionalities and forms but in a less dynamic media environment, such as telephone directories. Indeed, the media form shapes conditions for the form and functionality. Media forms operate conjointly with social norms (of the sciences, for our purposes) and rhetorical situations (inclusive of political, economic, and historical threads). Genre is a helpful tool to explore the database because the database functions as dialogic sites govern, by recurrent rhetorical situations and typified responses, continually participating not only in their design but also with each call or request that someone makes to the database. Database forms in the sciences are changing, and so too are the social actions they might perform, but they are "stabilized-for-now or stabilized enough" in a recognizable form that by theorizing them we can look closely at what ideologies or values are reproduced (Schryer, 1993, p. 208).

SUMMARY: GENRE HYBRIDITY IN DATABASES

Database design indeed inhabits the rhetorical, on multiple levels, ranging from the essential function of data in ontological and epistemological enterprises in science to trans-scientific problems and the legal and policy-based questions that we might more comfortably call rhetorical. Databases are rhetorical in that we decide what will be selected, segmented, represented, and stored. Effectively, we take these data as serving an argumentative function, and take that an argumentative function is a reality-building element. Thus, the way we identify data, structure databases, and decide what will be archived has significant implications for the ability to build high-quality and robust understandings about complex research problems and for the potentialities found in future research with our current data.

To understand the database and its related genre-ing activities is to acknowledge powerful rhetorical work involved in crafting a complex apparatus we use to construct knowledge. Design decisions are important, and we need a language in rhetorical studies of online science communications to talk about how disciplinary norms, discourse conventions, and argument shape the design features that are technically implemented. Indeed, the matters of argument that shape a database design and its ongoing use are valuable because the data that inhabit these organizational logics govern so much of how scientists explore and explain the world. Rhetorical study is relevant to these technologies and comes by way of rhetoric's capacity to articulate emerging technologies and their communicative functions in relation to more traditional forms (Geisler et al., 2001). Rhetorical genre studies have long been concerned with the study of written and oral expression, but the primary focus on these modes of expression should not be taken as wholly representative of genre studies. In addition to studies of delivery and performance, rhetorical studies have also considered the conceptual roots of our expressive modes, a variety of semiotic modalities not limited to auditory, aural, verbal, and visual expression, and indeed the media and technologies we employ for communicative functions. Ever-evolving expressive modes and associated media provide space to ask questions about rhetorical change: Are these new computational technologies and processes governed by rhetorical logics or something entirely different? Can we think of acts of composition and communication to create and use these technologies as rhetorical acts?

A researcher interested in providing open data will have a number of considerations to make, and many of these considerations exist outside the expected technical domain. Choices about audience, users, and the legality and ethics of sharing matter because databases are central to the mission of open science in that they allow sharing and redistribution of information that can advance research and scientific knowledge globally. However, because of the global and distributed nature of (open) science, and its mission to share information and knowledge broadly, attention to the rhetorical dimensions of databases is increasingly necessary. Because open data are designed to serve a larger stakeholder group, ensuring that those users' needs are anticipated requires expanded rhetorical work. Needs include traditional design-based questions, including what kinds of data might be useful, how those data will be related to one another, and also how a wider range of users will be able to access and make sense of the data that they did not collect. It is the audience that helps remind us that we are indeed engaging in rhetorical activities. As we have seen in previous chapters, an essential difference between these genres and their traditional counterparts is not simply the form, but the complex audience composed of a range of experts, amateurs, citizen scientists, and other engaged stakeholders. In the case of databases, we see the audience changes qualitatively and quantitatively. In terms of quantitative change, we see more researchers and scientists accessing data that they did not collect on their own. This might be for verification of a study or perhaps even expansion of a study. Data must be organized and structured in a way that this audience can access and use them appropriately, in particular, making constraints and limitations of the data apparent. The qualitative change is a little more difficult to account for, but when we open data to anyone who is interested, then the possibility for a more heterogeneous audience exists. This, again, can be addressed by providing good, structured, and rhetorically thoughtful design to help guide users in understanding the context of data, data collection, and appropriate constraints.

Although Safecast offers what Bazerman (2016) might caution is an exciting, perhaps exemplary, but not common case, what we learn from their work can be applied to broader trends. Consider Figshare, a data repository that allows researchers to share various kinds of data (data sets, figures, presentations, and so on). Researchers can do more than share data: they are also provided with a DataCite DOI for their contributions. Recall, similarly, successful Experiment projects also receive a DOI. A DOI allows research to be searched for and cited in a manner acceptable to most scientific disciplines. The purpose of sharing data through repositories such as Figshare extends beyond making one's research findable and, crucially, citable—it is also to make the data useful to other researchers, as did Safecast's efforts. With this framework, Figshare provides a platform for data sharing that is crucial for accessible data. The platform also frames itself as a place to host data specifically associated with published articles, and indeed even as a service for publishers to use so that their own infrastructures are not impacted by the growing interest in associating data with research articles (Figshare, 2017). Consider, for example, PLOS's integration with Figshare. PLOS is a nonprofit, born-digital, open-access publisher that has done much since its founding in 2003.[7] In 2013 PLOS and Figshare partnered to allow data to be hosted on Figshare and associated with articles in PLOS journals (Hahnel, 2013). Further, its infrastructure allows for data to be visualized alongside the article. This partnership underscores the value of providing data in an accessible, findable place online. Figshare and PLOS lead us into a discussion of the dissemination of research, the subject of the next chapter.

---

7. Although the company was in fact founded in 2003, the idea predates the founding. But the story is worth noting as the site's internal history reports a founding of 2001, when PLOS became a nonprofit, sprouting from its origins as a 2000 initiative by Harold Varmus, Patrick Brown, and Michael Eisen calling for scientists to make their articles freely available to everyone. In 2003, the organization began its publishing branch with its first journal, *PLOS Biology* (Public Library of Science, 2017b).

CHAPTER 4

Blogging

Genres for Scientific Engagement

BLOGS CONTINUE to challenge genre scholars' approaches to studying new and evolving media environments, serving as a reminder of the intimacy of technology, media, and genre. The relationship between genres and technologies—the medium through which genres are constituted and transmitted—can be exceedingly difficult to parse. As rhetoricians continue to investigate the influence of new media forms on our rhetorical worlds, blogs offer a well-considered and contested site to visit once more, with attention to the implications for writing and communication instruction in the sciences. In this chapter, a collection of Public Library of Science (PLOS) blog posts serve as the basis to characterize rhetorical dimensions of science blogs. The following analysis reveals a complex ecology for science blogs, an ecology where media and genre-ing activities shape a number of different forms of science blogging. It is striking that there are different forms of writing occurring in science blogs—multiple genres or proto-genres of science blogs—but without examining a number of different science blog posts, it is difficult to map the variety of genres. PLOS is a useful case for exploring questions of the broader ecologies within which science blogs operate because it is also the publisher of a range of open-access journals, including its flagship journal, *PLOS ONE*. Because of the size of the PLOS Blogs Network, the wide range of activities included in science blogs is also readily apparent, reminding us that science blogs are not a genre but rather themselves a space within which different genre-ing activities take place. Guiding this chapter is the question: What does science blogging illuminate about the relationship between genre evolution and speciation? And how can we understand the complex ecology blogs create and exist within? Attempting to answer these questions, the chapter gives some attention to technological change, but focuses most specifically on the rhetorical situation to which science blogs respond. Science blogs act to share information in a liminal—that is, trans-scientific—sphere of discourse. As the genre-ing activities that come to shape science blogs must navigate the domain of experts and the broader public, I argue these strategies are borrowed from both professional scientific communication and popularizations.

This question of a complex ecology is a thread that has been woven through this book, and blogs allow the question to be dealt with most directly. Crowdfunding offers an example of genre and platform tightly coupled and recursively informed. Databases offer an example of explicit articulation of platform as a pervasive governing logic, but a logic that is open to critique as its pragmatic application is disciplined by the norms of science. Investigating blogging about science is useful for understanding genre change online because we have a significant body of literature in genre studies theorizing blogging from its early days. This body of literature illustrates how the postmortem and situational approaches (Graham & Whalen, 2008) pose challenges to understanding genre evolution online. Theoretical characterizations of blogs, such as Miller and Shepherd's (2004) study, seemed to quickly lose their explanatory power even though they were not victims of poor execution or uncritical investigation. Rather, these theoretical accounts were the victims of online communications' resistance to stabilization with a temporal orientation rather than a spatial one (as *topos* or a material form). Once again applying move analysis, we learn something about the integration of platform and genre-ing activity, in particular how appeals are constructed in an interlinked media ecology (see Luzón, 2017).

BACKGROUND: SCIENCE BLOGGING AND SCIENCE BLOG NETWORKS

Science blogging describes a practice of writing, sharing, and discussing scientific subject matter online. Writers may be subject-matter experts, such as climate scientist Dr. Tasmin Edwards, the author of the PLOS blog *All Models Are Wrong*, or they may be science writers or journalists, such as investigative reporter Steve Silberman, who writes *NeuroTribes*. In the last decade, science blogging has been proliferating as a way to share one's research with other scientists and engage broader audiences, either from an interdisciplinary or a public engagement angle. Identifying a precise number of science bloggers is not especially helpful, or even possible. As Brian Trench (2012) informs us, "Because the definition of science blog or scientist blogger can never be unequivocally settled the numbers cannot be precise" (p. 276). A significant number of scientists report having blogged about science and their research. A 2015 Pew Research Center report on "How Scientists Engage the Public" provides some insight into scientists' blogging practices and how scientists view the blogging practices of science journalists. Surveying 3,748 scientists affiliated with the American Association for the Advancement of Science (AAAS), the Pew Research Center (2015) found that a majority of scientists—a significant majority, at 87 percent—believe scientists ought to be involved with policy debates and decisions. Moreover, a majority of scientists—a somewhat smaller majority, at 71 percent—agree that the public has "either some or a lot of interest in their specialty area" (p. 3). It is not surprising, then, that almost half of the scientists surveyed reported that they use social media to "discuss or follow science" (p. 4). And, relevant to our discussion in this chapter, Pew (2015) found that "24% of these AAAS scientists blog about science and research" (p. 4). Of these, about 10 percent reported writing for a blog "often/occasionally," while the other 14 percent reported they "rarely" write for a blog (p. 14). This, the report states, is about the same level of blog engagement scientists reported six years earlier, in a 2009 report (pp. 14–15).

Scientists write blogs, and they also write about blogging. Zivkovic (2012) offers an informal and internalist history of scientific blogging. Others, such as Shema, Bar-Ilan, and Thelwall (2012), consider the nature of scientific blogging, blogger demographics and disciplines, and languages represented, among other things. Their findings are significant because, as they note, "Science blogs can add to the transparency of the scientific process by reviewing and discussing the science culture in general and scientific research in particular" (Shema, Bar-Ilan, & Thelwall, 2012, p. 1). Many other scientists have published about science blogging both in blogs and in scholarly journals. Increasingly, blogging is part of the landscape of science communication, and scientists and science communication professionals are trying to characterize what science blogging looks like, who writes and reads science blogs, and just how science blogs function differently from other forms of science communication (Boon, 2016; Dunleavy, 2016). Science blogs can function as sites where specialists can intervene in contentious topics internal to science (Sidler, 2016) or public controversies. Smart (2016) studies the "discourse coalitions," borrowing from public sphere scholarship, of science blogs concerning climate change debate. He identifies that while several discourse coalitions shaped much of the conversation about climate change—as advocates, skeptics, and eco-optimists—the climate researchers had "sufficient agency to create a space for themselves in public discussions of climate change outside the narrow adversarial exchanges of the Advocates, Skeptics, and Eco-optimists" (p. 174). Pigg, Hart-Davidson, Grabill, and Ellenbogen (2016) also examine how experts and publics might engage in discussion online, focusing on how the Science Museum of Minnesota's *Science Buzz* blog facilitates such exchanges. Their study also reminds us that such discussion can in fact be a form of information learning, knowledge exchange, and engagement between experts and publics. Luzón (2017) provides a particularly valuable genre study of blogs, looking at thirteen Spanish research group blogs. Her analysis includes the variety of genres that are embedded within these research blogs (abstracts, biographical notes, video lectures), genres that are linked to by these blogs (home pages, conference websites, articles, calls for papers), and the purposes for the posts (showcasing research, event announcements, sharing outputs) (pp. 451–455). The value of understanding the complex ecology in which science blogs operate, she demonstrates, is that "they are hybrid texts where various genres are brought together, connected, and recontextualized, as part of an ecology of genres that function together to support the group's social and work activity" (p. 464). Luzón's analysis provides insight into the variety of genre-ing activities operating in blogs, as well as the motivations for researchers to run blogs (see, also, Luzón, 2013).

A number of questions arise from the current research on blogs. Are science blogs just for experts? Or are they for popularizing science? What kinds of science blogs exist, and are we able to call any of them typified? Many blogs serve a more heterogeneous audience than solely disciplinary experts, as we would see in traditional research genres; however, in line with trans-scientific genres, science blogs preclude neither disciplinary experts nor advance argument and in-field discussion. Almost a quarter of AAAS members reported that they have written for a blog (Pew Research Center, 2015). One study found more than half the readers surveyed from a variety of science blogs, including independent and more established network blogs, were over forty years old and one third were over fifty years old, with a 40:60 female-to-male breakdown for those who identified within the categories of female or male (Brown Jarreau, 2016; Jarreau & Porter, 2018). And, although the majority of respondents were educated in the sciences, more than half reported they never blogged about science themselves. PLOS, the case study for this chapter, conducted their own survey of readers and found that of the 966 respondents identified in non-mutually exclusive categories as researchers (65 percent), graduate students (28 percent), clinical workers (10 percent), citizen scientists (15 percent), and science writers (13 percent), 83 percent reported actively seeking "science-related information online" (Jarreau, 2016).

The PLOS Blogs Network is an illuminating example of the science blogs discussed here. PLOS (2015a) is a web-borne open-access publisher for research in science and medicine. Founded in 2000 as an initiative to advance the cause of accessible research, PLOS has, in the intervening fifteen years, established a reputation as an open-access publisher par excellence. In 2010, PLOS (2015d) established a blogs network. Other major science publishing outlets follow a similar structure for their blogs networks. *Scientific American,* the popular science magazine first published in 1845, expanded to a website, which includes a blogs network. The *Scientific American* blogs network is structured similarly to the PLOS Blogs Network, with staff blogs and an assortment of network blogs, the latter of which operate outside the editorial practices governing the magazine or the staff blog (*Scientific American,* 2015). Born of *Nature Magazine, Nature* blogs are primarily composed by staff. *Nature Magazine,* much like *Scientific American,* dates back to the 1800s, and thus is firmly situated within the traditional publishing landscape. Because I am interested in the genres that seem to be evolving online and outside (or, rather alongside) of traditional spheres of science communications, this chapter investigates the PLOS Blogs Network, which does not have the ties that *Nature* or *Scientific American* do to more long-standing traditional forms of publication.

PLOS's blogs network includes six blogs written by staff and more than sixteen blogs written by affiliates in the extended blogs network. Staff blogs include both general information blogs (*Official PLOS Blog, EveryONE, PLOS Tech, PLOS Opens*) and field-specific blogs (*PLOS Biologue* and *Speaking of Medicine*). Affiliated blogs,[1] include a range of intriguing titles, including *All Models Are Wrong, The Gleaming Retort, The Integrative Paleontologists, DNA Science Blog, Obesity Panacea, Mind the Brain,* and *NeuroTribes.*

Bloggers writing for these network blogs are typically scientists or science journalists interested in a particular topic, ranging from the science of the brain to paleontology, as indicated by the titles. PLOS (2015b) provides something of a disclaimer, reminding readers that "posts appearing on these blogs are not commissioned, pre-screened or edited by PLOS, thus opinions expressed belong solely to the blogger whose byline appears at the top of the

---

1. At the time of initially drafting this chapter, in the autumn of 2014, PLOS Blogs Network includes sixteen active blogs written by affiliates, and the "Guest Blog," which aggregates these posts. In addition to these blogs, there are twelve other blogs written by affiliates archived. As noted later in the chapter, some of this information has changed by the time of publication, but the general structure remains.

page." Each blog likely operates a little differently, but one example of how this kind of science writing looks behind the scenes might be useful. For a number of years I blogged for the PLOS *CitizenSci* blog. Much of what I wrote for the *CitizenSci* blog was of interest to me, and although I passed it by one of the *CitizenSci* blog's editors, a standard editorial practice was not in place. Much of this was outlined in an agreement I signed, provided by PLOS, which makes clear the author's responsibility for the material she posts. For academics and journalists, this kind of intellectual license is not especially different from what they do in traditional outlets, but it is different from the kind of vetting process they might encounter after producing drafts. Academic systems of peer review are designed to ensure a level of accountability, but book reviews and certain kinds of invited publications do not use these same mechanisms of review. For journalists the kind of vetting, fact-checking, and editorial oversight their work undergoes will likely be dependent upon the publication for which they are writing. However, somewhere in the intervening years since I began writing there and 2017, editors managed the system, and the processes for managing the blogs within PLOS changed. This is an unsurprising organizational shift as a community grows and as resources fall into place to better establish the discourse space. Indeed, this formalizing suggests that the blogs network is coming of age and crystalizing into a professionally managed resource. This assists the function of science blogs and demonstrates the communities' continued self-reflective and critical practices, designed to provide high-quality and accessible material. In fact, speaking from my own experience, the attention to a nonacademic audience is indeed serious, and I have rewritten material that attended to disciplinary expectations rather than speaking to a broader audience. Knowing something of the writers, we can now turn to the audience, or the imagined audience anyway, and try to better understand the rhetorical situation to which our PLOS bloggers respond.

Each blog offers a description of who the writer is and what she purports to write about. Taking all the descriptions together, blogs are not strictly aimed at either expert or nonexpert audiences. A sample of blog descriptions helps illustrate this point:

All Models Are Wrong . . . But Some Are Useful. Tamsin Edwards offers a "grown-up discussion about how to quantify uncertainties in modelling climate change and its impacts, past and future." (*All Models are Wrong*)

Where some see disparate and unrelated disciplines, At the Interface explores the expanding interaction between science and (mostly visual) art and culture. From artists working in labs, to scientists working in art museums, this blog explores how science can inspire great art and vice versa. (*At the Interface*)

Linking neuroscience research, psychological disorders, health and well-being. (*Mind the Brain*)

Our blog covers the latest paleontological research, with special attention to issues concerning open science, publishing, and fossils in the digital realm. (*The Integrative Paleontologists*)

Neuroanthropology examines the integration, as well as the breadth, of anthropology and neuroscience. Sometimes we do straight neuroscience, other times pure anthropology. Most of the time we'll be somewhere in the middle. (*Neuroanthropology*)

All Models are Wrong's description gives us a good degree of insight into the specific area of climate change research that will be discussed, namely how to "quantify uncertainties in modelling" (PLOS, 2015b). Likewise, *At the Interface* offers careful disciplinary situating, or rather interdisciplinary situating, in describing the focus of the blog. Such situating places the blog within the context of academic discourses about disciplinarity, but extends the focus beyond the academic realm to site venues such as museums. *Mind the Brain* makes similar moves to situate itself in relation to disciplines, but also with an outward focus on general issues such as "health and well-being" (PLOS, 2015b). Expanding the PLOS Blogs Network scope, *The Integrative Paleontologists* specifically cites open science and publishing as issues of interest, as well as disciplinary concerns. With more disciplinary concerns, *Neuroanthropology* describes a blogging program concerned with bringing together two areas of research. In these descriptions, numerous disciplinary concerns and foci are revealed, along with broader issues and connections for the sciences and arts. Given that contributors are often characterized in terms of their professional status and affiliation, it is not surprising that academic disciplinarity appears, but even so the focus is not strictly on specific disciplinary problems for internal or expert readers. Other blogs explicitly state their primary interest as extending their writing to broad public audiences. For example:

Translational Global Health facilitates the translation of findings from basic science to practical applications in Global Health practice and, thus, meaningful health outcomes for diverse populations and societies. (*Translational Global Health*)

The science blogs in the PLOS blogging network serve multiple and complex audiences that include experts and nonexperts—although we ought to always remind ourselves the nonexpert in one situation might very well be an expert in another, and qualifications and skills may translate across domains to help the nonexpert reason in a new context. Even the data regarding blog readers, cited early in this chapter, do not easily distinguish who is an expert or not since science is a large and diverse enterprise with an enormous amount of specializations that mark experts. The repertoire of discourse strategies to be found in these boundary-violating blogs will provide useful science communication lessons to be abstracted and used for better, broader, and more meaningful communication.

PLOS: AN EXAMINATION OF RHETORICAL MOVES

As noted in chapter 1, move analysis has been widely applied to scientific communications. Given that work, an assortment of moves that appear across scientific genres can help inform a move analysis of blogs. Moves, recall, identify "a section of a text that performs a specific communicative function. Each move not only has its own purpose but also contributes to the overall communicative purposes of the genre," and this helps us understand the rhetorical strategies at work in a genre (Connor et al., 2007, p. 23). For this study, two posts from each of the sixteen network blogs (table 3) were analyzed, for a total sample of thirty-two texts. Sampling for the posts from each blog used a simple selection method: the first and last posts from the total 680 network blog posts collected.

Taking a closer look at the thirty-two texts analyzed, it is first useful to note the different purposes they seem to serve as this provides us with a preliminary typology of science blog types. Reporting research is a common activity, where recent articles published in PLOS journals are described, which helps accommodate the research to a wider audience. Although books are less common in some STEM disciplines, book reviews do appear in science blogs and serve a similar function of sharing new research. Exploring the inner workings of science is also a subject appearing in science blogs, as exampled in the discussion of scientific methods or scientific process, STEM education, controversial science, and the challenges of communicating about science with broader publics. Also providing a glimpse behind the curtains are interviews with scientists, profiles of young scientists, and posts sharing a scientist's own personal learning experiences. Newsworthy subjects are also

TABLE 3. Summary of Blog Posts from PLOS Network Blogs

BLOG TITLE	NO. POST	NO. AUTHORS	AVG. WORDS	MENU
All Models Are Wrong	14	1	1130	Eco
Gleaming Retort	50	1	1946	Eco
Integrative Paleontologists	50	3	2003	Eco
DNA Science	50	1	2740	Health
Obesity Panacea	50	2	1306	Health
Public Health	50	3	1856	Health
Translational Global Health	50	20 (1 primary, 19 guests)	1727	Health
Mind the Brain	50	5	2319	Neuro
Neuroanthropology	10	2	2256	Neuro; Culture
Neurotribes	40	1	2878	Neuro; Culture
At the Interface	30	1	990	Culture
Citizen Sci	50	7	1597	Culture
MIT SciWrite	38	22	1077	Culture
On Science Blogs	48	1	2986	Culture
Sci-Ed	50	5	1928	Culture
The Student Blog	50	27	1936	Culture

reported, and we also find roundups of activities or projects and posts tackling common misconceptions about scientific topics. The range of activities in the thirty-two posts demonstrates that "science blogs" are not a singular genre.

Although we will return to the question of how to classify some of the genre-ing activities online, it is useful to also explore commonalities across blog posts to identify some of the features that characterize what we think of as a blog style and the broad social actions these posts serve. The next section charts moves in blogs to identify some of these features that give a blog its character. Hypothesizing that we might find some strategies from either internal or external kinds of writing, examining a selection of blog posts for both kinds of moves provides a useful way to eliminate or discover the rhetorical strategies at work. Three questions framed this analysis: What kinds of moves are made across blog posts? How are these moves made? How do these moves seem to function rhetorically to engage blog readers?

A similar approach to the one described in the analysis of crowdfunding proposals has been adopted here. Since we know that John Swales's CARS model appears across a range of scientific genres, these moves were incorporated into the analytical tool I initially designed for blogs. In addition to these moves, first by analyzing a few blog posts with my research assistant and then by discussing the strategies that appear to be at work, we have identified several other moves. We then crafted a coding sheet and analyzed more posts. After coding the large sample of texts from blogs noted above, we developed a list of moves that appear to be at work. The analysis included the textual content of the blog post, but images, videos, links to other sites, and comments all add richness.

Throughout the process of coding the blog posts, it became clear these posts have a number of complex moves designed to achieve different kinds of social action. But identifying the moves and the social action they are designed to enact is a challenging proposition given the relatively recent development of blogs—relative to, say, the experimental article—and the number of different blog authors contributing material. Even when we narrow the focus to science blogs, there remains a good deal of variation. To examine just what might be going on in these discursive environments, we will first look at the kinds of rhetorical moves made (table 4) and then explore how the range of moves might suggest various species of science blogs.

Establishing Interest is similar to a journalist's "hook" rather than the *Establishing Territory* move found in research introductions. Instead of a move that situates the argument in a tradition or community, a blog post often begins with a move that captures the reader's attention and interest. A striking statement such as "Our brains are alien technology" (Rennie, 2014) or a question such as "Do the words 'science class' evoke unhappy memories of struggling to memorize arcane facts unrelated to anything in the world you cared about?" (Lende, 2014) are good examples of how the *Establishing Interest* move is put to work to capture a reader's attention and imagination. However, the move can extend beyond a sentence to an entire paragraph, where an extended example or metaphor unfolds for similar effect. For example, the following paragraph works to establish interest:

> In the late 1990's, my grandmother who lived with my family was diagnosed with celiac disease. The experience of planning meals became mildly traumatic for all of us. My most vivid recollection that of [*sic*] is breakfast time: my grandmother pulling a heavy, spongey-looking, yellow loaf of bread out of the fridge and peeling apart two slices to toast and slather with jam to mask the (lack of) taste and awful sandy texture. (Kobayashi, 2014)

Often this move gives way to, sometimes overlapping with, a move to explain why a reader should remain interested in the topic after the hook.

TABLE 4. Rhetorical Moves in Science Blog Posts

MOVE	DESCRIPTION	STEPS
ESTABLISHING INTEREST	Establishes grounds for reader interest by appealing to 1) wonder or by appealing to 2) application (Fahnestock, 1986). Usually begins with a "hook" similar to a newspaper article.	Step 1A: Appealing to wonder Step 1B: Appealing to application
EXPLAINING SIGNIFICANCE	Indicates why the topic or issue should be considered important. Indicates the contribution that the current discussion intends to make to a broader conversation, including research-focused or socially or policy-driven discourses.	Step 1: Stating the topic or issue at hand Step 2A: Connecting related, newsworthy event or issue to the topic *or* Step 2B: Asking questions about the topic or issue
ILLUSTRATING THE CASE	Opens the body of blog by providing a vignette from which the problem articulated in the introduction can be elaborated upon. Following this move the body of the post may take on a narrative form, a list, or numerous other structures and accompanying moves.	Step 1: Applying a narrative account to the topic or issue *and* Step 2: Elaborating on how the narrative account illustrates some aspect of the topic or issue *and* Step 3 (optional): Repeating Steps 1 and 2
RE-ESTABLISHING INTEREST	Recalls the curiosity the author initially tried to spark in the reader by making concluding statements. In this manner, the move functions to "sum up" the article and suggest implications for the reader. It may re-invoke one of the appeals from *Establishing Interest*.	Step 1: Summarizing main points about the topic or issue *and* Step 2 (optional): Looking forward to new research or applications of research findings
ENCOURAGING ACTION	Asks reader to take action either conceptually (for example, read more, consider an issue) or materially (for example, follow a link, fund a crowdsourced project, participate in a study, or write letters to congress persons).	Step 1: Making an imperative *and* Step 2A (optional): Directing prospective participants to a study *or* Step 2B (optional): Recommending a resource
CITING SOURCES	References sources used in a blog post and may appear as a traditional works cited list, hyperlinks to sources, image captions, or a note contained within the blog post.	Step 1: Linking to external resources *and* Step 2 (optional): Including in-text citations to research *and/or* Step 3 (optional): Providing references for images, tables, and figures *and/or* Step 4 (optional): Listing full references
PERSONALIZING POSTS (OPTIONAL)	Includes two distinct but related steps. In the first use, personal information relates a story or establishes the importance of a topic in an everyday manner. In the second step, personal information is used in a biographical note to establish credibility.	Step 1A: Relating a personal *or* Step1B: Including biographical information

Adapted from Swales (1990), Connor (1998), Connor and Wagner (1998), and Connor and Mauranen (1999); see also Mehlenbacher (2017) for adaptations in crowdfunding proposals.

Explaining Significance, although related to *Establishing Interest,* advances the blog post by explaining why a topic is useful in terms of the community of practice. That is, where the move to *Establish Interest* may be playful, *Explaining Significance* is a move concerned with the factual issues the blog post will raise. It is a move that functions as a transition from introductory material to the main body of the blog post. Following the extended example of *Establishing Interest* above, the significance of the anecdote is explained thus:

> Fast forward ten years, and you could now throw a stone and hit someone with celiac disease or gluten intolerance, or who has tried a gluten-free diet for the sake of their health. Why have recent years seen a crazily rising prevalence of gluten intolerance in wealthy Western countries? I won't address this question today—but rather why eating gluten-free has risen in popularity, and why that's not a good thing. (Kobayashi, 2014)

Following from the paragraph that established interest is a personal narrative used to explain significance. Here, a marked change in the broadness of the issue is obvious, the importance of the issue is stated for the reader, and a clear indication about what exactly is going to be addressed and how is offered. Not all examples function quite so clearly, but this provides a good example of how moves function to structure the argument and eventually compel the reader to action. But compelling a reader to action requires more than a pithy statement and some claim about value, and that is where the turn to the body of the post begins.

Illustrating the Case is the move that begins the body of the blog post. Essentially, this is where the discussion, narrative, or study reported in the post begins, indicated by the end of the introductory moves and the beginning of an extended discussion. Considerable variation in how this occurs can be found. For example, some blog posts are presented in a question-and-answer format where introductory remarks lead directly into an interview. In list-style blog posts, several different topics are covered, and following a general introduction, each section has its own introduction. Personal narratives are another format that might structure the body of a post. Among all this variety are common strategies to explain an argument, invoke evidence, call for action, or persuade the reader. Just who the reader is shifts, imagined as a scientist in some blog spaces, a nonexpert in others, and some heterogeneous combination in many blogs. Such variation may be indicative of a range of science blog post types—or, perhaps, genres. Before considering variation in the types of science blog posts, strategies used to conclude a post merit attention.

Re-establishing Interest functions to summarize, restate, and reinvigorate the subject as the blog post concludes. In this way, the move functions traditionally in that it attempts to situate the importance of the issue and remind the reader of its significance to them. By reestablishing the reader's interest, the move creates an exigence to call the reader to action, a related but arguably distinct move.

Encouraging Action tends to function as part of the conclusion in a blog post and often appears toward the end of the conclusion, thus providing a kind of "takeaway" message for the blog reader to either consider further or to act on. Examples of the former, the conceptual action, include asking readers to be cautious about overreacting to public health threats, and to be weary of dubious scientific or health claims in the popular press. In the latter case, the physical or material action, there are numerous examples, such as participating in a research study or citizen science project, talking to senior colleagues, trying a science-based approach to improving one's life through health and fitness, or even purchasing a book. This move matters because it explicitly states in the post what the reader is supposed to use in the information and suggests how the reader might go about doing so.

Citing Sources is a move that may appear anywhere within a blog post. Citations may appear in a traditional reference list with full publication details included. Reference lists are not the only citation practice borrowed from the academy. Since blogs are sometimes reposted, a citation practice whereby the original source of the blog post is noted at the end of the text (for example, "This post first appeared in . . .") is used. Citing the original publication source is a practice common among academic genres such as articles that later appear reprinted in edited book collections. Moving outside of traditional citation practices, one example that relies on the affordances of the web is hyperlinks to external references, thus providing a direct path to source information. This in some ways mimics in-text citation practices and perhaps even footnote styles, but this activity also has a clear precedent in online genres, from online newspapers to blogs. Citation practices include not only the kinds of references we would find in a scholarly paper but also links to other blogs and websites, similar to how news sources link to other articles they have published. Such connections provide more than links to related articles, however. They, like traditional citations, also provide a strategy to situate an argument in a broader discourse. As well, and still similar to traditional citations, they provide the basis for a network of researchers through shared literature and community building through an engagement of this literature.

Another common citation practice is the textual accompaniment to a visual, which often cites the source of the image and potentially provides a description. While citing the source of images appears throughout the corpus, the practice of citing was better managed in some cases than others. Providing clear details about who produced the image, where the image was digitally copied from, and where to find the source image are all necessary to build a community where the exchange of ideas and the time-intensive work of image production are both given credit in an appropriate manner. While these citation practices differ in how they reference outwardly, they indeed are all engaged in the activity of situating and sourcing information. Several kinds of key rhetorical objectives are achieved by citing information in these multitudes of ways. For example, some rhetorical effects include demonstrating the blog authors are familiar with the research in a given community, that their own research is grounded in a body of scholarly literature, that they have done their due diligence in understanding the state of the field, and also that the blog authors value others' work and ideas enough to credit them. Sometimes, as well, references have a negative operation and instead point to an article that is being deconstructed for problems in thesis, method, or significance, which would be typical of posts specifically written to challenge findings of a study.

Personalizing Posts describes two rather different moves that both rely on the personal information of the author. In the first case, an author might tell a story (for example, about meeting an advisor and asking them to chair a dissertation project or, perhaps, explaining how the researcher came to learn a particular method would not work for their dissertation and how they then devised a new procedure). Telling personal stories helps the author provide a relatable narrative to draw in a reader. Another way personal information is provided in posts is through biographical notes, such as about credentials and institutional affiliations, although they seem to appear more commonly with guest authors, presumably because regular authors have their biographical information included on an "About" page connected with the blog.

All told, moves do not necessarily appear in a specific order, and their distribution varies. *Establishing Interest* appears in all of the sources, meaning that at least one of the two posts from each source/blog in the sample had this move, for a total of thirty-one coded references. Explaining significance only appeared in thirteen of the sixteen sources, with six sources only being coded once (meaning only one post of the two blogs featured this move), for a total of twenty-two references. *Illustrating the Case* appears in five notes, with six references. It is difficult from the sample to say why this is, but certainly the limited length of blog posts could be a factor. Some of the examples explain fairly simple concepts, some more complex. *Reestablishing Interest* appears in eleven sources, with fourteen references; *Encouraging Actions* appears in thirteen sources, with a total of twenty-four references; but five sources had one reference, meaning only one of the two blog posts was coded. *Citing Sources* likewise appears in thirteen sources, but as a reference—both image references and scholarly references—forty times. *Personalizing posts* only appeared in five sources, for a total of ten references, but this is unsurprising given the previously discussed trend for authors to have information on an "About" page.

Distribution of these moves demonstrates that with the range of topics and specializations across blogs, there are certain conventionalized forms at the level of a move. Although one could certainly begin a project to classify genres of blog posts, this is unlikely to serve our understanding of the recurrent rhetorical situation to which these blogs respond. For example, from the sample examined here, one could identify several types of blogs, including the "sharing research findings by summarizing a peer review journal article" genre, the "responding to a public controversy" genre, and the "discussing challenges to scientific research" genre. In addition to the difficulty in characterizing "genres" on such a granular scale, the enterprise serves a project in taxonomy rather than rhetorical awareness. Instead, when charting broad trends across these sixteen blogs, it is evident that they have many commonalities in form, and paired with their stated purpose, we see not disciplines represented, but problems or areas of interest. The problem-based work of blogs helps illustrate their broad rhetorical function, which is to engage readers with timely issues in science and society. Pairing this rhetorical account of blogs with a move analysis for new media environments, where genres are more nebulous, provides a lens to explore unfolding typifications. The usefulness of exploring unfolding typifications is that this approach attends more specifically to the "strategic genre performances" (Bawarshi, 2016, p. 246) through a diachronic lens, with proleptic sympathies. Although we can identify distinctions among blog posts (which suggests we are not looking at what we might characterize as a singular genre), we are indeed looking at a recurrent form of communication that shares typified forms. Notably, there are typified forms that are not deeply wed to the media form, the infrastructure, or the platform design specifically. Instead, blogs and blog posts can include a number of different forms, genres, and genre-ing activities. Contrast this freedom, for example, with crowdfunding on Experiment, where we see conventions formalized by the design of the platform itself.

It is notable that several other features are common to blog posts, and while they may not function as a move, they still serve useful rhetorical and relational purposes. One example is the use of hyperlinks or embedded social media. Elsewhere I have suggested this may be a move (A. R. Mehlenbacher, 2017), but now I speculate that the activity of linking serves different purposes, not limited to making or supporting an argument, establishing ethos or participation in a particular community, and so on. Twitter feeds can be integrated into a web page, allowing the blog to feature material written on the microblogging platform, and thus to network the blog with another platform and a wider community of readers. Social media may also be used as a means to share a blog post. By sharing a blog post through platforms such as Twitter or Facebook, the specific content of the post can be shared with a wider audience than the committed blog readership. Further, the post can also be contextualized by a brief note (for example, "Read this blog post that explains the recent NASA mission") or hashtags (for example, #science or #scicomm). The social function of such sharing is at least partially promotional and perhaps also part of popularizing science, once again reminding us of the liminal space between external and internal genres of science communication that blogs seem to inhabit.

Another recurrent contextualizing strategy is linking between blog posts in a series. For example, a blog author might write four related blog posts, but only post them once a week to keep reader engagement consistent. As the blog author posts each week's note, he or she provides a link to the previous post to either remind readers or point new readers to this other source. Commonly this kind of note appears toward the beginning of a post, or sometimes at the end, and reads, for example, "This is post 2 of 4 in an ongoing series about climate change modeling." Other kinds of notes include updates, and while this is not common among all blog posts, it certainly occurs often enough to mention. Updates might serve the function of correcting an oversight or wrong information, much like a newspaper issues a correction, or they might serve to provide additional information that came to light only after the original posting. A broader strategy of contextualizing is to ensure that blog posts can be seen as part of a larger project (the blog itself, and that blog within the PLOS Blogs Network), and one effective means to do that is through a visual branding. Indeed, it might be a promotional discourse, but as much as science is communicated through images, so too is the blog brand. In the next section, we turn from text-based strategies in blogs to explore visual elements.

Visual Strategies in Science Blogs

Images appearing in this book, reproductions of what appears online, are static, dull, and notable only as gestures toward the rich life of visuals in online environments. Pruning color and kinetics, what appears in figures 5 and 6 is, indeed, a postmortem of the complex and interactive visual environment that richly evolves in the PLOS Blogs Network.

FIGURE 5. *PLOS Biologue* Home Page.

FIGURE 6. *PLOS Ecology Community* Home Page.

In figure 5 and figure 6, two PLOS blog home pages are shown. Online these two pages are colorful landing pages filled with hyperlinks to take readers to particular blog posts. Blog posts may be featured or accessed through a tag cloud. Information about the blog can also be accessed. From the layout of the pages, it is evident that visuals are used as a promotional tool for blog posts. The range of visuals is striking: from familiar scenes such as a landscape or a bird to complex visualizations of data we cannot see without the assistance of scientific tools.

Were you to open the live and lively pages featured in figures 5 and 6, you would find an abundance of color: absolute zero blue, an alien armpit, lemon glacier, and magic potion, to approximate and borrow Crayola's terminology. Consider, for example, the *PLOS Biologue* or *Ecology Community*. Not only are the pages colorful, they are vibrant, with varying intensity, and draw attention to dramatic features of the natural world, visualizations, and illustrations. Logos for PLOS, along with directional cues that cut up the page, appear alongside these other kinds of visual elements, providing further visual complexity. Notably, text accompanies these visuals; however, the corresponding text does not serve to explain the image. Rather, a closer look reveals that the information appearing below the images in the middle of the page consists of blog post titles, author information, the date posted, and categories under which the blog post has been tagged.

The arrangement of images and text on the *PLOS Biologue* site impresses a puzzling message. The public audience is, presumably, drawn in by the exciting, colorful, and dynamic graphics that serve to promote the blog posts. Yet, the images and even the text descriptions advance specialized information, including a post about "non-coding RNAs" (Peng, 2016) and one about the "ASCB 2016 meeting" (Alvarez-Garcia, 2016). The images also present specialized knowledge that, without textual descriptions, is unlikely to be self-explanatory to a broad audience. Recall, however, that blog readers are typically well educated in the sciences, and many readers work professionally as scientists or in allied fields. As well, because these images appear on the landing page for *PLOS Biologue,* we might expect that they serve a promotional rather than informative function, drawing readers into the blog post itself.

In a blog post, we are likely to find markedly different kinds of images, particularly as we look across the various fields and topics that appear within the PLOS Blogs Network. Rather than attempt to create a taxonomic system for these images, I want to investigate one case. This post was chosen only because it is the most recent post appearing on the *PLOS Biologue* landing page at the time of writing. Titled "A Novel Prostate Cancer Risk Variant in African Americans, Dynamics of the Human Gut Microbiome, and Geno-Pheno Maps for Digital Organisms: The PLOS Comp Biol February Issue," from Chadwick (2017), the post helps to illustrate the complex audience addressed in these blogs: both experts and also an *engaged* broader readership. By *engaged* I mean readers who are not only interested in the subject but also willing to put their cognitive wetware to work to understand what they are reading. This is not science popularization, but equally it is not purely expert (visual) communication.

Let us explore how visualizations are handled within a blog post, where we can still expect some promotional efforts, but also a more content-rich appli-

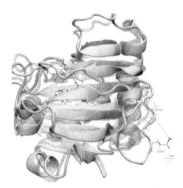

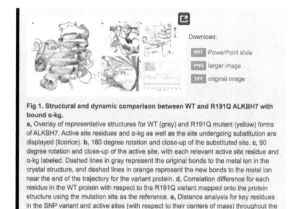

Overlay of representative structures for WT (gray) and R191Q mutant (yellow) forms of ALKBH7. Image Credit: Walker et al.

Fig 1. Structural and dynamic comparison between WT and R191Q ALKBH7 with bound α-kg.
a, Overlay of representative structures for WT (gray) and R191Q mutant (yellow) forms of ALKBH7. Active site residues and α-kg as well as the site undergoing substitution are displayed (licorice). b, 180 degree rotation and close-up of the substituted site. c, 90 degree rotation and close-up of the active site, with each relevant active site residue and α-kg labeled. Dashed lines in gray represent the original bonds to the metal ion in the crystal structure, and dashed lines in orange represent the new bonds to the metal ion near the end of the trajectory for the variant protein. d, Correlation difference for each residue in the WT protein with respect to the R191Q variant mapped onto the protein structure using the mutation site as the reference. e, Distance analysis for key residues in the SNP variant and active sites (with respect to their centers of mass) throughout the simulation trajectory.
https://doi.org/10.1371/journal.pcbl.1005345.g001

FIGURE 7. *PLOS Biologue* Blog Text and Graphic (left) and Original *PLOS Computational Biology* Article (right). Compare these two images, one from the blog (left) and one embedded in a PLOS research article (right). The complexity of both the image and the textual description becomes reduced. However, even in the blog description, the language remains expert, thus suggesting, again, that blogs are not simply popularizations but rather a complex form of science communication operating in the liminal space between expert and nonexpert discourse.

cation of visualizations. In our example post, an image appears at the top of the post, a kind of header. Typically, these images serve a promotional effort. When blogging for PLOS, I have been asked to provide such images, meant to draw readers into the material, and also useful attention-grabbers as the blog posts are shared across social media. Another kind of visual, however, operates much less as a promotional feature and more akin to the kind of explanatory aid expected in professional genres such as the research article. Figure 7 offers one such example, where a text–visual pairing offers a summary of the work being described in the body of the blog post. Still, the visual itself does not act on its own; instead, it underscores the object of study with the brief caption "Overlay of representative structures for WT (gray) and R191Q mutant (yellow) forms of ALKBH7. Image Credit: Walker et al." (Chadwick, 2017).

When the images in figure 7 (Chadwick, 2017), from a blog, are compared with the original source for the figure (Walker et al., 2017), a research article, the summary offered here becomes especially interesting. Work that is a great deal more descriptive is done in text in the original article, as we might expect if the function is more informative than promotional. But it is more than an image we encounter in the original PLOS article. Rather, this is an example of the kind of affordances that online journals such as PLOS have for interactive media. Figure 8 is a screen capture of the tool one can use to navigate the images embedded in the original PLOS article. This allows for a much more

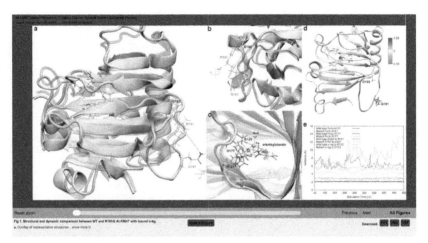

FIGURE 8. PLOS Image Viewer Technology. As noted in figure 7, the image in the original PLOS research article is more complex than the version appearing in PLOS blogs. Another interesting feature of the article is that it offers more complex ways of interacting with the image, as demonstrated by the image viewer here. A researcher might scroll in to further examine the details of this image, but given that only section (a) of this image travels to the blog, the complexity in the series is lost in the blog, as well as the granularity of the image. This suggests, perhaps, a promotional function in blogs rather than in the article.

serious study of the image, not because we can scroll in and about the images, but because we are invited by the technology to do so.

In the example from PLOS blogs, there appear to be multiple functions for the visuals that range from those we would expect to see in both popularizations of science and professional genres. The visuals function to advance, underscore, or illustrate arguments, but also serve clear promotional efforts. In blogs, images might function as cases of what appears in the full article, and although our case here is not exhaustive, it does demonstrate the point I want to make: visuals travel across genres, and as they do, they mean differently within them. In the case of the blog, the visuals may operate in the liminal space between professional and public, drawing from different sets of cultural (disciplinary or more broad) knowledge. Science blogs deploy visuals in interesting, creative, and varied forms, unsettling them from their original sanctioned context and delivering them to diverse readerships. As with crowdfunding proposals, the images provide us with a range of expressive possibilities afforded by the platforms crafted to share scientific knowledge, and like the database, those technologies are not bereft of rhetorical artistry.

Visuals[2] appear across different stages of scientific research, for instance, from funding a project, to collecting and organizing data and presenting find-

---

2. "Visual" is used throughout this chapter to describe a range of representational modes. "Scientific visualization" is a phrase used for a field of study itself and thus avoided to stave off confusion.

ings through blogs. In these examples, visuals are embedded within scientific genres, such as the research article or proposals or blog posts. Visuals, in addition to traveling across genres, travel through media and platforms, further complicating their functioning. Given the multimodal nature of scientific communications, particularly online, it is useful to talk about visuals in terms of where they travel within and the conventions that regulate those genres where visuals appear. And, grounding visuals in particular genres helps us avoid decontextualized interpretations of visuals in scientific genres. At the same time, examining visuals independently from the genres in which they appear is useful because visuals may travel across scientific genres, follow various conventions in their own right, and bring new kinds of representational modes to the genres they inhabit.

Visuals help us identify certain salient features of the data—for instance, where we find trends and patterns in data, where we locate the hidden meaning within data, or even where we uncover otherwise invisible phenomenon. When we rearticulate scientific visuals, they become more than a modality—more than a visual that exists within a text or with respect to a text—but rather a knowledge-making form. When we understand different kinds of scientific visuals as such, we can begin to understand how visuals do more than stand in as supporting features of a genre. "Different kinds" of scientific visuals mean more than charts or graphs, and include the fascinating "scientific portraiture," the kind of portraiture that presents scientists at work in the lab or the field, which Gigante (2015) argues is "a genre that lends itself to a range of visual messages *about scientists* and *science*" (p. 294; emphasis added). It is notable that researchers studying scientific visualizations have gone so far as to argue that certain kinds of visual forms operate not only as a part of knowledge-making genres, such as the scientific research article or blog, but as a genres themselves. Ross (2017) writes that "scientific illustrations constitute an identifiable scientific genre," and he continues, citing Miller's (1984) work on genre, echoing her argument, saying "genre itself is contextually relative because of its dependence on human action" (p. 148). These visuals, instead, act as genres themselves—and potentially as agents for genre change—to construct meaning and reflect values in our assessment of information and data. That is, scientific visuals are not merely representational vehicles that render data about the world visible; rather, they are epistemic objects that operate independently and in concert with other genres to construct meaning and knowledge about scientific subjects.

Although visuals are indeed born within their own context, by which they are shaped and, crucially, that they help to shape, they move about contexts online. When considering visuals as genre-ing activities themselves, new configurations of expression might be possible. Indeed, the context of creation shapes how an audience could understand and interpret a visual, how visuals work within different social contexts, and how novel exigencies and rhetorical situations afford opportunities for the evolution of new genres. We also learn how the visuals themselves shape the context of a scientific text and the production of scientific knowledge. Work on visuals is central to the question of trans-scientific genres because it helps us understand how a multiplicity of modalities craft new media environments out of which these genres emerge.

Having moved through the PLOS Blogs Network and charted some of its visual features, a case study of an individual blog post will be helpful to explore how the text that accompanies these images functions. Next, I illustrate how move analysis can help chart the textual rhetorical work in a blog post. However, it is helpful to remember that as science blogs continue to evolve, their purpose may change, and already there are multiple purposes for blogs and blog posts. Although there is some variation in science blogs, this chapter has detailed a set of moves that appear to broadly operate, as genreing features, across a variety of science blog forms.

CASE ANALYSIS: THE PLOS BLOGS NETWORK

The PLOS *SciComm* blog[3] offers a list of "Top 16 in 2016" blog posts from across the PLOS Blogs Network. Top posts are chosen for how much traffic they receive, and are then divided into themes deemed by the author to be salient in 2016 (e.g., "public health under pressure," "gene modification," and "meta-research—to address science's reproducibility problem") (Costello, 2017). Because health communication has some particular issues that I simply do not have the space to address in this book, and because "meta-research" on matters of reproducibility is method- and not content-focused, I opted to examine the "gene modification" theme to choose an exemplar. The first blog provided in this theme is from a PhD plant science student, Erin Zess, entitled "If 'Are GMOs Bad?' Is the Wrong Question, What's the Right One? And How Should Scientists Answer It?" It was shared on the *SciComm* blog after first being posted as "What We Talk about When We Talk about Genetic Modification" on the *PLOS Synbio Community* blog (Zess, 2016).

Zess's post begins with what we might traditionally call an *Establishing the Territory* move, in the Swalesian tradition:

---

3. This blog was not part of the network during the initial data collection period for this chapter, in 2014.

I would argue that the source of a transgene and its' [sic] method of introduction are irrelevant to the safety of the resulting plant. A gene is a gene—it is a sequence of DNA and, as a molecule, DNA has zero chance of harming you. The DNA can be from any organism—literally, any organism—and it is still just a sequence of the same chemical letters, A, T, G, and C. Moreover, the method of transgene introduction, be it by plant breeding or by transformation, has no effect on the action of the gene product in the cell. Either the gene is present and active, or it is not. (Zess, 2016)

Recall that *Establishing the Territory* includes a step to make generalizations about a topic, seen here through an explanation of what we know about transgenetics, which the author argues should be framed through a discussion of "action of the gene product in the cell" and not matters of donor or source. Where I suggest *Establishing Interest* may function alongside or in place of this first move, it is rather a matter of framing of the content. Intentionally provocative—"irrelevant to the safety of the resulting plant" or "a gene is a gene"—what we see is a move to generate interest not only in the topic, but in a specific argument. Here is it essential for the preconceptions about transgenetics creating monstrous hybrids (e.g., "frankenfood" metaphors) rather than new genetic combinations. Having set aside what *isn't* an important question—namely, the donor—Zess (2016) turns to what she believes is the matter in hand, functionality in the recipient:

What does matter to me, and what I find of critical concern, is how a transgene is read by the cell, what protein product it makes, how that protein acts in the cell, and how that action has consequences outside of the cell and, more generally, outside of the plant. I would argue that, when we debate genetic modification, our debates should be centered on these points. And, crucially, that these debates should be different for each and every GMO [genetically modified organism].

Every GMO has a different transgene or set of transgenes, and thus different protein products banging around the cell. Considering this fact, "Are GMOs safe?" is an asinine question.

Establishing a Niche, for Swales, includes steps counterclaiming, indicating a gap, raising questions, or continuing a tradition. By the end of the text quoted above, it is evident that counterclaiming is at work, specifically countering previous debate about the source of genes. Indeed, by the final sentence Zess advances an intentional conflagration to lay waste to moral absolutist arguments, which represent the values of a significant percentage of the public (Scott, Inbar, & Rozin, 2016). *Explaining Significance,* I have argued, helps to articulate a broader gap, whether related to social concerns or policy making, and in the above example we can see this at work. Further, a move Swales identified as *Occupying the Niche,* which announces the research or its central findings, is not made here. However, we can see some alignment—occupying—by advancing an argument and inhabiting that argument. The next move, then, is not part of a Swalesian model, but rather one that illustrates the argument.

> I'm certain that if I made a GM [genetically modified] plant that produced rat poison it would not be safe. However, if I made a GM plant that had a transgene to produce a protein from another plant, previous evidence would suggest that the resultant GMO is going to be harmless. Thus, sweeping generalizations about the safety of GMOs, whether #AntiGMO or #ProGM in their flavour, are insufficient and irresponsible. We need to ask more informative questions and, through this line of inquiry, start a new conversation about GMOs that reflects the complexity of the topic.

Illustrating the Case, recall, opens the body of a post by illustrating the matter raised in the introductory sections. Here another provocative statement is made to illustrate the point: modification techniques that result in poison are not safe, but this has nothing to do with the gene donor. Rather, it is the combination and the expression of the resulting combination that must be evaluated.

> Rather than, "Are GMOs bad?" we should ask a series of questions for each and every GM product: What is the cellular function of the transgene protein product? How does this cellular function affect the traits of the transgenic plant? Are there negative consequences—for humans, wildlife, or ecological systems—of these plant traits? Moreover, are there negative downstream effects of the way that this GMO will be used in agriculture? Lastly, do all of the negatives outweigh all of the benefits of using this GMO in agriculture?
>
> These are the questions that regulatory agencies (U. S., Europe) already ask in order to allow GM products on the market—but these are the questions that consumers need to ask, too. Moreover, industry scientists, academics, and government agencies need to be up to the task of answering these questions transparently and in understandable terms. The results of safety testing should be clearly communicated so that when a GMO is deemed "safe," consumers aren't left wondering what "safe" means.
>
> Rather than a climate of "hush, hush, trust" this shift would foster an environment of "ask, ask, understand,"—not as punchy to say, but far more powerful. If consumers are able to recognize the primacy of these questions

and access digestible information that satiated their inquisitive appetites, the GM debate as we know it would cease to exist. (Zess, 2016)

In the body of the post, the discussion breaks out points made in the introduction, cites sources via links, and further illustrates and reflects on the matter at hand. Above we can see how this blog post accomplishes making the case—which often must be done in fewer than 1,000 words for blog posts. Although it is certainly not the kind of lengthy and well-supported argument we would expect of a research article, supported arguments are made in the post.

> In place of garbage questions, oversimplified hashtags, and jargon-filled scientific placations, we'd be able to have a genuine, well-informed discussion about GM technology and the resulting GMOs.
>
> In the context of plant science, genetic modification (GM) technology is the introduction of transgenes into non-native host plant via biotechnology methods. With this now-understandable definition—which has plagued you throughout—I hope that when we talk about genetic modification, we talk about the technology and the safety of the products, leaving the oft-conflated issues (food security, industrial agriculture, Monsanto's policies) for another conversation.
>
> When we talk about genetic modification technology and the safety of the products, I hope that we also talk about the myriad of products and the diversity of GMOs. I hope that we forgo sweeping generalizations and, instead, opt to ask more nuanced questions and seek accurate answers. With clarity, we can break out of the current circular, unproductive argument and really talk about genetic modification when we talk about "genetic modification." (Zess, 2016)

Encouraging Action asks readers to exercise the knowledge they have gained, either conceptually or through social action. In our illustrative case, it appears the call to action is to shift the framing of discourse surrounding GMOs in order to focus on the science itself, setting aside matters of policy (for example, "food security, industrial agriculture, Monsanto's policies"). Months later, the National Academies of Science released a report that echoes the call to attend to the products of modification, and not the process per se (National Academies of Sciences and Medicine, 2016), underscoring the broader situation to which this rhetorical action responds. Finally, the biographical information appears at the conclusion of the post, as well as references for the associated image, and a standard disclaimer ("The views expressed in this post belong solely to its author and do not necessarily reflect those of PLOS").

With this illustrative analysis, I hope to show how to use moves for a qualitative analysis. A larger-scale analysis to test these moves might include a broader set of science blogs than those in the PLOS Blogs Network, such as those hosted by *Scientific American's* blogs network, and popular blogs that do not belong to blogs networks but have a wide readership. Blending move analysis with a somewhat more forgiving rhetorical orientation toward polysemy allows for blogs to be examined as they continue to change and find their niche among online genres of science communication. But it is worth considering that although the moves mapped nicely onto this example, there may be distinct genres or types of science blogs that simply will not fit this model. Next I turn to some research that helps unravel this problem, and provide possible heuristics for both analytical and instructive, pedagogical ends.

SUMMARY: A DIFFERENT KIND OF EVOLUTION AND SPECIATION

While there were good examples of moves and recurrent features across blog posts, few revealed a strong structure for the posts. Revealed by the move analysis are moves we can characterize generally to talk about a range of genre-ing activities that occur widely within science blogs. Moves are also helpful as pedagogical tools for novice blog writers. Certain conventional forms of science blogging appear to be taking shape, but categorizing them as genres rather than featuring genre-ing activities only serves to establish a closed set. Rather, some of the purposes to which blogging about science might be put are useful heuristics about what means of persuasion are available.

Science blogs include a number of different kinds, perhaps proto-genres, of blog posts. Some of those could be called "explanatory posts," which describe an assortment of writing that explains some scientific concept or finding, and may also discuss its current relevance or application. Explanatory posts may have some of the same features as their traditional counterparts. Blog posts may present the case with more detail and complex information and language than, say, a newspaper article. But specialized magazines, such as *Scientific American,* are a traditional form where similar complexity and nuance in argument could be expected. Another type of science blog proto-genre is the "roundup," which includes a list of top posts, favorite posts, and year-end highlights. This style of writing has certainly become popular online beyond science blogs, but nevertheless it has a distinct character in the science blogging sphere given the uniqueness of the content. Another interesting approach is the "take down," which reports flaws in a study, discusses a retraction, and may even report alternative analysis and findings. The "take down" draws from antecedents well established in internal science communication, but also has antecedents in more popular spheres of discourse, such as investigative journalism. A kind of "notice" genre might describe when blogs share calls to participate in studies requiring human subjects or citizen science projects. Another kind of rhetorical activity is the "autobiographical note," which may include a narrative about becoming a scientist, a memory of meeting a legend in the field, a personal experience recounted for the benefit of young scientists, an introduction of oneself to blog readers, or biographical information to sign off a blog. Other rhetorical activities could be characterized as "pedagogical lessons," including professional career advice, tips on writing and publishing, and even discussions on scientific methods themselves. By no means is this list inclusive of the wide range of science blogging activity; rather, these are some popular examples of the kinds of content found on science blogs. There are numerous options for the kinds of science blog posts one might write, and these sometimes blur the audience lines between scientists, nonscientists, scientists from another discipline, and combinations thereof.

Another way of cutting up PLOS blogs is offered by Jarreau (2016), who crafted a taxonomy for her survey of PLOS blog readers that included numerous "types" of science blogs:

- expert commentaries on current scientific issues,
- in-depth analyses of single research papers,
- basic explanatory science posts,
- science communication research updates / advice,
- issues facing scientific community,
- academic or career advice,
- behind the scenes stories on conducting research,
- news and views on open access publishing,
- about PLOS research collections,
- updates from meetings and conferences,
- interviews with thought leaders in scholarly publishing,
- career opportunities,
- health advice,
- media reviews, and
- posts revolving around multimedia or interactive content. (Jarreau, 2016)

The order in which this list appears is taken from Jarreau's chart of the ranking of respondents' favorite kind of post. While these insights into reader motives are fascinating, unfortunately they alone do not clarify how these genres function as rhetorical artifacts.

Across blog posts, there will be stylistic decisions and content coverage that challenge the traditional distinctions between internal and external genres of science writing. Fahnestock's (1986) observation that writing about scientific subjects undergoes a "genre shift" partially helps to explain why. Aristotle outlines three primary genres of speech: "forensic" (concerned with establishing the facts; past-oriented), "deliberative" (determining a course of action; future-oriented), and "epideictic" (celebrating; present-oriented). Scientists who write for other scientists are writing into forensic genres and are concerned with establishing and validating facts. Once the scientific issue is ready to be shared with the public, it must be *accommodated* by a genre shift into the epideictic genre, where the science can be celebrated. An accommodation in Fahnestock's sense must also change the way that information is framed, such as appealing to the "wonder" of the natural world. As this occurs, we see some changes in style, namely removing technical jargon, and although this removal of jargon is not the only change when an internal scientific text is accommodated to an external or popular text, the style change is easily notable. Likewise, the presence of jargon is notable. Texts from the PLOS Blogs Network, including some outside the corpus used in the move analysis, demonstrated numerous examples of jargon being used. From the *DNA Science Blog* there are, among other examples, "amino acid position," "bicarbonate transport," "adenosine deaminase deficiency" (Lewis, 2014), and over at *Mind the Brain* is some mathematical terminology, "positivity ratio," "factor analysis," "regression analyses predicting genomic expression," and so on (Coyne, 2014). While the use of jargon in these blogs suggests that writers expect their audience to be familiar with, or at least able to cope with, this sort of terminology, by no means do writers seem to be assuming the language does not present challenges. In addition to suggesting the internal/external distinction is eroding, the rhetorical activity refreshingly and decisively rejects a deficit model approach or presumptions of public (reader) incompetence. While the reader might not understand all of the content, the information is presented and summarized in different ways to accommodate a more heterogeneous audience than we might typically imagine for a popularization.

But the style gets more interesting as we put aside the internal/external distinction and begin to uncover boundary-violating examples. For instance, talking about the self-styled food "investigator" the "FoodBabe," Skwarecki (2014) writes specifically about the problem with colloquial language, noting that an example of bad science being shared is "when [the FoodBabe] makes a big deal about 'wood pulp' in your food. When you extract cellulose from anything, wood or otherwise, what you get is not chunks of trees in your food, but simply cellulose itself, better known as one type of dietary fiber, the stuff that veggies and whole grains are full of." Here we see where the shift to a more colloquial term has caused confusion, either intentionally or not, about the nature of cellulose in food. A somewhat similar, and often repeated, example is the "dihydrogen monoxide" hoax, where some members of the public are asked if the chemical should be banned, only to illustrate the significant degree of science illiteracy because, after all, it is just water. Similar to the wood pulp/cellulose example, the dihydrogen monoxide/water example aims to address the problem with accommodating language across the expert–public divide. But in contrast to the dihydrogen monoxide/water example, the wood pulp/cellulose example shows us that sometimes the colloquial word can mislead us as much as a chemical term such as "dihydrogen monoxide."

The linchpin here is the audience. I have argued that shifts in audience from internal to broader publics are characteristic of trans-scientific genres, and there appears to be a potential shift in audience among blog readership. Certainly, scientists represent a large percentage of PLOS science blog readers, but even our scientists may read beyond their disciplinary expertise, shifting them to a nonexpert role. Broader publics, such as citizen scientists or science communicators, who will be represented in the readership, demonstrate the heterogeneous audience for science blogs. When attending to such an audience, authors might attempt to accommodate their writing to as large an audience as possible, but the PLOS blogs examined here show us another way. Explaining complex scientific concepts in complex scientific language and structures can be blended with text that helps accommodate readers who may not be especially equipped for some of the more field-specific discussions. While a heterogeneous audience makes writing for it more difficult, it also presents an opportunity to uncover new ways of thinking about audience that reject deficit model and translationist approaches to science writing. Clear examples of how this can be accomplished are shown through the moves made by authors in PLOS blogs.

For the textual aspects of blogs, we can characterize certain moves that appear across a range of science blogs. These moves indicate that the suasive strategies used by blog authors are drawn from both internal and external or public discourses on science. It seems, then, blogs operate in an intermediary space between the internal sphere of science and the external sphere of popularization—although, certainly, with some bias toward scientists or at least those with some postsecondary education in the sciences. Inhabiting this liminal space, blogs not only function to advance science, the purpose of internal genres, or to popularize science, a primary purpose of external genres, but also to promote science with and through the public and to educate scientists to engage those publics in serious and considered ways. There appears to be a movement among scientists to authentically engage publics in scientific knowledge production and scientific discourse, and trans-scientific genres may be just the vehicles to do some of this work. However, consequences should also be considered. Brossard (2013) reminds us that blogs, in contrast to traditional media outlets such as newspapers, do not always make clear distinctions between what is "news" and what is "opinion" (p. 14097). Further, the media environments in which blogs are embedded could influence audience perception of content (How many "likes" does a post have from Facebook? How many retweets on Twitter?), and not only is the human audience potentially affected, but the algorithmic audience that decides, for instance, what posts will be amplified through other platforms (Brossard, 2013, p. 14097).

Other PLOS blogs provided good resources for analysis of blogging practices. The analysis in this chapter revealed some discourse strategies, highlighted the importance of visuals and multimodality, and explored the idea of networks in terms of platforms and hyperlinking. On the matter of visuals, it is worth remarking, images and videos can add richness to blogs and blog posts. Images are sometimes playful or attention grabbing and do not appear to demand the formality of traditional research genres of science communication. However, they certainly can be and sometimes are employed in a formal tradition. Similarly, videos can be incorporated, though they appear to be less common, but in the cases of both images and video, we see the multimodality of blogs allows for a multitude of strategies to share information.

Since I collected data for analysis, PLOS has introduced new blogs, including *SciComm*, mentioned earlier. *SciComm,* short for "Science Communication," marks a significant moment for how we think about these new and emerging genres of science communication. Rather than operating as fringe publications, the new and emerging genred spaces, such as those described in this book, are grounds where scientists are exploring possibilities and beginning new conversations with researchers interested in writing studies and science studies, publics and citizen scientists, science educators, and many others. *SciComm* puts it this way:

> In keeping with its mission to transform research communication, PLOS created SciComm as a forum for practitioners and readers of science to explore the art and science of science communication. Recognizing that as researchers and science communicators we serve a broad global community,

we will feature posts covering the exchange of information between scientists and with the general public. (PLOS, 2015c)

The mission for the blog reiterates the current distinction between internal and external audiences. There are some kinds of communication between scientists and some others between scientists and some imagined "general public." But, in fact, the blog's existence operates somewhere between the internal and external in an effort to better connect experts and broader publics. It is not a space entirely shaped for disciplinary debate, or even for interdisciplinary academic debate, but it also is not designed entirely for popular consumption. As a reflexive engagement, a blog about science communication serves a valuable function for writing studies scholars and science communicators.

There is, as well, a pedagogical lesson in our investigation of trans-scientific genres. When we teach students to write into traditional or trans-scientific genres, we are teaching them a way of constructing knowledge, about what counts as legitimate knowledge construction. The evolution of blogs helps us see how this process works even for the largely unsanctioned trans-scientific forms of communication. Blogs eventually became institutionalized through blogs networks such as *Scientific American*'s and PLOS's. Both of these powerful institutions have adopted this new approach to science communication. Certainly, others can and do write for blogs outside of this institutional context, but those who do will likely need to cultivate authority differently. Authors of nonaffiliated blogs do not benefit from the ethos of publishing institutions, so they might rely on academic affiliation or scholarly credentials. Again, the principles from the rhetorical tradition—building credibility, for instance—are central concepts for these online forms of science communication.

CONCLUSION

WHEN CAROLYN MILLER articulated the rhetorical importance of genre in 1984, she told us that by understanding genre and genres we learn "what ends we may have" (p. 165). Our ends include the ability to "eulogize, apologize, [and] recommend one person to another," and thus, we "learn to understand better the situations in which we find ourselves and the potentials for failure and success in acting together" (p. 165). In this book's account of trans-scientific genres, there is new potential for acting together. Through crowdfunding, researchers find new ways to persuade broad audiences that their research is valuable enough to support with one's own financial weight. And through the collection, aggregation, and sharing of data sets, researchers can convey that their data are meaningful beyond the confines of a particular study or lab. Researchers can, likewise, present their work through blogging, where they can share research rapidly and engage experts across fields as well as publics interested in their scholarly investigations. All of these genres have antecedents in traditional scientific genres. Researchers ask for funding, share data in traditional academic and scientific work, and share results. At once trans-scientific genres provide us with new expressive possibilities and with opportunities for acting together, all the while grounded in tradition. This is an essential point to consider when investigating new modes of typified responses because it underscores how these typifications constrain the way knowledge is produced and shared.

When Miller and I set out to expand Kaplan and Radin's (2011) notion of para-scientific media, we examined genres operating within new media environments, notably those made possible by the internet/web, GPS technologies, and global mobile networks and their associated technologies and personal devices. Kaplan and Radin (2011) provided the foundations for this work describing para-scientific communications, noting that "para-scientific media include trade journals such as C&EN [*Chemical & Engineering News*] as well as semi-popular science periodicals such as *Scientific American*" (p. 459). Miller and I argued that, further to this account, para-scientific genres are those that operate alongside research process genres and that these para-scientific genres borrow scientific authority and epistemic commitments from the realm of science without being wholly subsumed within gatekeeping discourses. We first examined what we might call expository genres in Kelly and Miller (2016), and I later took up argumentative genres (Kelly, 2016). Although Miller and I expanded Kaplan and Radin's use of "para-scientific" to describe genres that inhabit online semipopular and popular sources, including social media sites and even projects generated by citizen scientists, we did not trace the prospects for such genres much beyond a single exigency. This exigency, however, revealed genres—or proto-genres, as we argued—that exist somewhere between or outside of the internal/external division of science communication. Some features aligned with Swales's research process genres, but practices that traditionally build epistemic authority in science appeared more inconsistently, and different kinds of authority-building practices took their place. Ultimately, we suggested a great potential in para-scientific spheres for new ways of producing scientific knowledge and facing the complex rhetorical situations at the nexus of science and its publics.

This book continues investigating these emerging forms of science communication as trans-scientific communication. It has attempted to theorize genre-ing activity online in terms of rhetorical situations and exigencies, antecedent genres, and the media platforms and media ecologies that shape the structure and use of emerging forms of communication. Tracing where these genres come from throughout this book has shown there is significant import of internal scientific discourse strategies, and thus we might see trans-scientific genres extending the kind of epistemic work that scientific research participates in or even allows. In their most ideal imaginings, these trans-scientific genres might provide for more inclusive deliberation about complex techno-scientific problems by engaging different communities in knowledge making, but we must attend to the kind of boundary work happening even in our liminal trans-scientific spaces and who may be excluded by our rhetorical efforts (Carolan, 2006). Along with antecedents in scientific genres and communities, there appear to be strategies taken from external genres of science communication, including those we might often attribute to genres that popularize science, such as a newspaper article about a wondrous scientific discovery. It seems, then, that we are watching new kinds of science communication unfold across the web, and as these communications evolve, they become typified and respond to recurrent rhetorical situations. But these genre spaces are also emerging and unfolding at a rapid pace, and we can watch blogs speciate into science blogs, and science blogs into genres of science blogs. Similarly, we can watch crowdfunding proposals specialize, from their origins in generic platforms such as Kickstarter to science-specific sites such as Experiment, sites that have codified certain norms of crowdfunding alongside the discursive norms of internal science communication. Evolution of trans-scientific genres reflects a trend in an open, deliberative approach to science communication. Rather than a one-way transmission model of communication, trans-scientific genres describe a conversational approach, with genres evolving along with new technologies and rhetorical situations—and, indeed, there has been a dramatic shift in rhetorical situation, including media forms, for those communicating science.

Becoming rhetorically attuned to diverse audiences through trans-scientific genres has significant pedagogical consequences for young scientists and science writers. Although the rhetorical strategies found in trans-scientific genres depart in some ways from traditional genres of science communication, they also appear to employ some similar strategies—or, at least, trans-scientific genres appear to be influenced by some of the strategies present in established genres. Throughout the book, the examples analyzed have shown that trans-scientific genres inhabit a sphere *alongside* scientific genres as genre researchers presently theorize them, inhabited by scientists, students, citizen scientists, and activists. For young scientists and junior researchers, the rhetorical strategies we have found in trans-scientific genres may be of help in crafting a blog post or pitching a project for a crowdfunding initiative. But more crucially than any particular strategy we have considered is the idea that these trans-scientific genres reveal to us a way forward for science communication as engagement. Boundaries between internal and external genres of science communication can be productively challenged to address wicked problems that defy purely scientific approaches. Science cannot be set apart from the moral and ethical, the social, economic, or political. But traditional internal genres are ill-equipped to address these other dimensions of our challenging problems because those genres are narrowly designed for a small, technical, and specialized audience. This is not to say those genres do not serve a worthy function: they do. Popularizations also serve critical functions.

But the complexities we face demand more rhetorical possibilities than the binary of internal and external genres of science communication provides. Thus, trans-scientific genres are more than the constellation of their strategies. They are rhetorically sophisticated responses and offer a promising resource for science communication.

Trans-scientific genres, drawing on scientific genres and the evolution and massive proliferation of technology, are deeply rooted in techno-scientific modernity. While these genres promise new ways of collecting and sharing data, collaboratively funding and producing scientific research, and sharing the findings of that research, these genres also remain firmly within the epistemic world of science. These genres do not significantly represent production of scientific knowledge through other epistemologies, for instance, traditional knowledges. Primarily, the examples of trans-scientific genres in this book show that traditional forms of science communication significantly influence these genres. Indeed, many of the same actors and audiences participate in trans-scientific genres, and although there is a push to broaden the audience for these genres, the epistemic system all this work operates in has not changed much. We should be mindful, then, that in many ways these trans-scientific genres are necessarily exclusionary genres as much as they expand the sphere in which discourses and discourse participants are involved in the epistemic work of science—a significant constraint to remember as we talk about democratizing knowledge. As each chapter has illustrated, numerous rhetorical strategies are at work in trans-scientific genres, and many of these strategies borrow from antecedent forms in scientific genres. These genres also underscore the challenges faced by scientists and science communicators today. For example, through crowdfunding scientists find new ways to persuade broad audiences that their research is meaningful enough to support financially. However, the turn toward private rather than public funding is marked by concerning economic trajectories for research, and the enterprise of science is certainly vulnerable in both traditional and crowdfunding models to political and cultural influences that might be at myopic or malicious. Although crowdfunding platforms are available to a somewhat international audience, in Experiment's list of institutions (currently, 218 are listed), those in the United States seem to outnumber those in other nations. My home institution in Canada recently listed Experiment as a funding opportunity in our list of funding resources; however, it reports only one University of Waterloo researcher has secured funding this way. In the notes about this opportunity, prospective applicants are told it is "predominantly a U. S. audience" (University of Waterloo Office of Research, 2018). The University of Waterloo (2018) also notes that some areas of research are more likely to secure funding, and this is dependent, they suggest, on "interest and *attention* of the common person." Attention is, as I suggested, crucial to this model of funding, and although it certainly plays a role in traditional funding proposals, too, garnering attention in the web-based ecology in which crowdfunding is embedded is challenging. Open data sets and the apparatus of genres around them let researchers convey that their data might be reused. Other researchers can access data, run replication studies, or even allow publics to access data for citizen science or civic science. However, open data sets require considerable resources to sustainably support them, and the possibility for commercial interests to shape them should be a concern for researchers, as we have learned watching how publishers can severely limit access and even encourage promotional efforts of journals, such as increasing impact factors (as opposed to focusing on good science itself). Blogging allows researchers to share research rapidly, engage experts across fields for more multidisciplinary thinking, and also engage publics interested in their scholarly investigations. Science blogs, however, still seem to cater to a well-educated audience already interested in science. Although blogs might serve to more seriously engage those audiences in the enterprise of science, their reach is nevertheless rather limited.

Complexities in the economic and social conditions from which these genres arise are crucial to understanding their relative advantages and disadvantages. Consider, then, for a moment longer the possible disadvantages of these trans-scientific genres. Crowdfunding provides a powerful case for how what may seem a positive form of engagement with science can undermine the enterprise itself. Although traditional granting mechanisms have posed problems for researchers, the problems associated with crowdfunding should not be underestimated. Those participating in crowdfunding also risk participating in the replication of a system that may shift funding responsibilities from government organizations, perpetuating a kind of erosion of our cultural and intellectual commons. Or perhaps the evolution of crowdfunding marks a sensible response to a space created by that erosion. That is to suggest that whatever mechanisms provided, for example, seed funding through institutions no longer address the kinds of matters researchers require funding for, or perhaps the frequency with which this funding is required. It is unsurprising, then, that an industry would capitalize on these struggles to respond to changing funding situations and career demands.

While increasing demands for external support have become the norm, access to those funds is not equally or necessarily equitably distributed. Crowdfunding, it has been argued, is especially helpful for researchers who may not have access to government or even foundation funding, including more junior researchers or researchers in developing nations (Vachelard, Gambarra-Soares, Augustini, Riul, & Maracaja-Coutinho, 2016). Interest may also be field-dependent, as it is increasingly difficult to secure funding in some areas. The National Institutes of Health (NIH), for example, saw a 22 percent decrease in funding capacity between 2003 and 2015, with some modest increases following, although the certainty of continued increases or budgets cannot be assumed (Federation of American Societies for Experimental Biology, 2016). Indeed, major funding cuts are expected for U.S. agencies such as the NIH, Environmental Protection Agency, and Department of Energy and for specific programs such as the National Oceanic and Atmospheric Administration Sea Grant program (Reardon, Tollefson, Witze, & Ross, 2017). Although the cuts are suspected to be significant, they are not all settled at the time of writing, and the Senate Appropriations Committee has recently approached the Energy and Water Appropriations Bill, which restores funding for the U.S. Department of Energy (Fares, 2017). It is likely an intervention for NIH funding will be made, too (Kaiser, 2017). Crowdfunding sites already acknowledged, before the threat of budget cuts in 2017, the challenges traditional funding allocation poses for researchers. In a welcoming interview for a new employee, the Experiment blog reports data on the decreased funding from the NIH and NSF. Specifically, the new employee cites these reductions as a key motivation for Experiment, saying, "The World Wide Web was invented by a scientist about 25 years ago in a Physics lab. It kicked off a tech industry that became incredibly prosperous, while funding for science in America plunged (NIH's funding decreased by 20% since 2004, NSF by 9% since 2012)." The employee continues, "Grants are more competitive and fewer risky experiments get funded. I want there to be a place in our society for new and independent and more of every kind of science, and I believe enough people also want it that we can find each other on the web and make it happen," citing both the Federation of American Societies for Experimental Biology (2016) on the NIH data and the NSF itself (Ray, 2015).

Another rationale may be that with the change in the participants or audience for scientific research, a rhetorical situation emerged to which there was no recurrent response. Federal or state funding has various kinds of restrictions on who might apply, requiring status as student or faculty or other institutionally affiliated researcher, excluding some researchers based on their resident status in a nation, and so on. If we take seriously that the growth of citizen science, DIYBio, and other grassroots science movements are changing who might participate in research, along with the growing numbers of students encouraged to undertake publishable research, then there is certainly a case for crowdfunding as a response to traditional or institutional science's lag in adapting to a changing, more open, public, and proto-expert community's investment in conducting research.

Whatever the case for its evolution, scientists would do well to hear artists' concerns about this revised patronage model. Presently, crowdfunding seems to model seed grants or other small funding mechanisms, and typically cannot be compared to federal funding dollars, which often count by millions, not thousands, of dollars. But the issues pointed to by these small funding amounts are not only a matter of scale; they are a matter of sustainability. Federal grant dollars are not significant because researchers who secure them spend a large sum on a single project or because universities take a percentage off the top, but rather because the kinds of long-term research projects that truly advance our understanding of complex problems typically take decades to solve. Multimillion-dollar labs undergo intense scrutiny both in the initial phases when funding is secured and on an ongoing basis, by their home institution and by the granting agency. A university will attend carefully to resource matters, including space, fairly funding hired researchers, and providing "benefits," including health care in the United States. In addition, federal agencies have serious regulatory structures for spending and mechanisms for accountability that labs must answer to.

Questions about oversight in crowdfunding remain, both in terms of long-term scientific vision and in the pragmatics of spending and ethical oversight. Several different types of oversights might occur. First, there is the general notion that science progresses with incremental steps toward some large problem. Kuhn's "normal science" is this program of tackling a major problem in a field for a number of years, perhaps even decades, and normally by many researchers and teams. Undertaking such efforts is predicated upon an idea that scientific problems are shared and that while the vision about how to solve them might vary, there is indeed a shared vision. Everyone will work toward solutions in some principled ways that other researchers working in the field can understand and, crucially, replicate. Open Collins and Pinch's introductory science and technology studies (STS) textbook, the *Golem,* for numerous examples of what happens when this model is not followed—cold fusion being a prime example, or, less dramatically, chemical transfer of memory in worms (Collins & Pinch, 1998). These tales are the floundering and flopping of scientific research. At a broad level, the need for shared disciplinary oversight is one of the problems these tales illustrate. Such visions are shared through research agendas, disciplinary conversations, apprenticeships, and other socio-discursive work. How might crowdfunding participate in these conversations and in the oversight provided by long-established traditions for shaping disciplinary cultures, problems, and approaches to problems? To some degree, the research may fit pretty much the same way as it always has; yet, one cannot assume certain kinds of affiliations, training, or expertise. If the process of vetting a project relies on popularity as much as domain-specific experts making decisions about what kinds of research ought to be funded, is there something lost, not simply in scientific rigorousness, but in the sense of a culture of scientific research that propels us forward, together, to solve our most pressing problems?

Once a project is funded, pragmatic questions about oversight must be asked. Is the money going to be spent where the researchers have promised? Has the researcher followed through on the full project? Did the researcher provide the promised outputs? For federal grant dollars, certainly in the United States, and likewise in Canada, numerous mechanisms are in place to ensure that grant support is used responsibly. Even before grant funding is awarded, these sorts of measures ensure that dollars are allocated from appropriate sources for appropriate kinds of work. Oversight such as this raises its own problems, but the principles behind these mechanisms remain crucial. Without oversight, it is difficult to measure whether or not research programs are followed through to completion. What does Experiment say to this point? On their website, they tell prospective proposal writers, "There is no requirement for when you post a result, only that you do share your research findings and outcomes with your backers in an engaging way. This can be data, abstracts, preprints, presentations, or more" (2017b). The norms of science, and indeed general honesty, would demand researchers follow through on projects with goodwill. However, there are certainly a small number of problematic cases. These serious cases harm not only the agency that provided the funds but also the taxpayers who have supported the agency. Such acts harm researcher communities more broadly, as they are built on a significant degree of trust and communalism. For example, researchers may follow through with goodwill to a point, but for lack of guidance or poor planning, a project falls through the cracks. This is why part of the oversight provided by traditional granting mechanisms considers a researcher's past accomplishments. If you doubt there are problems, there are numerous cases of lawsuits and confusing matters that the U.S. Federal Trade Communication and even Internal Revenue Service have taken up (Cohen, 2015).

Further, concerns about oversight may also extend to ethical realms. Because universities and other research institutions abide by research ethics oversight, there is some mechanism to ensure research is designed to minimize risks to human and other animal participants. In Canada, the Tri-Council agencies—the Social Science and Humanities Research Council (SSHRC), the Canadian Institutes of Health Research (CIHR), and the Natural Science and Engineering Research Council of Canada (NSERC)—manage ethical concerns under their "Responsible Conduct of Research," for example. This is a framework that details policies surrounding the conduct of research funded by tri-council agencies, as well as expectations and regulations for universities and other research institutions falling under tri-council guidance (Tri-Agencies, 2016). Perhaps journals will be a notable site to ensure appropriate protocols have been followed, but with the rise of predatory journals, such assumptions certainly do not provide much confidence. These ethical concerns extend beyond research itself, and certainly have implications for those concerned with where their funds come from and the other kinds of projects that platforms allow. Platforms must be called upon to develop policies that ensure the environment broadly operates under strong ethical frameworks, and this includes deciding whether or not to support them by one's participation.

Taken together, our analyses give us insights into how crowdfunding platforms operate, how proposals on these sites are configured, and the challenges this new form of science communication brings to our economic and ethical decision making. On the one hand, researchers from a variety of backgrounds—including citizen and civic scientists—have opportunities to fund projects that are meaningful to communities. On the other hand, many problems arise from the seeming divestment of public funds for research, attunement to free market orientations, and numerous underdeveloped frameworks for ethical oversight. Not only are rhetorical modes changing, but the actors and agents participating and shaping the spaces for new rhetorical situations and responses, as well as social and economic conditions, are changing as well.

Changes to media, in addition to changes in genre, audience, and broader social context, also generate a moment to reflect on the rhetorical decisions that become "black boxed," or have their inner workings taken for granted in a particular discourse community. Media change is implicated in the information and data that compose the content of our genres. Changes to our media underscore how information and data contained within said media are always already prescribed and proscribed. Because data are always translations, they shape and structure the meaning and interpretation a user or audience takes away from a particular data context. Thus, we can understand how media we use to store and share our information and data is a function of specific human decision making and design—and, importantly, how it is rhetorically crafted.

In the introduction to her book *Close Up at a Distance: Mapping Technology and Politics*, Laura Kurgan (2013) illustrates how media change and modes of visualization coevolve. She begins with two striking images: NASA's

AS8–14–2383 and AS17–148–22727, otherwise known by their iconic vernacular labels—*Earthrise* and *The Blue Marble*. *Earthrise* offers a compelling origin narrative about the Apollo 17 astronauts who captured the image in 1972, an image that became part of our cultural consciousness and collective memory (Kurgan, 2013 p. 9). *The Blue Marble,* however, has a starkly different origin, one that supremely illustrates the effects of media change on scientific visualizations. Set of images with the same name were produced in 2002, 2005, and 2012, offering different continental perspectives and different modes of production. Photos produced in 2002 were composites of satellite images; the 2005 images used the same principle but captured high-resolution images. In 1972 astronauts captured photos with a camera, and in 2002 and 2005, satellites captured a number of images that could then be processed into one. In 2012, new satellites equipped with Visible/Infrared Imager Radiometer Suite (VIIRS) technology collected data to be used in the production of another set of these iconic images. However, Kurgan (2013) reminds us, these later images "are not simply photographs taken by a person traveling in space with a camera. They are composites of massive quantities of remotely sensed data collected by satellite-borne sensors" (p. 11). Radical media change allowed the production of this image. The image is "not the integrating vision of a particular person standing in a particular place or even floating in space," but rather "an image of something no human could see with his or her own eye," and this matters to its rhetoricity (Kurgan, 2013, p. 12). It matters because the image is crafted by human ingenuity and argument—a crafted, a rhetorical object—and the image persuades us to see and understand the world in a way that profoundly alters how we understand our relations with one another.

SCIENCE'S SOCIAL ACTION

Not every scientist is partial to the nature of the political responses we have been witness to in 2017, voicing concerns about the "politicization" and "polarization" of science (see, for examples, Ghorayshi, 2017; Young, 2017). Geologist Robert S. Young (2017), taking up a more traditional form of media, the op-ed, wrote in the *New York Times* that he felt that politically charged events, such as the "March for Science," could be detrimental to science. He has reason for believing this to be the case: Young was a coauthor of the North Carolina's Coastal Resources Commission report that indicated coastal sea level rises of thirty-nine inches before the end of the century, which would have devastating consequences to the state. The state legislature advanced House Bill 819, which temporarily barred scientists from using the kind of predicative modeling Young used, instead relying on historical linear modeling. Work such as Young's was seen as a threat to well-established economic stakeholders in the state who have interests in real estate and progress narratives counter to conservation efforts. The backlash against climate change research and reporting is similarly symptomatic of neoliberal trends that resist serious engagement with the science itself. With such neoliberal influences on policy making, it is crucial that scientists do more than simply report data, and rather connect with constituents and policy makers to demonstrate their goodwill and their care for the regions and peoples affected by climate change. Young's caution, then, is essentially an ethotic caution:

> A march by scientists, while well intentioned, will serve only to trivialize and politicize the science we care so much about, turn scientists into another group caught up in the culture wars and further drive the wedge between scientists and a certain segment of the American electorate. (Young, 2017)

The whole idea that the march only serves to cement a community in partisan politics is astute. Instead of offering an ethos of the expert, still distant and part of a large collective or group, Young (2017) suggests a more direct rhetorical action:

> Rather than marching on Washington and in other locations around the country, I suggest that my fellow scientists march into local civic groups, churches, schools, county fairs and, privately, into the offices of elected officials. Make contact with that part of America that doesn't know any scientists. Put a face on the debate. Help them understand what we do, and how we do it. Give them your email, or better yet, your phone number.

It seems what Young argues against aligns with what Miller (2003) cautioned in the "substitution of expertise for ethos" in her account of risk analysis and communication related to nuclear energy (p. 201). Marching alongside community groups shows eunoia, goodwill, as does providing one's time to talk to others about one's work and its process. Through the kind of direct contact Young advocates, it is possible to demonstrate one's arête, moral virtues, and indeed the virtues of the discipline in which one works. All of this effort is to rebuild trust among broader publics and scientists, which, as Young suggests, has certainly been fueled by partisan politics and the neoliberal motivations that drive both sides of the party line. Miller (2003) warned of such a circumstance as Young experienced, and her lesson certainly merits continued consideration; she cautions that "success is limited by the loss of trust—that is, precisely by the poverty of their ethos" (p. 202).

Certainly, scientists are working to address their ethotic poverty by putting social media technologies to work. Yet, what Young reminds us is that while all these technologies can play useful roles in the funding, organization, research, and sharing of science, it is our attention to the needs and responses of our audience, and our ability to connect with and engage that audience, that become the measure of our success. And, further, "audience" must be understood in broad terms because science touches almost everyone's everyday life in some way. However, there are reasons someone would rather believe the science is wrong rather than that their future is uncertain. For example, fear about the erosion of coastal land and the possibility of losing one's home must feel much worse than thinking maybe scientists have it all wrong, or at least some of it wrong. A climate scientist might not think this is a good reason to ignore the evidence, and that facts speak for themselves, but this is a dangerous position to take. Attending to dissenting voices is important precisely because those are the members of one's audience that often require the most attention in how one shares a message and engages in a dialogue. This is not to suggest one ought to waver in one's message, but rather should craft that message so the intended audiences receive it, which can then spur on productive discourses. It almost seems a truism to reference research on filter bubbles, selective exposure to information, echo chambers, and so on (Bakshy, Messing, & Adamic, 2015; Pariser, 2011), but they are indeed powerful, and scientific discourse must operate outside these technological constraints because the messages scientists bring us are urgent and have global significance.

Such interactions can be broadened by engaging in partisan politics in a serious manner: running for office (see: Zamudio-Suaréz, 2017). A nonprofit called 314 Action is a kind of call to arms for scientists or others with a STEM background to run for elected office in the United States. The group explains it is "a 501(c)(4) organization who intends to leverage the goals and values of the greater science, technology, engineering and mathematics community to aggressively advocate combating the all-too-common attacks on basic scientific understandings, research funding, and climate change" (314 Action, 2017). To do this, its website offers a sign-up for an online information session about running for office, a place to nominate someone, and a blog for continued discussion. Remember the Public Library of Science from our discussion of databases and of blogs? One of its founders, Michael Eisen, intends to run for the U.S. Senate in 2018 (Reardon, 2017).

All told, driving the response of scientists is that old rhetorical concern of civic discourse. In a moment when all those rhetorical tools of argument, even the most basic modes of persuasion—logos (good reason), and even ethos (credibility) and pathos (emotions, dealing with responsibility)—have fallen aside, replaced by coercion or force in politics, there is promise in the efforts scientists have undertaken to challenge what is not true or just.[1] While the forms of science communication I have detailed in this book have significant implications for scientists who hope to share the process and products of science, it is ultimately the job of scientists and science communicators to choose how they will deploy the available means these genres afford them. Following the current efforts, the most promising rhetorical strategies seem to be when we think not simply of readership but of audience, not of network reach but of representation, not of influence but of *eunoia,* and not of unidirectional communication but of engagement and dialogue.

---

1. Drawing from Aristotle Rh. 1355a: "Rhetoric is useful, because the true and the just are naturally superior to their opposites, so that, if decisions are improperly made, they must owe their defeat to their own advocates; which is reprehensible. Further, in dealing with certain persons, even if we possessed the most accurate scientific knowledge, we should not find it easy to persuade them by the employment of such knowledge. For scientific discourse is concerned with instruction, but in the case of such persons instruction is impossible; our proofs and arguments must rest on generally accepted principles, as we said in the Topics, when speaking of converse with the multitude. Further, the orator should be able to prove opposites, as in logical arguments; not that we should do both (for one ought not to persuade people to do what is wrong) but that the real state of the case may not escape us, and that we ourselves may be able to counteract false arguments, if another makes an unfair use of them. Rhetoric and Dialectic alone of all the arts prove opposites; for both are equally concerned with them. However, it is not the same with the subject matter, but, generally speaking, that which is true and better is naturally always easier to prove and more likely to persuade." From *Aristotle in 23 Volumes,* Vol. 22, translated by J. H. Freese. Cambridge and London: Harvard University Press; William Heinemann Ltd., 1926. Also available online via Perseus at Tufts.

REFERENCES

314 Action. (2017). Mission. Retrieved March 18, 2017, from http://www.314action.org/mission-1/

Academia.edu. (2014). Mission. Retrieved August 1, 2014, from https://www.academia.edu/hiring/mission

Acheson, K. (2013). *Visual Rhetoric and Early Modern English Literature.* Burlington, VT: Ashgate Publishing Company.

Adam. (2017). First They Came . . . Retrieved September 14, 2017, from http://knowyourmeme.com/memes/first-they-came

Aldrich, D. P. (2015). The Emergence of Civil Society: Networks in Disasters, Mitigation, and Recovery. In U. Fra.Paleo (Ed.), *Risk Governance* (pp. 135–48). Dordrecht, Netherlands: Springer Netherlands.

Alvarez-Garcia, I. (2016). ASCB 2016 meeting (San Francisco, Dec 3–7). Retrieved from http://blogs.plos.org/biologue/author/ialvarez-garcia/

Andersen, J. (2017). Genre, the Organization of Knowledge and Everyday Life. In "Proceedings of the Ninth International Conference on Conceptions of Library and Information Science, Uppsala, Sweden, June 27–29, 2016," *Information Research, 22*(1).

Applegarth, R. (2017). Genre Emergence and Disappearance in Feminist Histories of Rhetoric. In C. R. Miller & A. Kelly R. (Eds.), *Emerging Genres in New Media Environments* (pp. 275–89). London: Palgrave Macmillan.

Applegarth, R. (2014). *Rhetoric in American Anthropology: Gender, Genre, and Science.* Pittsburgh, PA: University of Pittsburgh Press.

Aristotle. (2013). *Politics* (C. Lord, Trans.). Chicago, IL: University of Chicago Press.

Arsenault, D. J., Smith, L. D., & Beauchamp, E. A. (2006). Visual Inscriptions in the Scientific Hierarchy: Mapping the "Treasures of Science." *Science Communication, 27*(3), 376–428. doi:10.1177/1075547005285030

Auken, S. (2015). Genre and Interpretation. In S. Auken, P. S. Lauridsen, & A. J. Rasmussen (Eds.), *Genre and . . .* (Vol. 2, pp. 154–83). Copenhagen: Ekbátana.

Bakhtin, M. M. (1986). The Problem of Speech Genres. In C. Emerson & M. Holquist (Eds.), *Speech Genres and Other Late Essays* (pp. 60–102). Austin, TX: University of Texas Press.

Bakshy, E., Messing, S., & Adamic, L. A. (2015). Exposure to ideologically diverse news and opinion on Facebook. *Science, 348*(6239), 1130–32. doi:10.1126/science.aaa1160

Bawarshi, A. (2016). Beyond the Genre Fixation: A Translingual Perspective on Genre. *College English, 78*(3), 243–49.

Bazerman, C. (1988). *Shaping Written Knowledge: The Genre and Activity of the Experimental Article in Science*. Madison, WI: University of Wisconsin Press.

Bazerman, C. (1994). Systems of Genres and the Enactment of Social Intentions. In A. Freedman & P. Medway (Eds.), *Genre and the New Rhetoric* (pp. 79–101). London: Taylor and Francis.

Bazerman, C. (2009). Genre and Cognitive Development: Beyond Writing to Learn. *Pratiques: Linguistique, Littérature, Didactique, 127–38.

Bazerman, C. (2016). Afterword: Social Changes in Science Communication: Rattling the Information Chain. In A. G. Gross & J. Buehl (Eds.), *Science and the Internet: Communicating Knowledge in a Digital Age* (pp. 267–82). Amityville, NY: Baywood Press.

Bawarshi, A. S., & Reiff, M. J. (2010). *Genre: An Introduction to History, Theory, Research, and Pedagogy*. West Lafayette, IN: Parlor Press.

Beer, D. (2008). Social Network(ing) Sites . . . Revisiting the Story So Far: A Response to danah boyd & Nicole Ellison. *Journal of Computer-Mediated Communication, 13*(2), 516–529. doi:10.1111/j.1083-6101.2008.00408.x

Berkenkotter, C., & Huckin, T. N. (1993). Rethinking Genre from a Sociocognitive Perspective. *Written Communication, 10*, 475–509.

Berkenkotter, C., & Huckin, T. N. (1995). *Genre Knowledge in Disciplinary Communication: Cognition/Culture/Power*. Hillsdale, NJ: Lawrence Erlbaum.

Berkenkotter, C., Huckin, T., & Ackerman, J. (1991). Social Context and Socially Constructed Texts: The Initiation of a Graduate Student into a Writing Research Community. In C. Bazerman & J. Paradis (Eds.), *Textual Dynamics of the Professions: Historical and Contemporary Studies of Writing in Professional Communities*. Madison, WI: University of Wisconsin Press. Retrieved from https://wac.colostate.edu/books/landmarks/textual-dynamics/

Bhatia, V. K. (1993). *Analysing Genre: Language Use in Professional Settings*. London: Longman.

Bhatia, V. K. (1996). Methodological Issues in Genre Analysis. *Hermes, Journal of Linguistic, 16*, 39–59.

Bhatia, V. K. (1998). Generic patterns in fundraising discourse. *New Directions for Philanthropic Fundraising, 1998*(22), 95–110.

Binkowski, B. (2017). Twitter's Alts and Rogues. *Snopes*. Retrieved from https://www.snopes.com/news/2017/06/01/alts-and-rogues/

Bitzer, L. F. (1968). The Rhetorical Situation. *Philosophy & Rhetoric, 1*(1), 1–14.

Bonner, S. (2011a). New Map on Safecast.org. Safecast.org. Retrieved from http://blog.safecast.org/2011/06/new-map-on-safecast-org

Bonner, S. (2011b). New Visualizations. Safecast.org Blog. Retrieved August 10, 2011, from http://blog.safecast.org/2011/08/new-visualizations/

Bonner, S. (2011c). Safecast Drives as of May 29. Safecast.org Blog. Retrieved May 29, 2011, from http://blog.safecast.org/2011/05/safecast-drives-as-of-may-29/

Bonner, S. (2012). Safecast: DIY and Citizen-sensing of Radiation. Retrieved from http://media.ccc.de/browse/congress/2012/29c3-5140-en-safecast_h264.html

Bonner, S. (2014). Useful data. *Safecast Blog*. Retrieved from https://blog.safecast.org/2014/01/useful-data/

Boon, S. (2016.) Science Blogging 101. *Canadian Science Publishing Blog*.

Bowker, G. C., Baker, K., Millerand, F., & Ribes, D. (2010). Toward Information Infrastructure Studies: Ways of Knowing in a Networked Environment. In J. Hunsinger, L. Klastrup, M. Allen, & M. Matthew (Eds.). *International Handbook of Internet Research* (pp. 97–117). Dordrecht, Netherlands: Springer.

boyd, d. (2006). A Blogger's Blog: Exploring the Definition of a Medium. *Reconstruction, 6*(4).

Breslin, P. (2018, January 5). Next Generation Conservation Strategies for Endangered Plants. New York, NY: Experiment.com. Accessed March 27, 2018. http://doi.org/10.18258.10273

Brock, K., & Mehlenbacher, A. R. (2017). Rhetorical Genres in Code. *Journal of Technical Writing and Communication, 48*(4), 383–411. doi: 10.1177/0047281617726278

Brossard, D. (2013). New Media Landscapes and the Science Information Consumer. *Proceedings of the National Academy of Sciences, 110* (Supplement 3), 14096–101. doi:10.1073/pnas.1212744110

Brown Jarreau, P. (2016). The Results Are In: Who Reads Science Blogs? The Highlights. *Experiment.* New York, NY: Expertiment.com. Retrieved from https://experiment.com/u/eO4zuQ

Brunk, C. G. (2006). Public Knowledge, Public Trust: Understanding the "Knowledge Deficit." *Public Health Genomics, 9*(3), 178–83.

Bruss, M., Albers, M. J., & McNamera, D. (2004). *Changes in Scientific Articles over Two Hundred Years: A Coh-Metrix Analysis.* Paper presented at the SIGDOC'04: Proceedings of the 22nd Annual International Conference on Design of Communication, New York, NY.

Buehl, J. (2014). Toward an Ethical Rhetoric of the Digital Scientific Image: Learning From the Era When Science Met Photoshop. *Technical Communication Quarterly, 23*(3), 184–206. doi:1 0.1080/10572252.2014.914783

Buehl, J. (2016). Revolution or Evolution? Casing the Impact of Digital Media on the Rhetoric of Science. In A. G. Gross & J. Buehl (Eds.), *Science and the Internet: Communicating Knowledge in a Digital Age.* (pp. 1–9). Amityville, NY: Baywood Press.

Byrnes, J. E. K., Ranganathan, J., Walker, B. L. E., & Faulkes, Z. (2014). To Crowdfund Research, Scientists Must Build an Audience for Their Work. *PLoS ONE, 9*(12), e110329. doi:10.1371/journal.pone.0110329

Cadogan, D. (2014). Funding for Research? Look to the Crowd: Crowdfunding Resources for Academia. *College & Research Libraries News, 75*(5), 268–71.

Campbell, J. A. (2015). Citizen Science in Lower Hood Canal: The Emergence of the Lower Hood Canal Watershed Coalition (LHCWC) as a Forum for Environmental Education, Policy Development and the Shaping of Political Will. In A. T. Demo (Ed.), *Rhetoric Across Borders* (pp. 187–98). Anderson, SC: Parlor Press.

Carolan, M. S. (2006). Science, Expertise, and the Democratization of the Decision-Making Process. *Society & Natural Resources, 19*(7), 661–68. doi:10.1080/08941920600742443

Casper, C. F. (2016). The Online Research Article and the Ecological Basis of New Digital Genres. In A. G. Gross & J. Buehl (Eds.), *Science and the Internet: Communicating Knowledge in a Digital Age* (pp. 77–98). Amityville, NY: Baywood Press.

Ceccarelli, L. (2001). *Shaping Science with Rhetoric: The Cases of Dobzhansky, Schrodinger, and Wilson.* Chicago, IL: University of Chicago Press.

Ceccarelli, L. (2011). Manufactured Scientific Controversy. *Rhetoric & Public Affairs, 14*(2), 195–228.

Chadwick, B. (2017). A Novel Prostate Cancer Risk Variant in African Americans, Dynamics of the Human Gut Microbiome, and Geno-Pheno Maps for Digital Organisms: the PLOS

Comp Biol February Issue. Retrieved from http://blogs.plos.org/biologue/2017/03/07/ploscompbiol-feb-2017-issue/

Chambers, C. D., Dienes, Z., McIntosh, R. D., Rotshtein, P., & Willmes, K. (2015). Registered Reports: Realigning Incentives in Scientific Publishing. *Cortex, 66,* A1–A2.

Cohen, R. (2015, July 2). The Feds Take Action against Crowdfunding Fraud, and It's About Time! *Nonprofit Quarterly.* Retrieved from https://nonprofitquarterly.org/2015/07/02/the-feds-take-action-against-crowdfunding-fraud-and-its-about-time/

Collins, H. M., & Pinch, T. (1998). *The Golem: What You Should Know about Science.* Cambridge, UK: Cambridge University Press.

Condit, C. (2012). Recent Rhetorical Studies in Public Understanding of Science: Multiple Purposes and Strengths. *Public Understanding of Science, 21*(4), 386–400.

Connor, U. (1998) Comparing Research and Not-for-profit Grant Proposals. In *Written Discourse in Philanthropic Fund Raising: Issues of Language and Rhetoric* (pp. 98–113). Indianapolis, IN: Indiana University Center on Philanthropy.

Connor, U. (2000). Variation in Rhetorical Moves in Grant Proposals of US Humanists and Scientists. *Text, 20*(1), 1–28.

Connor, U., & Mauranen, A. (1999). Linguistic Analysis of Grant Proposals: European Union Research Grants. *English for Specific Purposes, 18*(1), 47–62.

Connor, U., Upton, T., & Kanoksilapatham, B. (2007). Introduction to Move Analysis. In D. Biber, U. Connor, & T. Upton (Eds.), *Discourse on the Move: Using Corpus Analysis to Describe Discourse Structure* (pp. 23–41). Philadelphia, PA: John Benjamins Publishing Company.

Connor, U., & Wagner, L. (1998). Language Use in Grant Proposals by Nonprofits: Spanish and English. *New Directions for Philanthropic Fundraising, 1998*(22), 59–74.

Costello, V. (2017). Where Did Science Go Last Year? PLOSBLOGS' Top 16 in 2016. Retrieved from http://blogs.plos.org/scicomm/2017/01/03/where-did-science-go-last-year-plosblogs-top-16-posts-in-2016/

Coyne, J. (2014). Reanalysis: No Health Benefits Found for Pursuing Meaning in Life Versus Pleasure. *Mind the Brain.* Retrieved from http://blogs.plos.org/mindthebrain/2014/08/25/reanalysis-health-benefits-found-pursuing-meaning-life-versus-pleasure/

Crawley, G. M., & O'Sullivan, E. (2015). *The Grant Writer's Handbook: How to Write a Research Proposal and Succeed.* London: Imperial College Press.

Creative Commons. (2014). About CC0—"No Rights Reserved." Retrieved from http://creativecommons.org/about/cco

Cross, P. (2018, January 11). Alpine Invaders in the Greater Yellowstone. New York, NY: Experiment.com. Accessed March 27, 2018. http://doi.org/10.18258/9163

Courtenay, S., Brightsmith, D. J., Trauco, G. V., Regelmann, K., & Boyd, J. (2018, January 07). Increasing Survival of Macaw Chicks Using Foster Macaw Parents in the Wild. New York, NY: Experiment.com. Accessed March 27, 2018. http://doi.org/10.18258/10020

Dalton, C., & Thatcher, J. (2014). What Does a Critical Data Studies Look Like, and Why Do We Care? *Society and Space.* Retrieved from http://societyandspace.org/2014/05/12/what-does-a-critical-data-studies-look-like-and-why-do-we-care-craig-dalton-and-jim-thatcher/

Danisch, R., & Mudry, J. (2008). Is It Safe to Eat That? Raw Oysters, Risk Assessment and the Rhetoric of Science. *Social Epistemology, 22*(2), 129–43.

Devitt, A. J. (1991). Intertextuality in Tax Accounting: Generic, Referential, and Functional. In C. Bazerman & J. Paradis (Eds.), *Textual Dynamics of the Professions: Historical and Contemporary Studies of Writing in Professional Communities* (pp. 336–55). Madison, WI: University of Wisconsin Press.

Devitt, A. J. (2015). Genre Performances: John Swales' Genre Analysis and Rhetorical-Linguistic Genre Studies. *Journal of English for Academic Purposes, 19,* 44–51.

Devitt, A. J. (2017). Post-Rhetoric? Retrieved from http://www.amydevitt.com/genre-colored-glasses/post-rhetoric

Ding, H. (2008). The Use of Cognitive and Social Apprenticeship to Teach a Disciplinary Genre: Initiation of Graduate Students into NIH Grant Writing. *Written Communication, 25,* 3–52.

Dolezal, N. (2015). Development: Real-Time Interpolation. Safecast.org Blog. Retrieved January 14, 2015, from http://blog.safecast.org/2015/01/rt-interpolation/

Dunleavy, P. (2016). How to Write a Blogpost from Your Journal Article in Eleven Easy Steps. Retrieved from http://blogs.lse.ac.uk/impactofsocialsciences/2016/01/25/how-to-write-a-blogpost-from-your-journal-article/

Eilperin, J., & Dennis, B. (2017, January 24). Federal Agencies Ordered to Restrict Their Communications. *The Washington Post.* Retrieved from https://www.washingtonpost.com/politics/federal-agencies-ordered-to-restrict-their-communications/2017/01/24/9daa6aa4-e26f-11e6-ba11-63c4b4fb5a63_story.html?utm_term=.605e01bfa8c5

Experiment. (2014). Experiment.com. Retrieved from https://www.experiment.com

Experiment. (2017a). Community Statistics. Retrieved January 14, 2017, from https://experiment.com/stats

Experiment. (2017b). Your Scientific Discovery Awaits. Retrieved January 20, 2017, from https://experiment.com/start

Fahnestock, J. (1986). Accommodating Science: The Rhetorical Life of Scientific Facts. *Written Communication, 3,* 275–96.

Fahnestock, J. (1999). *Rhetorical Figures in Science.* Oxford, UK: Oxford University Press.

Fairclough, N. (1993). Critical Discourse Analysis and the Marketization of Public Discourse: The Universities. *Discourse & Society, 4*(2), 133–68.

Fares, R. (2017). Senate Advances Bill Undermining Trump Administration's Energy Research Cuts. Retrieved from https://blogs.scientificamerican.com/plugged-in/senate-advances-bill-undermining-trump-administrations-energy-research-cuts/

Farley, K. (2016). How Do Post-industrial Landscapes Affect American Woodcock Breeding Success? Retrieved January 21, 2017, from https://experiment.com/projects/how-do-post-industrial-landscapes-affect-american-woodcock-breeding-success

Federation of American Societies for Experimental Biology. (2016). NIH Research Funding Trends. Retrieved February 2, 2017, from http://www.faseb.org/Portals/2/PDFs/opa/2016/Factsheet_Restore_NIH_Funding.pdf

Feng, H., & Shi, L. (2004). Genre Analysis of Research Grant Proposals. *LSP and Professional Communication, 4,* 8–32.

Figshare. (2017). Figshare for Publishers. Retrieved February 4, 2017, from https://figshare.com/services/publishers

Freadman, A. (2012). The Traps and Trappings of Genre Theory. *Applied Linguistics, 33*(5), 544–63.

Freedman, A. (1993). Show and Tell? The Role of Explicit Teaching in the Learning of New Genres. *Research in the Teaching of English* 27, 222–51.

Freese, J. H. (Trans.) (1926). *Aristotle: Art of Rhetoric*. Cambridge and London: Harvard University Press; William Heinemann Ltd. Retrieved September 23, 2018, from Perseus at Tufts.

Gagne, A. (2017, June 7). The Gopher Tortoises of Cumberland Island—Is Beach Life All It's Cracked Up to Be? New York, NY: Experiment.com. Retrieved March 27, 2018, from http://doi.org/10.18258/9325

Garzone, G. (2012). Where Do Web Genres Come From? The Case of Blogs. In S. Campagna, G. Garzone, C. Ilie, & E. Rowley-Jolivet (Eds.), *Evolving Genres in Web-mediated Communication* (pp. 217–42). Bern, Switzerland: Peter Lang.

Ghorayshi, A. (2017, Febuary 4). Scientists Are Arguing About Whether the March for Science Will Be Too Political. *BuzzFeedNews*. Retrieved March 18, 2017, from https://www.buzzfeed.com/azeenghorayshi/is-science-political?utm_term=.rploobABdm—.tuj99a6W4v

Gieryn, T. F. (1983). Boundary-Work and the Demarcation of Science from Non-Science: Strains and Interests in Professional Ideologies of Scientists. *American Sociological Review, 48*(6), 781–95. doi:10.2307/2095325

Gieryn, T. F. (1999). *Cultural Boundaries of Science: Credibility on the Line*. Chicago, IL: University of Chicago Press.

Gigante, M. E. (2012). Accommodating Scientific Illiteracy: Award-Winning Visualizations on the Covers of Science. *Journal of Technical Writing and Communication, 42*(1), 21–38. doi:10.2190/TW.42.1.c

Gigante, M. E. (2015). A Portrait of Exclusion: The Archetype of the Scientist at Work in Life Magazine. *Rhetoric Review, 34*(3), 292–314. doi:10.1080/07350198.2015.1040305

Giltrow, J. (2002). Meta-genre. In R. Coe, L. Lingard, & T. Teslenko (Eds.), *The Rhetoric and Ideology of Genre: Strategies for Stability and Change* (pp. 187–205). Cresskill, NJ: Hampton Press.

Giltrow, J., & Stein, D. (2009). *Genres in the Internet: Issues in the Theory of Genre*. Amsterdam, Netherlands: John Benjamins.

Gitelman, L. (2013). *"Raw Data" Is an Oxymoron*. Cambridge, MA: MIT Press.

Geisler, C., Bazerman, C., Doheny-Farina, S., Gurak, L., Haas, C., Johnson-Eilola, J., . . . Yates, J. (2001). IText: Future Directions for Research on the Relationship between Information Technology and Writing. *Journal of Business and Technical Communication, 15*, 269–308.

Glass, T. (2018, Jan 15). Why Do Wolverines Need Snow? New York, NY: Experiment.com. Retrieved March 27, 2018, from http://doi.org/10.18258/7257

Grafton, K., & Maurer, E. (2007). Engaging with and Arranging for Publics in Blog Genres. *Linguistics and the Human Sciences, 3*, 47–66.

Graham, S. S., & Whalen, B. (2008). Mode, Medium, and Genre: A Case Study of Decisions in New-Media Design. *Journal of Business & Technical Communication, 22*, 65–91.

Gries, L. E. (2015). *Still Life with Rhetoric: A New Materialist Approach for Visual Rhetorics*. Boulder, CO: University Press of Colorado.

Gross, A. G. (1994). The Roles of Rhetoric in the Public Understanding of Science. *Public Understanding of Science, 3*(1), 3–23. doi:10.1088/0963-6625/3/1/001

Gross, A. G., & Buehl, J. (2016). *Science and the Internet: Communicating Knowledge in a Digital Age*. Amityville, NY: Baywood Press.

Gross, A. G., & Harmon, J. E. (2014). *Science from Sight to Insight: How Scientists Illustrate Meaning*. Chicago, IL: University of Chicago Press.

Gross, A. G., & Harmon, J. E. (2016). *The Internet Revolution in the Sciences and Humanities*. Oxford, UK: Oxford University Press.

Gross, A. G., Harmon, J. E., & Reidy, M. (2002). *Communicating Science: The Scientific Article from the 17th Century to the Present*. Oxford, UK: Oxford University Press.

Ha, J., & Fritscher, S. J. (2017, June 18). Cat and Human Personality Interaction Project. New York, NY: Experiment.com. Retrieved March 27, 2018, from http://doi.org/10.18258.8590

Hahnel, M. (2013). Figshare Partners with Open Access Mega Journal Publisher PLOS. Retrieved from https://figshare.com/blog/figshare_partners_with_Open_Access_mega_journal_publisher_PLOS/68

Harmon, J. E. (2016.) The Scientific Journal: Making It New? In A. G. Gross & J. Buehl (Eds.), *Science and the Internet: Communicating Knowledge in a Digital Age* (pp. 33–58). Amityville, NY: Baywood Press.

Harris, R. A. (1997). Introduction. In R. A. Harris (Ed.), *Landmark Essays on Rhetoric of Science* (pp. xi–xlv). Mahwah, NJ: Hermagoras Press.

Harris, R.A. (2017). *Landmark Essays on the Rhetoric of Science: Case Studies,* 2nd edition. New York, NY: Routledge.

Herring, S. C., & Paolillo, J. C. (2006). Gender and Genre Variation in Weblogs. *Journal of Sociolinguistics, 10,* 439–59.

Herring, S. C., Scheidt, L. A., Bonus, S., & Wright, E. (2004). Bridging the Gap: A Genre Analysis of Weblogs. In R. H. Sprague, Jr. (Ed.), *Proceedings of the 37th Annual Hawaii International Conference on System Science* (pp. 101–11). Los Alamitos, CA: IEEE Computer Society Press.

Herring, S. C., Scheidt, L. A., Bonus, S., & Wright, E. (2005). Weblogs as a Bridging Genre. *Information, Technology & People, 18,* 142–71.

Hyon, S. (1996). Genre in Three Traditions: Implications for ESL. *TESOL Quarterly, 30,* 693–722.

International Atomic Energy. (2014). Fukushima Monitoring Database. Retrieved from http://ec.iaea.org/fund

Iliadis, A., & Russo, F. (2016). Critical Data Studies: An Introduction. *Big Data & Society, 3*(2), 2053951716674238. doi:doi:10.1177/2053951716674238

Ito, J. (2011). Safecast and CC0. *Joi Ito*. Retrieved September, 2014, from http://joi.ito.com/weblog/2011/09/05/safecast-and-cc.html

Jack, J. (2009). *Science on the Home Front: American Women Scientists in World War II*. Champaign, IL: University of Illinois Press.

Jaffe, D. A., Hof, G., Malashanka, S., Putz, J., Thayer, J., Fry, J. L., . . . Pierce, J. R. (2014). Diesel Particulate Matter Emission Factors and Air Quality Implications from In-service Rail in Washington State, USA. *Atmospheric Pollution Research, 5*(2), 344–51

Jamieson, K. M. (1975). Antecedent Genre as Rhetorical Constraint. *Quarterly Journal of Speech, 61,* 406–15.

Jarreau, P. (2016). New Roles for Science Blogs in Shifting Sci-pub Landscape: Paige Jarreau Scrubs Data from 2016 PLOSBLOGS Reader Survey. *PLOS SciCom Blog*. Retrieved from https://blogs.plos.org/scicomm/2016/06/21/new-roles-for-science-blogs-in-shifting-sci-pub-landscape-paige-jarreau-scrubs-data-from-2016-plosblogs-reader-survey/

Jarreau, P. B., & Porter, L. (2018). Science in the Social Media Age: Profiles of Science Blog Readers. *Journalism & Mass Communication Quarterly, 95(1)*, 142–68. doi:10.1177/1077699016685558

Jasanoff, S. (2017). Virtual, Visible, and Actionable: Data Assemblages and the Sightlines of Justice. *Big Data & Society, 4(2)*, 1–15. doi:10.1177/2053951717724477

Jiang, B. (2017, June 17). The Ideal Molecular Barcode for Identifying Freshwater Green Algae (Chlorophyceae). New York, NY: Experiment.com. Retrieved July 5, 2018, from http://doi.org/10.18258/9257

Kaiser, J. (2017). Senate Spending Panel Approves $2 Billion Raise for NIH in 2018. *Science* (News). Retrieved from http://www.sciencemag.org/news/2017/09/senate-spending-panel-approves-2-billion-raise-nih-2018

Kaplan, S., & Radin, J. (2011). Bounding an Emerging Technology: Para-scientific Media and the Drexler-Smalley Debate about Nanotechnology. *Social Studies of Science, 41(4)*, 457–85.

Kelly [now Mehlenbacher], A. R. (2014, March). *Hacking Science: Emerging Para-scientific Genres and Public Participation in Scientific Research*. Dissertation, NCSU Institutional Repository, Raleigh, NC.

Kelly [now Mehlenbacher], A. R. (2016). Emerging Genres of Science Communication and Their Ethical Exigencies. In B. Vanacker & D. Heider (Eds.), *Ethics for a Digital Age* (pp. 3–18). New York, NY: Peter Lang.

Kelly [now Mehlenbacher], A. R., & Kittle Autry, M. (2013). Access, Accommodation, and Science: Knowledge in an "Open" World. *First Monday, 18(6)*.

Kelly [now Mehlenbacher], A. R., Kittle Autry, M., & Mehlenbacher, B. (2014) Considering Chronos and Kairos in Digital Media Rhetorics. In *Digital Rhetoric and Global Literacies: Communication Modes and Digital Practices in the Networked World* (pp. 227–47). Hershey, PA: IGI Global.

Kelly [now Mehlenbacher], A. R., & Miller, C. R. (2016). Intersections: Scientific and Parascientific Communication on the Internet. In A. G. Gross & J. Buehl (Eds.), *Science and the Internet: Communicating Knowledge in a Digital Age* (pp. 221–45). Amityville, NY: Baywood Press.

Killingsworth, M. J. (1992). Discourse Communities—Local and Global. *Rhetoric Review, 11(1)*, 110–22. doi:10.1080/07350199209388990

Kinsella, W. J. (2005). Rhetoric, Action, and Agency in Institutionalized Science and Technology. *Technical Communication Quarterly, 14(3)*, 303–10. doi:10.1207/s15427625tcq1403_8

Kinsella, W. J., Kelly, A. R., & Kittle Autry, M. (2013). Risk, Regulation, and Rhetorical Boundaries: Claims and Challenges Surrounding a Purported Nuclear Renaissance. *Communication Monographs, 80(3)*, 278–301.

Kobayashi, L. (2014). Gluten-free Does Not Equal Healthy. But the Food Industry Doesn't Want You to Know That. *Public Health Perspectives*. Retrieved from http://blogs.plos.org/publichealth/2014/08/25/gluten-free/

Kostelnick, C., & Kostelnick, J. (2016). Online Visualizations of Natural Disasters and Hazards: The Rhetorical Dynamic of Charing Risk. In A. G. Gross & J. Buehl (Eds.), *Science and the Internet: Communicating Knowledge in a Digital Age* (pp. 157–90). Amityville, NY: Baywood Press.

Kronick, D. A. (1976). *A History of Scientific and Technical Periodicals: The Origins and Development of the Scientific and Technical Press, 1665–1790*. Lanham, MD: The Scarecrow Press.

Kuhn, Thomas. (1970). *The Structure of Scientific Revolutions*. Chicago, IL: University of Chicago Press.

Kurgan, L. (2013). *Close Up at a Distance: Mapping, Technology, and Politics*. Brooklyn, NY: Zone Books.

Kurtzleben, D. (2017). With "Fake News," Trump Moves From Alternative Facts To Alternative Language. *NPR*. Retrived from https://www.npr.org/2017/02/17/515630467/with-fake-news-trump-moves-from-alternative-facts-to-alternative-language

Lanham, R. A. (2006). *The Economics of Attention*. Chicago, IL: University of Chicago Press.

Lefèvre, W., Renn, J., & Schoepflin, U. (Eds.). (2003). *The Power of Images in Early Modern Science*. Basel, Switzerland: Birkhäuser Verlag.

Lende, D. (2014). Our Brains as Alien Technology. *Neuroanthropology*. Retrieved from http://blogs.plos.org/neuroanthropology/2014/07/19/brains-alien-technology/

Lewis, J. (2016). Content Management Systems, Bittorrent trackers, and Large-scale Rhetorical Genres: Analyzing Collective Activity in Participatory Digital Spaces. *Journal of Technical Writing and Communication, 46*(1), 4–26.

Lewis, R. (2014). Medical Success Stories: From Cystic Fibrosis to Diabetes. *DNA Science Blog*. Retrieved from http://blogs.plos.org/dnascience/2014/08/24/medical-success-stories-cystic-fibrosis-diabetes/

Li, P., & Marrongelle, K. (2013). *Having Success with NSF: A Practical Guide*. Hoboken, NJ: John Wiley & Sons.

Lora, S. O. (2017, October 20). Ecosystem Services Loss Due to Impacts of Hurricanes Irma and Maria in San Juan Residential Trees. New York, NY: Experiment.com. Retrieved March 27, 2018, from http://doi.org/10.18258.10080

Luzón, M. J. (2013). Public Communication of Science in Blogs: Recontextualizing Scientific Discourse for a Diversified Audience. *Written Communication, 30*(4), 428–57.

Luzón, M. J. (2017). Connecting Genres and Languages in Online Scholarly Communication: An Analysis of Research Group Blogs. *Written Communication, 34*(4), 441–71.

Lynch, M. (2005). The Production of Scientific Images: Vision and Re-Vision in the History, Philosophy, and Sociloqy of Science. In L. Pauwels (Ed.), *Visual Cultures of Science Rethinking Representational Practices in Knowledge Building and Science Communication* (pp. 26–40). Lebanon, NH: University Press of New England.

Mackenzie Owen, J. (2007). *The Scientific Article in the Age of Digitization*. Dordrecht, Netherlands: Springer.

Mahrt, M., & Puschmann, C. (2014). Science Blogging: An Exploratory Study of Motives, Styles, and Audience Reactions. *Journal of Science Communication, 13*(3), A05.

McNeill, L. (2003). Teaching an Old Genre New Tricks: The Diary on the Internet. *Biography, 26*, 24–47.

Mehlenbacher, A. R. (2017). Crowdfunding Science: Exigencies and Strategies in an Emerging Genre of Science Communication. *Technical Communication Quarterly, 26*(2), 127–44. doi:10.1080/10572252.2017.1287361

Mehlenbacher, B. (1992). *Rhetorical Moves in Scientific Proposal Writing: A Case Study from Biochemical Engineering*. Pittsburgh, PA: Carnegie Mellon University. Unpublished dissertation.

Mehlenbacher, B. (1994). The Rhetorical Nature of Academic Research Funding. *IEEE Transactions on Professional Communication, 37*(3), 157–62.

Mehlenbacher, B. (2010). *Instruction and Technology: Designs for Everyday Learning*. Cambridge, MA: MIT Press.

Miller, C. R. (1979). A Humanistic Rationale for Technical Writing. *College English, 40*(6), 610–17.

Miller, C. R. (1984). Genre as Social Action. *Quarterly Journal of Speech, 70*, 151–76.

Miller, C. R. (2003). The Presumptions of Expertise: The Role of Ethos in Risk Analysis. *Configurations, 11*, 163–202.

Miller, C. R. (2012). Foreword: Rhetoric, Technology, and the Pushmi-Pullyu. In *Rhetorics and Technologies: New Directions in Writing and Communication* (pp. ix–xii). Columbia: University of South Carolina Press.

Miller, C. R. (2017). Where Do Genres Come From? In C. R. Miller & A. R. Kelly (Eds.) *Emerging Genres in New Media Enivronments* (pp. 1–34). London, UK: Palgrave Macmillan.

Miller, C. R., & Fahnestock, J. (2013). Genres in Scientific and Technical Rhetoric. *Poroi, 9*(1).

Miller, C. R., & Kelly [now Mehlenbacher], A. R. (2016). Discourse Genres. In *Verbal Communication* (pp. 269–86). Berlin, Germany: Mouton-De Gruyter.

Miller, C. R., & Shepherd, D. (2004). Blogging as Social Action: A Genre Analysis of the Weblog. In L. Gurak, S. Antonijevic, L. Johnson, C. Ratliff, & J. Reymann (Eds.), *Into the Blogosphere: Rhetoric, Community, and the Culture of Weblogs.* Minneapolis, MN: University of Minnesota Libraries. Retrieved from http://blog.lib.umn.edu/blogosphere/blogging_as_social_action.html

Miller, C. R., & Shepherd, D. (2009). Questions for Genre Theory from the Blogosphere. In J. Giltrow & D. Stein (Eds.), *Genres in the Internet: Issues in the Theory of Genre* (pp. 263–90). Amsterdam: John Benjamins.

Moeller, R. M., & Christensen, D. M. (2010). System Mapping: A Genre Field Analysis of the National Science Foundation's Grant Proposal an Funding Process. *Technical Communication Quarterly, 19*, 69–89.

Mole, B. (2013). NSF Cancels Political-Science Grant Cycle. *Nature* (News). Retrieved from https://www.nature.com/news/nsf-cancels-political-science-grant-cycle-1.13501

Molina, H. R., & Monge, O. (2017, July 13). DNA to the Rescue: A First Genetic Approach for the Conservation of the Endangered Great Green Macaw. New York, NY: Experiment.com. Retrieved March 27, 2018, from http://doi.org/10.18258.9359

Morrison, A. (2010). Autobiography in Real Time: A Genre Analysis of Personal Mommy Blogging. *Cyberpsychology: Journal of Psychosocial Research on Cyberspace, 4*(3), A.5.

Morrison, A. (2011). Suffused by Feeling and Affect: The Intimate Public of Personal Mommy Blogging. *Biography, 34*(1), 37–55. doi:10.2307/23541177

Morrison, A. (2019). Laughing at Injustice: #DistractinglySexy and #StayMadAbby as Counternarratives. In D. Parry & C. Johnson (Eds.), *Digital Dilemmas: Transforming Gender Identities and Power Relations in Everyday Life* (23–52). London: Palgrave MacMillan. doi: 10.1007/978-3-319-95300-7_2

Myers, G. (1990). *Writing Biology: Texts in the Social Construction of Scientific Knowledge.* Madison, WI: University of Wisconsin Press.

Myers, G. (1997). Words and Pictures in a Biology Textbok. In T. Miller (Ed.), *Functional Approaches to Written Text: Classroom Applications* (113–26). Washington, DC: United States Information Agency.

Myers, G. (2003). Discourse Studies of Scientific Popularization: Questioning the Boundaries. *Discourse Studies, 5*(2), 265–79. doi:10.1177/1461445603005002006

nallen. (2018). r/science Will No Longer Be Hosting AMAs. Reddit.com. Retrieved from https://www.reddit.com/r/science/comments/8khscc/rscience_will_no_longer_be_hosting_amas/

Nardi, B. A., Schiano, D. J., & Gumbrecht, M. (2004). *Blogging as Social Activity, or, Would You Let 900 Million People Read Your Diary?* Paper presented at the Proceedings of the 2004 ACM Conference on Computer Supported Cooperative Work, Chicago, Illinois, USA.

National Academies of Sciences, Engineering, & Medicine. (2016). *Genetically Engineered Crops: Experiences and Prospects.* Washington, DC: National Academies Press.

National Science Board. (2016). *Science and Technology: Public Attitudes and Understanding Science and Engineering Indicators* (Vol. NSB-2016–1). Arlington, VA: National Science Foundation. Retrieved from https://www.nsf.gov/statistics/2016/nsb20161/uploads/1/nsb20161.pdf

National Science Foundation. (2016). NSF Funding Profile. In FY 2016 Budget Request. Retrieved from https://www.nsf.gov/about/budget/fy2016/pdf/04_fy2016.pdf

National Science Foundation. (2018). NSF Funding Profile. In FY 2018 Budget Request to Congress. Retrieved from https://www.nsf.gov/about/budget/fy2018/pdf/04_fy2018.pdf

Natural Sciences and Engineering Research Council of Canada. (2017). 2017 Competition Statistics Discovery Grants (DG) and Research Tools and Instruments (RTI) Programs. Retrieved from http://www.nserc-crsng.gc.ca/_doc/Professors-Professeurs/2017DG-RTI_e.pdf

Nelson, B. (2009, September). Empty Archives. *Nature* (News), *461*(2009),160–63. Retrieved from https://www.nature.com/news/2009/090909/full/461160a.html

Orlikowski, W. J., & Yates, J. (1994). Genre Repertoire: The Structuring of Communicative Practices in Organizations. *Administrative Science Quarterly, 39,* 541–74.

Ortega, J. L. (2016). *Social Network Sites for Scientists: A Quantitative Survey.* Cambridge, MA: Chandos Publishing.

Pariser, E. (2011). *The Filter Bubble: What the Internet Is Hiding from You.* London, UK: Penguin UK.

Peng, J. C. (2016). Molina n-coding RNAs. *PLOS Blogs Biologue.* Retrieved from http://blogs.plos.org/biologue/2016/11/17/understanding-images-animal-fertility-governed-by-small-non-coding-rnas/

Pew Research Center. (2014). *World Wide Web Timeline.* Washington, DC: PEW. Retrieved from http://www.pewinternet.org/2014/03/11/world-wide-web-timeline/

Pew Research Center. (2015). *How Scientists Engage the Public.* Washington, DC: PEW. Retrieved from http://www.pewinternet.org/2015/02/15/how-scientists-engage-public/

Pew Research Center, Barthel, M., Mitchell, A., & Holcomb, J. (2016). *Many Americans Believe Fake News Is Sowing Confusion.* Washington, DC: PEW.

Pew Research Center & Kennedy, B. (2016). *Most Americans Trust the Military and Scientists to Act in the Public's Interest.* Washington, DC: PEW. Retrieved from http://www.journalism.org/2016/12/15/many-americans-believe-fake-news-is-sowing-confusion/

Pew Research Center, Mitchell, A., Gottfried, J., Barthel, M., & Shearer, E. (2016). *The Modern News Consumer.* Washington, DC: PEW. Retrieved from http://www.journalism.org/2016/07/07/the-modern-news-consumer/

Pew Research Center & Smith, A. (2016). *Shared, Collaborative and On Demand: The New Digital Economy.* Washington, DC: PEW. Retrieved from http://www.pewinternet.org/2016/05/19/the-new-digital-economy/

Pigg, S., Hart-Davidson, W., Grabill, J, & Ellenbogen, K. (2016). Why People Care about Chickens and Other Lessons about Rhetoric, Public Science, and Informal Learning Environments. In A. G. Gross & J. Buehl (Eds.), *Science and the Internet: Communicating Knowledge in a Digital Age* (pp. 247–65). Amityville, NY: Baywood Press.

Porter, J. E. (1986). Intertextuality and the Discourse Community. *Rhetoric Review, 5*(1), 34–47. doi:10.1080/07350198609359131

Public Library of Science. (2015a). History. Retrieved August 12, 2015, from http://www.plos.org/about/plos/history/

Public Library of Science. (2015b). A List of PLOS BLOGS. Retrieved August 12, 2015, from http://blogs.plos.org/blogosphere/

Public Library of Science. (2015c). Welcome Science Communicators and Readers. Retrieved August 12, 2015, from http://blogs.plos.org/scicomm/sample-page/

Public Library of Science. (2015d). What Is PLOS? Retrieved August 12, 2015, from https://www.plos.org/about/plos/

Public Library of Science. (2017a). Home Page. Retrieved February 4, 2017, from https://www.plos.org/

Public Library of Science. (2017b). The PLOS Story. Retrieved February 4, 2017, from https://www.plos.org/history

Ray, Kate. (2015). Hello Kate! Retrieved September 22, 2018, from http://blog.experiment.com/post/130631790282/hello-kate

Reardon, S. (2017, January 27). Geneticist launches bid for US Senate, Q&A. *Nature*. Retrieved from http://www.nature.com/news/geneticist-launches-bid-for-us-senate-1.21381

Reardon, S., Tollefson, J., Witze, A., & Ross, E. (2017). US Science Agencies Face Deep Cuts in Trump Budget. *Nature, 543*, 471–42.

Reddit Science. (n.d.). Science AMA Series Submission Guide. Retrieved from Reddit.com

Reeves, C. (2011). Scientific Visuals, Language, and the Commercialization of a Scientific Idea: The Strange Case of the Prion. *Technical Communication Quarterly, 20*(3), 239–73. doi:10.1080/10572252.2011.578237

Reiff, M. J., & Bawarshi, A. (Eds.). (2016). *Genre and the Performance of Publics*. Logan, UT: Utah State University Press.

Rennie, J. (2014). Passion and 3D printers Reinvent STEM Learning. *PLOS Blogs The Gleaming Retort*. Retrieved from http://blogs.plos.org/retort/2014/07/17/passion-3d-printers-can-reinvent-stem-learning/

ResearchGate. (2014). About Us. Retrieved August 2014 from http://www.researchgate.net/about

Riesch, H., & Mendel, J. (2013). Science Blogging: Networks, Boundaries and Limitations. *Science as Culture, 23*(1), 51–72. doi: 10.1080/09505431.2013.801420.

Rosenberg, D. (2013). Data Before the Fact. In L. Gitelman (Ed.), *"Raw Data" Is an Oxymoron* (pp. 15–40). Cambridge: MIT Press.

Ross, D. G. (2017). The Role of Ethics, Culture, and Artistry in Scientific Illustration. *Technical Communication Quarterly, 26*(2), 145–172.

Rulyova, N. (2017). Russian New Media Users' Reaction to a Meteor Explosion in Chelyabinsk: Twitter Versus YouTube. In C. R. Miller & A. R. Kelly (Eds.), *Emerging Genres in New Media Environments* (pp. 79–97). London, UK: Palgrave Macmillan.

Safecast. (2017). The Safecast Report. Retrieved from https://blog.safecast.org/the-safecast-report/

Schake, S. & Peuramaki-Brown, M. (2014). City Growth and Trade at the Ancient Maya Site of Alabama in Belize. New York, NY: Experiment.com. Retrieved March 27, 2018, from http://doi.org/10.18258/2289

Scheibler, R. (2014). Safecast bGeigie library. *GitHub*. Retrieved from https://github.com/Safecast

Schimel, J. (2012). *Writing Science: How to Write Papers That Get Cited and Proposals That Get Funded*. New York, NY: Oxford University Press.

Schryer, C. F. (1993). Records as Genre. *Written Communication, 10,* 200–34.

Schryer, C. F. (1994). The Lab vs. the Clinic: Sites of Competing Genres. In A. Freedman & P. Medway (Eds.), *Genre and the New Rhetoric* (pp. 105–24). London: Taylor and Francis.

Schryer, C. F. (2000). Walking a Fine Line: Writing "Negative News" Letters in an Insurance Company. *Journal of Business and Technical Communication, 14,* 445–97.

Scientific American. (2015). About the Scientific American Blog Network. Retrieved August 12, 2015, from http://blogs.scientificamerican.com/about-the-network/

Scott, S. E., Inbar, Y., & Rozin, P. (2016). Evidence for Absolute Moral Opposition to Genetically Modified Food in the United States. *Perspectives on Psychological Science, 11*(3), 315–24. doi:10.1177/1745691615621275

Segal, Judy Z. (2000). What Is a Rhetoric of Death? End-of-life Decision-making at a Psychiatric Hospital. *Technostyle, 16*(1), 65–86.

Shanahan, M.-C. (2011). Science Blogs as Boundary Layers: Creating and Understanding New Writer and Reader Interactions through Science Blogging. *Journalism, 12*(7), 903–19. doi:10.1177/1464884911412844

Shema, H., Bar-Ilan, J., & Thelwall, M. (2012). Research Blogs and the Discussion of Scholarly Information. *PLoS ONE, 7*(5), e35869. doi:10.1371/journal.pone.0035869

Sidler, M. (2016). The Chemistry Liveblogging Event: The Web Refigures Peer Review. In A. G. Gross & J. Buehl (Eds.), *Science and the Internet: Communicating Knowledge in a Digital Age* (pp. 99–116). Amityville, NY: Baywood Press.

Skwarecki, B. (2014). Why It's So Easy to Believe Our Food Is Toxic. *Public Health Blog.* Retrieved from http://blogs.plos.org/publichealth/2014/04/29/easy-believe-food-toxic/

Smart, G. (2003). A Central Bank's Communications Strategy: The Interplay of Activity, Discourse Genres, and Technology in a Time of Organizational Change. In C. Bazerman & D.R. Russell (Eds.), *Writing Selves and Societies: Research from Activity Perspectives* (pp. 9–61). Fort Collins, CO: The WAC Clearinghouse and Mind, Culture, and Activity.

Smart, G. (2016). Discourse Coalitions, Science Blogs, and the Public Debate on Global Climate Change. In M. J. Reiff & A. Bawarshi (Eds.), *Genre and the Performance of Publics* (pp. 157–77). Logan, UT: Utah State University Press.

Sokół, M. (2012). Metadiscourse and the Construction of the Author's Voices in the Blogosphere: Academic Weblogs as a Form of Selfpromotion. In S. Campagna, G. Garzone, C. Ilie, & E. Rowley-Jolivet (Eds.), *Evolving Genres in Web-mediated Communication* (pp. 265–87). Bern, Switzerland: Peter Lang.

Spinuzzi, C. (2002). *Modeling Genre Ecologies.* Paper presented at the 20th Annual International Conference on Computer Documentation (pp. 200–207), October 20–23, 2002, Toronto, Canada. doi:10.1145/584955.584985

Spinuzzi, C. (2003a). Compound Mediation in Software Development: Using Genre Ecologies to Study Textual Artifacts. In C. Bazerman & D. Russell (Eds.), *Writing Selves/Writing Societies: Research from Activity Perspectives* (pp. 97–124). Fort Collins, CO: The WAC Clearinghouse and Mind, Culture, and Activity.

Spinuzzi, C. (2003b). *Tracing Genres through Organizations: A Sociocultural Approach to Information.* Cambridge, MA: MIT Press.

Spinuzzi, C. (2004). Four Ways to Investigate Assemblages of Texts: Genre Sets, Systems, Repertoires, and Ecologies. *Proceedings of the 22nd Annual International Conference on Design of Communication, SIGDOC 2004*, 110–16.

Spinuzzi, C. (2008). *Theorizing Knowledge Work in Telecommunications*. Cambridge: Cambridge University Press.

Star, S. L. (1988). The Structure of Ill-structured Solutions: Boundary Objects and Heterogeneous Distributed Problem Solving. In M. Huhns & L. Gasser (Eds.), *Readings in Distributed Artificial Intelligence* (37–54). Menlo Park, CA: Kaufman.

Star, S. L. (2010). This Is Not a Boundary Object: Reflections on the Origin of a Concept. *Science, Technology & Human Values, 35*(5), 601–17. doi:10.1177/0162243910377624

Strasser, C., Cook, R., Michener, W., & Budden, A. (2012). *Primer on Data Management: What You Always Wanted to Know*. DataONE. Retrieved from https://www.dataone.org/sites/all/documents/DataONE_BP_Primer_020212.pdf

Swales, J. M. (1990). *Genre Analysis: English in Academic and Research Settings*. Cambridge: Cambridge University Press.

Swales, J. M. (2004). *Research Genres: Explorations and Applications*. Cambridge: Cambridge University Press.

Swarts, J. (2006). Coherent Fragments: The Problem of Mobility and Genred Information. *Written Communication, 23*, 173–201.

Tardy, C. M. (2003). A Genre System View of the Funding of Academic Research. *Written Communication, 20*, 7–36.

Taylor, C. A. (1991). Defining the Scientific Community: A Rhetorical Perspective on Demarcation. *Communication Monographs, 58*, 402–20.

Thrift, N. (2005). *Knowing Capitalism*. London: Sage.

Trayf. (2017). First They Came for the Scientists . . . Retrieved September 14, 2017, from https://www.reddit.com/r/PoliticalHumor/comments/5quwfi/first_they_came_for_the_scientists/

Trench, B. (2008). Internet: Turning Science Communication Inside-out. In *Handbook of Public Communication of Science and Technology* (pp. 185–98). New York, NY: Routledge.

Trench, B. (2012). Scientists' Blogs: Glimpses Behind the Scenes. In S. Rödder, M. Franzen, & P. Weingart (Eds.), *The Sciences' Media Connection–Public Communication and its Repercussions* (Vol. 28, pp. 273–89). Dordrecht, Netherlands: Springer Netherlands.

Tri-Agencies. (2016). Tri-Agency Framework: Responsible Conduct of Research. *Canadian Institutes of Health Research, Natural Sciences and Engineering Research Council of Canada, & Social Sciences and Humanities Research Council of Canada*. Ottawa, ON: Secretariat on Responsible Conduct of Research. Retrived from http://www.rcr.ethics.gc.ca/policy-politique/files/Framework2016-CadreReference2016_eng.pdf

University of Waterloo Office of Research. (2018). Experiment.com Crowdfunding Opportunity. Retrieved from https://uwaterloo.ca/research/find-and-manage-funding/find-funding/experimentcom-crowdfunding-opportunity

Upton, T. A., & Connor, U. (2001). Using Computerized Corpus Analysis to Investigate the Text-linguistic Discourse Moves of a Genre. *English for Specific Purposes, 20*(4), 313–29.

Vachelard, J., Gambarra-Soares, T., Augustini, G., Riul, P., & Maracaja-Coutinho, V. (2016). A Guide to Scientific Crowdfunding. *PLOS Biology, 14*(2), e1002373. doi:10.1371/journal. pbio.1002373

Walker, A. R., Silvestrov, P., Müller, T. A., Podolsky, R. H., Dyson, G., Hausinger, R. P., & Cisneros, G. A. (2017). ALKBH7 Variant Related to Prostate Cancer Exhibits Altered Substrate Binding. *PLOS Computational Biology, 13*(2), e1005345. doi:10.1371/journal.pcbi.1005345

Wardlaw, S. (2016). Radiolab and Parasites: Podcasting Horror and Wonder to Foster Interest in Science. In A. G. Gross & J. Buehl (Eds.), *Science and the Internet: Communicating Knowledge in a Digital Age* (143–56). Amityville, NY: Baywood Press.

Weinberg, A. M. (1972). Science and Trans-science. *Minerva, 10*(2), 209–22. doi:10.1007/ BF01682418

Weinberg, A. M. (1987). Science and Its Limits. In C. Whipple (Ed.), *De Minimis Risk* (Vol. 2, pp. 27–38). New York, NY: Springer US.

Weinberg, A. M. (1992). *Nuclear Reactions: Science and Trans-science.* New York, NY: American Institute of Physics.

White, W. J. (2017). Optical Solutions: Reception of an NSF-Funded Science Comic Book on the Biology of the Eye. *Technical Communication Quarterly, 26*(2), 101–15. doi:10.1080/10572252. 2017.1285962

Williams, M., & Gill, J. (2017, June 29). 10,000 Years of Climate and Environmental Changes in Jamaica, a Biodiverse Tropical Island. New York, NY: Experiment.com. Retrieved March 27, 2018, from http://doi.org/10.18258/9322

Woolgar, S. (1988). *Science, the Very Idea.* Ann Arbor, MI: University of Michigan Press.

Wynn, J. (2016). Meltdowns in the Media: Visualization of Radiation Risk from the Printed Page to the Internet. In A. G. Gross & J. Buehl (Eds.), *Science and the Internet: Communicating Knowledge in a Digital Age* (pp. 191–219). Amityville, NY: Baywood Press.

Wynne, B. (2006). Public Engagement as a Means of Restoring Public Trust in Science—Hitting the Notes, but Missing the Music? *Public Health Genomics, 9*(3), 211–20.

Yates, J. (1989). The Emergence of the Memo as a Managerial Genre. *Management Communication Quarterly, 2(4),* 485–510.

Yates, J., & Orlikowski, W. (1992). Genres of Organizational Communication: A Structurational Approach to Studying Communication and Media. *Academy of Management Review, 17,* 299–326.

Young, E. (2012). Scattered Reflections about ScienceOnline 2012 (#sci012). Retrieved from http://blogs.discovermagazine.com/notrocketscience/2012/01/22/scattered-reflections -about-scienceonline-2012-sci012/

Young, E. (2017, January 25). Professor Smith Goes to Washington. *The Atlantic.* Retrieved from https://www.theatlantic.com/science/archive/2017/01/thanks-to-trump-scientists -are-planning-to-run-for-office/514229/

Young, R. S. (2017, January 31). A Scientists' March on Washington Is a Bad Idea [Op-ed]. *The New York Times.* Retrieved from https://www.nytimes.com/2017/01/31/opinion/a-scientists- march-on-washington-is-a-bad-idea.html?_r=0

Zachry, M. (2000). Communicative Practices in the Workplace: A Historical Examination of Genre Development. *Journal of Technical Writing and Communication, 30,* 57–79.

Zamudio-Suaréz, F. (2017, February 2). Sensing New Threats, Scientists Entertain Political Ambitions. *The Chronicle of Higher Education*. Retrieved from http://www.chronicle.com/article/Sensing-New-Threats/239082

Zess, E. (2016). What We Talk about When We Talk about Genetic Modification. Retrieved from http://blogs.plos.org/synbio/2016/04/25/what-we-talk-about-when-we-talk-about-genetic-modification-medium/

Zivkovic, B. (2012). Science Blogs—Definition, and a History. *Scientific American Blogs: A Blog Around The Clock*. Retrieved on August 13, 2015 from https://blogs.scientificamerican.com/a-blog-around-the-clock/science-blogs-definition-and-a-history/.

INDEX